RADICAL POSSIBILITIES
2nd Edition

The core argument of Jean Anyon's classic *Radical Possibilities* is deceptively simple: If we do not direct our attention to the ways in which federal and metropolitan policies maintain the poverty that plagues communities in American cities, urban school reform as currently conceived is doomed to fail. With every chapter thoroughly revised and updated, this edition picks up where the 2005 publication left off, including a completely new chapter detailing how three decades of political decisions leading up to the "Great Recession" produced an economic crisis of epic proportions. By tracing the root causes of the financial crisis, Anyon effectively demonstrates the concrete effects of economic decision-making on the education sector, revealing in particular the disastrous impacts of these policies on black and Latino communities.

Going beyond lament, *Radical Possibilities* offers those interested in a better future for the millions of America's poor families a set of practical and theoretical insights. Expanding on her paradigm for combating educational injustice, Anyon discusses the Occupy Wall Street movement as a recent example of popular resistance in this new edition, set against a larger framework of civil rights history. A ringing call to action, *Radical Possibilities* reminds readers that throughout U.S. history, equitable public policies have typically been created as a result of the political pressure brought to bear by social movements. Ultimately, Anyon's revelations teach us that the current moment contains its own very real radical possibilities.

Jean Anyon was Professor of Social and Educational Policy in the Doctoral Program in Urban Education at the Graduate Center of the City University of New York. Her publications include the best-selling and critically acclaimed *Ghetto Schooling: A Political Economy of Urban School Reform*.

The Critical Social Thought Series
Edited by Michael W. Apple
University of Wisconsin–Madison

Political Spectacle and the Fate of American Schools
Mary Lee Smith with Walter Heinecke, Linda Miller-Kahn, and Patricia F. Jarvis

Rethinking Scientific Literacy
Wolff-Michael Roth and Angela Calabrese Barton

High Stakes Education: Inequality, Globalization, and Urban School Reform
Pauline Lipman

Learning to Labor in New Times
Nadine Dolby and Greg Dimitriadis, editors

Working Method: Research and Social Justice
Lois Weis and Michelle Fine

Class Reunion: The Remaking of the American White Working Class
Lois Weis

Race, Identity, and Representation in Education, Second Edition
Cameron McCarthy, Warren Crichlow, Greg Dimitriadis, and Nadine Dolby

Radical Possibilities: Public Policy, Urban Education, and a New Social Movement
Jean Anyon

Could It Be Otherwise? Parents and the Inequities of Public School Choice
Lois André-Bechely

Reading and Writing the World with Mathematics
Eric Gustein

Market Movements: African American Involvement in School Voucher Reform
Thomas C. Pedroni

Rightist Multiculturalism: Core Lessons on Neoconservative School Reform
Kristen L. Buras

Unequal By Design: High-Stakes Testing and the Standardization of Inequality
Wayne Au

Black Literate Lives: Historical and Contemporary Perspectives
Maisha T. Fisher

Hidden Markets: The New Education Privatization
Patricia Burch

Critical Perspectives on Bell Hooks
Maria del Guadalupe Davidson and George Yancy, editors

Advocacy Leadership: Toward a Post-Reform Agenda in Education
Gary L. Anderson

Race, Whiteness, and Education
Zeus Leonardo

Controversy in the Classroom: The Democratic Power of Discussion
Diana E. Hess

The New Political Economy of Urban Education: Neoliberalism, Race, and the Right to the City
Pauline Lipman

Critical Curriculum Studies: Education, Consciousness, and the Politics of Knowing
Wayne Au

Learning to Liberate: Community-Based Solutions to the Crisis in Urban Education
Vajra Watson

Critical Pedagogy and Social Change: Critical Analysis on the Language of Possibility
Seehwa Cho

Educating Activist Allies: Social Justice Pedagogy with the Suburban and Urban Elite
Katy Swalwell

RADICAL POSSIBILITIES

Public Policy, Urban Education, and a New Social Movement

2nd Edition

Jean Anyon

Routledge
Taylor & Francis Group

NEW YORK AND LONDON

Second edition published 2014
by Routledge
711 Third Avenue, New York, NY 10017

and by Routledge
2 Park Square, Milton Park, Abingdon, Oxon, OX14 4RN

Routledge is an imprint of the Taylor & Francis Group, an informa business

First edition published 2005 by Routledge

Library of Congress Cataloging in Publication Data
Anyon, Jean.
Radical possibilities: public policy, urban education, and a new social
movement / by Jean Anyon. – Second edition.
pages cm. – (Critical social thought)
Includes bibliographical references and index.
1. Education, Urban–Social aspects–United States. 2. Educational change–
United States. 3. Social change–United States. I. Title.
LC5131.A56 2014
370.9173'2–dc23
2013033323

ISBN: 978-0-415-63557-8 (hbk)
ISBN: 978-0-415-63558-5 (pbk)
ISBN: 978-0-203-09296-5 (ebk)

Typeset in Bembo and ITC Stone Sans
by Cenveo Publisher Services

CONTENTS

ACKNOWLEDGEMENTS

Without my daughter Jessie at my side throughout a recent illness I wouldn't have been able to complete this project. It is to her that I dedicate this book with enormous love and appreciation.

My doctoral students past and present have been an intellectual inspiration to me, and my love for them has grown each year: Kiersten Greene, Michael Dumas, Madeline Perez, Kathleen Nolan, Amy Moran, Edwin Mayorga, Liza Pappas, Shannon Allen, Jeremy Benson, Joanna Yip, John Wenk, Mikela Bjork, Kylah Torre, Jennifer Stoops, Ashleigh Thompson, Sara Zaidi, Nelson Flores, Roberto Martinez, Brian Jones, Danny Volotch, Erica Chutuape, Darla Linville, Jen Weiss, Tahir Butt, and Danny Walsh in particular were always a delight.

Colleagues in academia who I have learned from and cared deeply for over the years include Tony Picciano, Ofelia Garcia, Wendy Lutrell, Nick Michelli, Lois Weis, Greg Dimitriadis, Michelle Fine, Mike Apple, Geoff Whitty, Roz Mickelson, Alan Sadovnik, and Sherry Giles.

I could not have finished this book without the encouragement and support of my dear friends Janet Miller, Kathryn Herr, Gary Anderson, Jane Califf, Florence Tager, Dolores Bentham, Kathleen Livingston, Renate Bridenthal, Joan Farber, Michael O'Brien, MaryAnn Peterson, and Jerry Fauchet.

My brother Bob and sister-in-law Joan stood by me in all the best ways. My niece Yolanda Anyon and nephew Tyler Anyon sent love I could feel.

Last but certainly not least, my editor Catherine Bernard has been—as always—amazing.

To all these people I love I say thank you for everything.

INTRODUCTION

I opened the first edition of *Radical Possibilities* with the following personal narrative:

> Born in the 1940s to parents who had been active in the radical social movements of the 1930s, I was a "red-diaper baby." Both parents had been labor organizers, and continued their activism during my youth. In the mid-1950s, Senator Joseph McCarthy called my father to Washington, D.C., on charges that he had been a member of the Communist Party almost twenty years before. The president of the elite university where my father was by then a tenured faculty member stepped in, and McCarthy desisted, but had my father's passport revoked.
>
> Early on I imbibed the family passion for social justice. I believed I should, and could, fight against the racial and class oppression I observed. During my high school and college years, the Civil Rights Movement deeply engaged me, and I became active in a Northern branch of CORE (Congress of Racial Equality)—picketing, marching, and sometimes organizing. I raised money for the movement in Mississippi during "Freedom Summer" of 1964. Three years later, political activist Abbie Hoffman and I opened a store in New York City where we sold leather and cotton goods made by an African American women's collective in South Carolina; we sent the proceeds south to support the collective and civil rights activity.
>
> During the late 1960s and early '70s I taught elementary grades in inner city schools in Washington, D.C., and Bedford Stuyvesant, Brooklyn—ever hopeful for black civil rights, as victories followed major protests in the South. During those years I joined protests against the Vietnam War, and rejoiced when the 10-year-old movement met with success and U.S. troops were withdrawn from Vietnam in 1973.

After seven years, I left city classrooms for doctoral studies, and then a position in the Teacher Education Department of Rutgers University in Newark, NJ—wanting very much to make a difference in the struggle against what I perceived to be racial and class oppression of a systemic nature in urban schools. I wrote *Ghetto Schooling: A Political Economy of Urban Educational Reform*, in part to demonstrate that the failure of city school systems such as Newark was a function of 100 years of urban political and economic history, rather than a result of an influx of black Southern families in the 1950s and '60s—as many whites assumed.

Radical Possibilities is another attempt to intervene against injustice. In it, I examine ways in which the current political economy maintains the damage that U.S. history has inflicted on cities. While historical decisions and policies severely delimited the capacity of cities to support their schools, current public policy maintains this disadvantage.

Now, as I rewrite this book for a second edition, I must add another, more public, chapter to the story. Since the book's publication in 2005, the world's economies have been shaken—and some toppled—by an economic catastrophe euphemistically called the Great Recession. The Great Recession, officially from 2007 to 2009 (but continuing for most of the U.S. population in 2013 as I write this), destroyed millions of jobs, debased home values, wiped out nearly 40% of the wealth of middle-class families, collapsed employment prospects, slashed education and other public spending, increased inequality, and deepened and expanded poverty in the U.S. and many other countries as well. The years leading up to the economic collapse, during which the financial sector was let loose to graze freely on people's mortgages and other assets, the implosion itself, and its handling by the federal government, culminated in a tiny 1% of the population controlling 40% of the wealth in the country, and taking home nearly a *quarter* of all the income. Post-crash mergers encouraged by the federal government among the five biggest banks created behemoths that now hold assets amounting to more than *half* of the nation's economy. Using tax havens and loopholes, many of the largest and most profitable corporations have basically stopped paying federal taxes, and some—like General Electric, Verizon, and Kraft Foods, among others—get billions in refunds from U.S. taxpayers. The Great Recession increased inequality in the U.S. to the point that one of every three Americans is either poor or near poor.

These developments are important not only because of the pain they have caused, but because they underscore the destructive power of recent iterations of the political economy—policies put in place over the last four decades, many of which I described in the first edition of this book. These policies—and others to be introduced in this new edition—reveal how both Democratic and Republican administrations, basing many of their decisions on the needs of an increasingly demanding corporate class, created a situation between 1980 and the mid-2000s that made the 2007 economic explosion and its effects seem inevitable. But the crash was not inevitable; nor did it just "happen"—as I suggest above, it was created by federal policies and corporate behavior. And I believe that if we act together, these policies and behavior can be changed.

One hundred years ago, during the first two tumultuous decades of the 20th century, and then especially after the 1930s Depression began, social movements against the power of robber barons and big banks—and for a populist program of economic supports for working people—were strong and continuous. By the end of the Depression, the public pressure of these social movements had successfully forced the federal government to pass progressive legislation that inaugurated a period of "gentler, kinder, capitalism"—an iteration of the political economy that lasted 40 years. Between the 1940s and about 1980, business and finance were controlled and highly regulated, and could not gamble with other people's money; unions were a federally supported, countervailing force to corporate power; the rich were charged high taxes and paid for much of the expansive local and national infrastructural development; and the middle class expanded because good jobs were available. (Most African Americans, however, especially those living in the South, were excluded from policies that created this "Golden Age.")

This 40-year period of our history is examined in the following pages because it is highly instructive. The history shows the power of social movements to bring about fundamental progressive change, and—if corrected for racial exclusion, this earlier period also demonstrates that there are indeed plausible alternatives to recent excesses of economic policy—alternatives that provided widely based prosperity and economic stability for nearly half a century.

But since the 1980s we have lived in a fragile, recession-prone political economy—a society in which the spread of income in 2011 was as unequal as in "Russia with its Oligarchs and Iran" (Stiglitz, 2011). The policies described in the first edition of *Radical Possibilities*, and updated in later chapters here (regarding minimum wages, lack of decent jobs, taxes, etc.), have been instrumental in contributing to this inequality. Extreme inequality matters not only for humanistic reasons but for reasons of economic health.

> Although inequality did not directly cause the [2007–2009] crisis, it is no coincidence that the 1920s—the last time inequality of income and wealth in the United States was so high—ended with the Great Crash and the Depression. The International Monetary Fund has noted the systematic relationship between economic instability and economic inequality.
>
> *(Stiglitz, 2013b, p. 1)*

And the latest Recession, in turn, has exacerbated the trends of increasing inequality and joblessness I described in 2005. In order to mount a successful social movement against the banks and hedge funds, and the politicians who so often seem beholden to them, we need to understand what caused the Great Recession.

In this edition of *Radical Possibilities* I have added a chapter that traces the deregulation and financial developments that were culpable.

I then return to the policies I described in 2005, and examine them in their current form—those regulating the minimum wage, job availability, tax rates, federal public transportation, and affordable housing (for example). For these policies continue, and remain crucial to the creation of the extreme inequality that contributes to the fragility of the political economy and potential future financial implosions.

In addition to contributing to a highly unequal and therefore fragile economy, the policies I described in 2005 (regarding minimum wage, lack of jobs, taxation, for instance) are connected to the financial and banking practices and policies that triggered the Great Recession in another way. Policies that tax the rich at effectively lower rates than the middle class; keep the minimum wage at fractions of its former strength; prevent the establishment of jobs with decent wages, affordable housing, and public transportation to where the jobs are located are part and parcel of the same neoliberal paradigm that freed the wealthy from their tax responsibilities and cut loose corporations, banks, and hedge funds from oversight. The neoliberal paradigm (also described in the next chapter) assumes that free markets—labor, monetary, financial, educational, and housing markets, for example—will regulate and stabilize themselves without government regulation or the need for taxation to support them, and the resulting prosperity will "lift all boats." In the neoliberal model, no welfare is necessary because individuals can find jobs if they obtain skill training or education; unions must be weakened and wages lowered to increase business profits; and investment is concentrated in exotic financial products rather than, as heretofore, in the production of goods and services (which creates jobs). Also part of the neoliberal paradigm is the application of the corporate logic of profits and privatization to as many spheres of life as possible, such as public education, in order to eradicate the need for taxes.

Effects on Urban Education

It is an important part of my argument here, as in the first edition of *Radical Possibilities*, that the political economic policies I discuss have a determining effect on the fortunes of education in urban areas. This book is not "about" education— in the typical sense of gazing inside schools to assess how they work, or fail to work. This book, rather, is about the macroeconomic policies regulating wages, jobs, tax rates, federal transportation, and affordable housing (among others) that create conditions in urban areas that no existing educational policy or urban school reform can transcend. If anything, the Great Recession has cemented, in the politically powerful players, a belief in corporate sponsored reforms like educational privatization, charter schools, accountability focused on individual teachers, and high-stakes testing. These also lie under the neoliberal, free-market, no-taxes-needed umbrella.

But in my view, low-achieving urban schools are not primarily a consequence of failed education policy, urban family dynamics, underprepared teachers, or too few tests—as mainstream analysts and public policies typically imply. Failing public schools in cities are, rather, a logical consequence of the U.S. political economy—and the federal and regional policies and practices that support it. Teachers, principals, and urban students are not the culprits—as reform policies that target high stakes testing, educator quality, and the control of youth assume. Rather, an unjust economy and the policies through which it is maintained create barriers to educational success that no teacher or principal practice, no standardized test, and no "zero tolerance" policy can surmount for long. It is for this reason that I argue that *macroeconomic mandates continually trump urban educational policy and school reform.*

Policies such as minimum wage statutes that yield poverty wages, housing and transportation policies that segregate low-income workers of color in urban areas, and industrial and other job development in far-flung suburbs where public transit does not reach, all maintain poverty in city neighborhoods and therefore the schools. In order to solve the systemic problems of urban education, then, we need not only school reform, but the reform of these public policies. If, as I am suggesting, the macroeconomy deeply affects the quality of urban education, then perhaps we should rethink what "counts" as educational policy. Rules and regulations regarding teaching, curriculum, and assessment certainly count; but perhaps policies that maintain high levels of urban poverty and segregation should be part of the educational policy panoply as well—for these have consequences for urban education at least as profound as curriculum and pedagogy (Anyon, 2005a).

We have been attempting educational reform in U.S. cities for over 40 years—and there is little significant district-wide improvement that we can point to. As a nation, we have been counting on education to solve the problems of unemployment, joblessness, and poverty for many years. But education did not cause these problems, and education cannot solve them. An economic system that chases profits and casts people aside (especially people of color) is culpable.

How can a successfully reformed urban school benefit a low-income student of color whose graduation will not lead to a job on which to make a living because there are not enough such jobs, nor lead to the resources for college completion? New curriculum, standardized tests, or even nurturing, democratic small schools do not create living wage jobs, and do not provide poor students with the funds and supports for enough further education to make a significant difference in their lives. Only government policy can mandate that jobs provide decent wages; and adequate family income or public provision (such as the 1944 GI Bill that paid for the education of 8 million veterans) are necessary to guarantee funds for college degrees—to the millions of urban poor who want, and need them.

I acknowledge that even though economic justice may be a prerequisite for educational justice, more equitable macroeconomic polices will not by themselves create high-quality urban schools. Macroeconomic policy will need to be augmented by educational reform. Providing economic opportunity and realistic hope in urban neighborhoods will be necessary to create the conditions that allow for and support successful urban schools, but these nurturing conditions will have to be supplemented by reforms that prevent racial tracking, low-level curriculum, and provides supports for teachers (for example).

Despite my serious criticism of public policy as legislated by the political and economic coalitions that govern, I have great faith in the American people. U.S. history demonstrates—and my experience in two social movements confirms for me personally—that the most egregious social policies can be replaced by significantly more equitable ones by the power of a people who are united and organized. From the American Revolution (fought in part against economic policies perceived as unjust) to the labor movements of the 19th and 20th centuries, to the civil rights, women's, bilingual, and disability movements, the most unjust policies have been replaced by liberal and sometimes radical legislation. Today, despite the brief eruption of Occupy Wall Street in 2011, the radical, well-funded Right has weakened many of those mandates, and we need a set of public policies that will protect and support—and provide economic and educational justice for—residents of urban America.

The strength of governing political and economic elites—and the power of mass movements to challenge them—do not imply that single individuals have no agency. They do; we each can make a difference wherever we "cast down our buckets," as civil rights leader Ella Baker used to say. But to actually change federal polices that amply benefit the groups that govern, individual agency needs to be compounded by the joint efforts of hundreds of thousands of citizens who are "street-marching mad," and who voice their demands for change together.

The fruits of a social movement for economic justice would not just benefit urban minorities. The many millions of white families who are poor, working class, or even lower-middle class would benefit as well. These families are not well served by the 21st century U.S. economy—and would certainly profit from policies (such as a doubling of the minimum wage) that substantially improved the economic milieu in which they—and their black and brown brothers and sisters—struggle to make a living.

I am aware that the presence of just policies does not guarantee equitable implementation or permanent success. As we have seen, civil rights victories such as affirmative action, and even minority voting rights, mostly in the South, are not secure. The end of the Vietnam War did not prevent the federal government from waging other unnecessary or unjust wars. Constant vigilance is necessary. *But it is considerably more likely that equitable practice will follow from good policy than from bad.*

Finally, it may be that some readers will feel that in arguing for a new social movement I am indulging in utopian thinking. To that charge I reply that *the utopian thinking of yesteryear becomes the common sense of today.* Imagine the late 19th century/early 20th century dreams of workers and labor organizers, and know that those utopian schemes for an eight-hour workday, a minimum wage, and some sort of financial assistance when fired, became federal policy in the 1930s, and are accepted as common sense by most Americans today. A million black American slaves were legally forced to walk across the South in 1805 to populate and cultivate fields in the new Louisiana Purchase. More black people were displaced during this journey than during the passage from Africa to the shores of the Atlantic (Berlin, 2003). Utopian dreams of freedom must have filled the thoughts of those enslaved men and women. Yet 60 years later, slavery was abolished, and black freedom was inscribed in the U.S. Constitution. I conclude from examples such as these that, far from useless, visionary thinking may be a necessary, prescient prelude to social progress.

Overview

In order to place current social policies and their antecedents in perspective—and to demonstrate how they were part and parcel of the lead up to the Great Recession—Part I describes the specific rules and regulations that led, ultimately, to a financial crisis of epic proportions. Part I also provides a historical understanding of how different things were during the post-World War II period, when social equality and widely spread prosperity were goals and practices of federal policy. I argue that many of these policies could be reinstated today.

Part II, Federal Policies that Maintain Poverty, demonstrates that during the last three to four decades, even in periods of strong economic growth, such as the late 1990s, a number of federal policies kept people—especially people of color—poor. Analysts typically do not link federal policies to the maintenance of poverty, to the lack of jobs that bedevils American workers, or to the increasingly large portion of employment that pays poverty and near-poverty wages. Yet federal policy is determinant. Congress, to take a blatant example, set the first minimum wage in 1938 at $3.05 (in 2000 dollars). When I wrote the first edition of *Radical Possibilities*, the minimum wage stood at $5.15—a mere two dollars more than in 1938. In 2013, the federal minimum wage is $7.25. In real terms the minimum wage is substantially lower than it was in the 1960s. Yet worker productivity has doubled. The minimum wage ensures that full-time year-round minimum-wage work (yielding $15,080) will not raise people out of poverty. As Chapter Four reports, minimum wage standards directly affect the wages of almost 10% of the workforce; and when we include those making one dollar more an hour than the minimum wage, this legislation affects the wages of almost one-fifth of the workforce.

There are other macroeconomic policies with consequences that produce hardship. These especially burden the lives of African Amerians and Latinos. Chapters Four and Five describe a number of federal policies that have egregious consequences. Among the policies considered (in addition to minimum wage legislation) are job training as a predominant federal anti-poverty policy when there have been too few jobs for graduates; ineffective federal implementation of policies that outlaw racial discrimination in hiring and housing; regressive income taxes that charge wealthy individuals less than half the rate charged during most of the first 60 years of the 20th century, yet substantially raise the payroll taxes paid by the working poor and middle class; and corporate tax policies in recent years that allow 60% of large U.S. corporations to pay no federal taxes at all (and in some cases to obtain billions in rebates); harsh anti-union laws and lack of federal protection for labor organizing; Federal Reserve Bank pronouncements that ignore its mandate to maintain a high level of employment; free trade agreements that send thousands of corporations—and their job opportunities—to other countries; and more. All these are part of the "free market" paradigm that led to the Great Crash in 2007.

Also important are policies that would help, but are conspicuous by their absence; for example, regulation of the minimum wage that kept low-paid workers' income at the median of highly-paid, unionized workers in the decades after World War II; federal programs for urban youth that would support college completion; a program of job creation in cities; and policies to enforce laws against discrimination in hiring. These and other alternative policy choices are advanced throughout the chapters of Part II.

Chapter Five closes Part II with an examination of the results of federally induced poverty and low-wage work on urban children and schools. It examines empirical research demonstrating ways in which conditions of few or no financial resources can undermine opportunities for children's educational success. Importantly, however, the chapter also describes the increasingly robust body of research documenting that when minority urban low-income families are provided with financial resources and support, the educational achievement of the children typically improves significantly.

Part III, Metro Area Inequities, moves the focus from federal policy to regional arrangements—and ways these inequitable distributions of decent housing, public transit, and entry-level jobs contribute to the maintenance of poverty, particularly for families of color.

While states are defined by geographic and political boundaries, metropolitan areas are shaped by regional markets—for jobs, housing, investment, and production. Metro areas account for over 80% of national output, and drive the economic performance of the nation as a whole. Each metro area is anchored by one or more cities.

Today, metropolitan regions are characterized by population growth, extensive inequality, and segregation. More than half of all poor people live in fiscally stressed suburbs or towns outside the central city, with an increasing number of neighborhoods of *concentrated* poverty there.

A number of social scientists concerned about poverty have investigated the unequal distributions of public and private investment, production, labor, and housing markets that characterize U.S. metro areas. They have found the following:

Most entry-level jobs for which those with limited education are qualified are located in the outlying suburbs; federal and state public transportation systems do not connect these job centers to areas where low-income minorities live, thus preventing poor people from commuting to the jobs there; state-allowed local zoning on the basis of income prevents affordable housing in most suburbs where entry-level jobs are located; failure to enforce anti-racial discrimination statutes confines most blacks and Latinos to central cities and segregated suburbs; and federal and state taxes paid by residents throughout metro regions (including inner cities) support profit-producing development that takes place primarily in the affluent suburbs. These inequitable regional arrangements contribute in important ways to joblessness and poverty in cities and urbanized suburbs, and to the poor quality of services such as public education there.

Chapters Six, Seven, and Eight chronicle the field of metropolitan studies and the consequences inequities there hold for urban education. Metro area inequities also imply an approach to urban problems that considers regional arrangements as in part determinant of local distress—in both neighborhoods and schools. The spread of concentrated poverty outside the central core also suggests that coalitions between inner cities and urbanized, segregated suburbs could produce powerful political constituencies for education and other reform.

The tendency of federal and regional policies and arrangements to maintain urban poverty and metropolitan inequities suggests that local neighborhoods are not isolated from these forces. Instead, urban neighborhoods—like urban schools—are not just "local"; they are extremely vulnerable to federal and regional mandates and practices. The local is not only a product of neighborhood and city cultures, and municipal regulations and policies, but is also shaped by federal and regional decisions both current and historical. Federal policies that sustain urban minority poverty, and metropolitan arrangements that spread resources unequally through regions, have been formative of the problems that plague urban neighborhoods and schools today.

Since the mid-1960s, the federal government has placed hundreds of programs in urban neighborhoods, ostensibly to ameliorate problems of poverty, unemployment, and inadequate housing—with little progress to show for it (although commercial downtowns often thrive). Philanthropic foundations and community-based organizations have also devoted time and energy to improving neighborhoods. There are major disappointments in these latter efforts as well, although there are some interesting successes. Chapter Eight closes Part III with an assessment of the efforts of regional coalitions of community organizations in metro areas, and finds that most of the successful endeavors arise from local groups that *join with others in metro-wide coalitions* to challenge federal or regional policies that maintain inequities. The results of these coalitions affirm the potential of alliances among inner-city and urbanized suburban educational interests.

Part IV, Social Movements, New Public Policy, and Urban Educational Reform, places the focus squarely on educators and ways in which they might join with others to make the fundamental changes that would ensure an equitable political economy, and equitable schooling, for all children.

Most books that critique aspects of the social system end with a list of policy recommendations. I want to go considerably further. I want to provide historically and theoretically based suggestions for ways we could obtain the policies I will recommend.

My reading of U.S. history tells me that social movements have been the most efficacious—if not the only—method of obtaining public policies that offer basic civil and economic rights to African Americans, Latinos, the white working class, and women (for example). Over a century of active political struggle has been necessary to obtain the most fundamental civil rights for black Americans. At least 20 years of activism were required before (white) women were permitted to vote in 1920. Three decades of labor battles were necessary before legislation in 1938 finally provided the legal end to child labor, an eight-hour day, a 40-hour week, and a minimum wage. This decades-long, vociferous advocacy also culminated in the 1930s in the right to overtime pay, unemployment insurance, social security, and the freedom to organize unions—many of the policies that led to the Golden Age of widespread prosperity and expanding equality.

And social movements have changed education. The radical tumult of the Progressive Era opened public schools to the community in many cities, and increased educational opportunity for immigrant families in the form of kindergartens, vacation schools, night schools, social settlement programs, and libraries. As a result of the Civil Rights Movement, "Head Start"—a radical innovation by activists in Jackson, Mississippi, these issues moved to center stage in federal educational policy—segregation of blacks in public schools became illegal.

In the 1970s and '80s, the women's, disabilities, and bilingual education movements also had significant impacts on schooling—opening up opportunities previously denied great numbers of students. Lastly, in recent years a movement of an invigorated and political Right has pushed both America and its schools in conservative directions: Education, economic opportunity, and civil rights have all been weakened by the rise of an organized, corporate-funded political Right.

Chapter Nine uses early civil rights activism (between 1900 and 1950) as an example of the historical, but insufficiently acknowledged, relationship between political contention and more equitable public policy. From NAACP Supreme Court victories before 1920, to the outlawing of all-white primaries in 1944, President Truman's Comprehensive Civil Rights Bill in 1946, and the *Brown* decision in 1954, social justice policy followed upon (and indeed, incited increased) public contention and activism by black Americans.

The South was an extremely dangerous place to publicly protest Jim Crow segregation. What allowed early activists to take on public contestation when it would almost certainly lead to fierce economic and physical reprisals? And later, what allowed southern sharecroppers, maids, cooks, beauticians, and day laborers—who may have spent entire lives accommodating their resistance—to take part in, no, to build, the massive public rebellions that began in the early 1950s? Chapter Nine attempts to answer these questions by utilizing innovations in social movement theory. This theorizing makes clear that raising people's consciousness about their oppression through reflection and talk (as in critical pedagogy classes) is not enough: Physical and emotional support for *actual participation in public contention is required.*

Chapter Ten, Building a Social Movement, applies this and other theoretical lessons to the current scene. How can we, in an era as ostensibly conservative as our own, motivate the active involvement of hundreds of thousands of Americans in a movement to change unjust economic and educational policies? Throughout, I make suggestions for what might have made the Occupy movement more successful. How can we make use of the finding that individual and group identities as agents of change develop not primarily because of educators' use of critical pedagogy or other consciousness raising (as crucial as these are), but because of actual participation in situations of political contention? Chapter Ten takes up these questions and suggests a variety of answers.

The final chapter puts urban educators at the center of attempts to build a politically progressive movement. One theoretically strategic reason for the centrality of urban educators is that *inside poverty-stricken city schools is the congealed result of economic and other social hardships impinging on urban families.* An enlightened focus on urban education and its practitioners could, therefore, highlight poverty wages, joblessness, and housing injustice as well as the lack of educational opportunities.

Moreover, placing educators at the center of a unified campaign is strategic logistically, because concerned city teachers and administrators are well positioned for movement-building in poor neighborhoods. They are in close proximity to, and able to have continual contact with, community adults and youth. Educators who have built up trust with these community members are in a perfect position to work with them in planning and implementing social activism.

The main task of Chapter Eleven, then, is to provide concrete activities that educators in various positions can utilize to make classrooms and schools progressive movement-building spaces. An important goal is to offer ways in which equity-seeking school reform groups (those working to maintain nurturing small schools, for example) and community organizers could join forces. Low-income parents are rarely told about school reforms being planned, and the changes typically have had little community support. If mainstream school reform groups listened, and adapted, to projects that education and other community organizers are engaged in, a synergy could be created that would propel reform outward into the community, and deeper into the school.

Among the most important participants in the process of movement building are urban youth. New research on youth organizations nationwide demonstrates an important consequence of young people's engagement in civic activism: Urban students involved in overt political struggle for their educational and other rights not only improve their schools and communities, but typically end up enhancing their own psychological development and educational achievement in the process. Chapter Eleven offers extensive protocols for working with students on progressive issue campaigns and direct political action.

Ghetto schools are often distressing places—toilets and sinks overflow, students are angry and sometimes violent, teachers appear worn down and cynical, computer rooms are full of broken machines, and academic achievement is depressingly low (Anyon, 1997). We understandably want to fix the problems we see—so we police and counsel students, provide staff development for the teachers, create smaller classes and schools, and mount court challenges for increased funding to pay for resources, new programs, and school buildings.

Sometimes these reforms work to make urban schools less stressful, disturbing places—and achievement scores may tick upwards. But if truth be told, these educational improvements rarely affect the material trajectory of most students' lives. A better K–12 education does not increase a child's life chances when there is no decent job the diploma will attract, and no funding that will stay with the graduate through a college degree.

Thus, public policies that concentrate on poverty, delimiting wages to bare subsistence, and supporting economic development in unreachable suburban job centers can make a mockery of safer, cleaner, better financed urban schools. The fact that macroeconomic and other public policies trump educational policy and urban school reform challenges us to attend to the larger social issues. As advocates for students we need to work for equity-seeking school change, but in order to measurably improve their futures we must enlarge the geographic and policy terrain over which we claim dominion.

This means that we need to reconsider what counts as educational policy. The elimination of economic, housing, and other public policies responsible for urban poverty and segregation must become companion goals of urban educational reform. Moreover, we need to contemplate the strategic strength that will be required to put humane public policies in place. I believe a social movement for economic and educational rights will be necessary to instantiate justice in legislative, judicial, and regulatory decisions. I have re-written this book to provide analyses that assist in understanding the ways egregious public policies undermine the urban educational enterprise, and to solicit educator activity for fundamental change.

PART I

The Great Recession

1

FINANCIALIZATION, ECONOMIC DISASTER, AND AN ALTERNATIVE

The enormous losses of money, homes, jobs, retirement income, and wealth during the Great Recession were a result of economic policies with long histories. These developments came to a head in the fall of 2008.

On September 18, 2008, the Chairperson of the Senate Banking Committee informed Congressional leaders that "We are literally days away from a complete meltdown of our financial system, with all the implications here at home and globally" (Herszenhorn, 2008). Despite an emergency infusion of federal money, lending by banks and other institutions soon ceased, and the financial system of the U.S. ground to a halt. Because the credit system was frozen (with no one willing to lend money), many industries and businesses—which typically depend on loans and other forms of credit to operate—were forced to slow or stop production. In the last three months of 2008, over a million and a half jobs were lost—the largest quarterly loss as a percentage of employment since the first quarter of 1975 (Shierholz, 2009; Uchitelle, 2009).

This implosion of the financial system shattered financial institutions that Nobel laureate economist Paul Krugman and others have identified as an extensive unregulated "shadow banking system" (2009, p. 177) that spun out of control. In a financialized economy, corporate profits that hitherto were invested in the "real" economy (for production and the provision of services) are used for speculation (e.g., placing bets) in stock, mortgage, currency, and other markets. While investment in industry and services (e.g., in teachers, school buildings, student services, and textbook production) spreads jobs and income around, financial speculation propels income upwards, to the relatively small handful of investors with sufficient wealth to invest in the private equity markets.

In this chapter I describe the main determinants of the Great Recession. Then, in order to contextualize developments that led to the crisis, I describe the

Keynesian post-World War II political economy that produced widespread prosperity and economic stability. I contrast this Golden Age to the recent free market/neoliberal configuration that led to the Great Recession. The purpose of describing and contrasting these historical periods is to show that the way things are now is not the way they have been or have to be. For the U.S. had—during the decades between World War II and the late 1970s—an economic system that grew a large middle class, and spread income and wealth widely among the population.

Financialization of the U.S. Economy

The bursting of an unsustainable housing bubble, during which U.S. house prices had for several years risen faster than the rate of inflation for the first time in a century, was the immediate trigger of the crisis (Shiller, 2006). The bubble burst in 2007, as the home and office building boom led to such over-supply that higher prices could no longer be supported (Baker, 2008).

But what allowed and encouraged the bubble and eventual economic trauma was the extreme financalization of the U.S. economy. Financialization is typically defined as the shift of economic activity from the production of goods and the provision of services to the accumulation of profits through interest, dividends, and capital gains accumulated through speculation and other forms of profit-making from debt (Kripner, 2005; Foster, 2007). Companies and banks, instead of investing profits in production, which spurs economic growth, spend the surplus on speculation. (In 2008, net U.S. investment in business production was half of what it was in 1965.) Funds spent on factory expansion, teachers, or interstate highways provide more widespread economic activity (i.e., stimulus) than money spent on speculation, whose activity and profits remain within the relatively small group of wealthy investors.

Increasingly, profits of U.S. companies have derived from financial speculation rather than production. In the 1960s, profits from finance were only 15% of all profits of companies in the U.S.; in 2006, almost half (41%) of all profits of U.S. companies came from finance; "a remarkable indication of the growth of finan-cialization in the U.S. political economy" (Tabb, 2008, p. 5).

From 1973 to 1985, the financial sector earned about 16% of all domestic corporate profits. In 1986, the figure was 19%. Between 2000 and 2009 the share of financial sector profits reached 41%—almost half of all domestic corporate profits (Johnson, 2009).

A primary method by which economic transactions are financialized is through securitization of debt and debt payment flows—the transformation of various types of financial assets and debts that are not convertible to cash into instruments that can be sold at a profit, or used to make speculative bets on the direction of asset prices of stocks, interest rates, currency levels, the price of oil or gas, etc. A prime example in the recent crisis is the securitization of home mortgages, which proceeds as follows. A bank or other mortgage issuing institution lends money to a home buyer in the form of a mortgage. Then, the bank sells the debt to a hedge fund or other entity that combines the mortgage with thousands of others. These bundles of mortgages are securities. Other investors then purchase the right to part of the income flow that results from the bundle as people pay their monthly mortgage fees. This risk has been passed on to the hedge fund or other investor who typically passes it on to others as they purchase rights to part of the mortgage payment flows. In addition to mortgages, the banks and hedge funds bundled and sold tranches of credit card holders' debt, student loans, life insurance policies, town and county assets, the price of wheat and gas, and just about any asset they could "securitize." Many of the banks targeted poor and immigrant communities in their mortgage schemes (Baker, 2008; Ferguson, 2012a).

Federal Deregulation of Banking

An important reason that financialization grew to dangerously large proportions was the gradual abandoning of rules that had prevented extreme financial risk-taking after the crash in 1929.

After the bank failures of the early 1930s, Congress passed the Glass-Steagall Act of 1933, which mandated the separation of commercial and investment banking. This separation would protect depositors in commercial banks from the hazards of risky investment and speculation—because while investment banks (which did not take deposits) could speculate with their funds, commercial banks could not (Zandi, 2008). Banks were prohibited from speculating with depositors' FDIC (Federal Deposit Insurance Corporation) insured moneys.

The banking industry had begun lobbying for the repeal of the Glass-Steagall Act during the 1980s. At President Bill Clinton's urging, a bipartisan vote (90–8) during his second term repealed the separation. The repeal, signed into law by Clinton in 1999, enabled deposit-taking banks such as Citibank, which was the largest U.S. bank by assets, to invest in financial instruments like mortgage-backed securities and collateralized debt obligations. The large banks began to make risky bets not only with wealthy investors' money, but with the contents of depositors' accounts.

A culmination of the drive toward deregulation occurred in 2004, during President Clinton's tenure, when the Securities and Exchange Commission voted unanimously to change the "net capital rule" so that major investment banks could borrow more (without commensurate increases in collateral like cash and assets) than regulations had previously allowed (Labaton, 2008). As a result, the major banks were soon highly leveraged. Before the deregulation of the net capital rule, leverage of $12 of debt to $1 of collateral was typical; the ratio soon shot up to 33 to one.[1]

Complex Investment Technologies

These financial products—particularly derivatives, so named because their value derives from underlying assets like stocks or loans—were created and utilized by private entities in the shadow banking system (the hedge funds, investment banks, hedge funds set up within banks, by loan companies like Countrywide Financial, by GMAC, the financial arm of General Motors, etc.). Because these entities had no public stock offering, they were completely unregulated (Krugman, 2009). Even the Sarbanes-Oxley Act, passed in 2002 in an attempt to restore confidence in the nation's securities markets (after Enron, WorldCom, and other accounting scandals cost investors billions of dollars), did not apply to hedge funds and other equity groups because they were private.

The derivatives market is exceptionally large—the value of derivatives traded is $3.3 trillion, and the value of the goods that are the subject of those derivatives trades in 2011 was $600 trillion (Fitz-Gerald, 2011). Ninety-six percent of the derivatives market is housed in five banks. The three biggest derivatives traders are also three of the biggest banks that take individual deposits: Bank of America, Citigroup, and JP Morgan Chase. The fact that these institutions have FDIC protection on most of their deposits makes the derivative contracts these banks sell attractive to investors. (Federal Deposit Insurance was intended to protect the content of depositors' bank accounts, never to protect banks that use their deposit base to engage in speculation.) (See Johnson, 2010.)

I have described the "hyper-financialization" (Minsky, 2008b) of our economy and other developments in the political economy that brought on the 2008 crisis. Because investment funds have gone primarily to speculation (rather than to investment in industry, public services, or infrastructure), in the last few decades, the latter three have weakened (Wallace-Wells, 2004; Mishel, Bernstein, and Allegretto, 2006). In regard to infrastructure—for example bridges, public toll roads, transit equipment, electric power plants, and sewer systems which are in disrepair nationwide—in order to make up for disappearing state taxes before and during the recession, some states, cities, and towns have put public properties up for sale, sold them to hedge funds or banks, or leased them in quasi-privatization speculative deals involving swaps and other fancy financial products (Morcroft, 2008; Morgenson, 2008; Stempel, 2008). When the deals collapsed, as many did during the Recession, the public authorities were placed in dire financial straights, continuing to owe the banks huge sums despite the collapse of the arrangement (Morgenson, 2008; Krugman, 2009). And the banks imposed enormous termination fees should the public entities want to extricate themselves from the deals. New York State, for example, has paid $243 million in recent years to extricate itself from swaps-related debt. "That money went straight from taxpayers' pockets to Wall Street" (Morgenson, 2012).

Education districts have lost significant sums as a result of complicated swap arrangements. Districts in Colorado, Pennsylvania, and California, among others, entered into complicated swap arrangements to attempt to lower their interest payments with J.P.Morgan (for example) and are, since the Recession, paying huge fees to the banks (Morgenson, 2010).

A recent analysis by the Service Employees International Union (SEIU) estimated that between 2008 and 2010, state and local governments have paid banks that arranged these transactions $28 billion to get out of the deals. SEIU estimates that New Jersey would have to pay $536 million to get out of its derivatives contracts, while California faces $234 million in such payments. Chicago is looking at $442 million in termination fees to unwind its transactions, and Philadelphia would have to pay $332 million (ibid.).

Federal Action to Stem the Crisis

When President Obama composed his economic rescue team in 2008, he appointed to regulatory positions executives from the largest banks and banking organizations that had been complicit in bringing about the crisis. These officials first prepared the Housing and Economic Recovery Act in June 2008, and then TARP—the Troubled Asset Relief Program—that gave and lent the largest banks $700 billion so that they would have cash on hand to make loans (which they basically did not do) and pay those who came collecting debts.

The amount grew, however, and by 2010 estimates were that the total amount of the bailout was $2 trillion to $3 trillion. And on November 27, 2011, Freedom of Information Act filings by Bloomberg News discovered that during the crisis, assistance to the largest banks by the Federal Reserve Board had been far larger. The federal government had not disclosed the larger figures. The actual amount,

> including loans, loan guarantees, securities purchases, and other commitments, was *$7.8 trillion,* with several hundred billion dollars in loans outstanding at any given time during the height of the crisis. *These low-interest loans generated at least $13 billion in additional profits for the banks that received them.* None of the banks had disclosed the size of these loans or their impact on profits.
>
> *(Ferguson, 2012a, p. 205)*

A federal economic stimulus of $787 billion by the federal government followed in due course, to attempt to jump start economic activity. Paul Krugman points out that "[t]he slumps that follow a financial crisis are usually nasty, brutish, and long. A realistic assessment was that the stimulus would have to deal with three or more years of severe economic pain" (2012, p. 122). And the U.S. economy is enormous, producing close to $15 trillion worth of goods and services every year.

> If the U.S. economy was going to experience a three-year crisis [which is what the federal officials thought], the stimulus was trying to rescue a $45 trillion economy—the value of output over three years—with a $787 billion plan, *amounting to well under 2 percent of the economy's total spending over that period.*

Thus, the stimulus, while it did create some jobs, was not nearly enough to prime the economic pump and put the millions of people who needed jobs back to work (ibid.).

Concerning the bailout of the large banks with taxpayer money, and the (at least) $13 billion in profit they accrued from it, former Labor Secretary Robert Reich was moved to ask why Americans didn't get equity in the firms when we bailed them out (that is, get part of the profits when things got better) like Warren Buffett did when he bailed out Goldman Sachs.

Bank Influence

Throughout the financial reform debate, the finance industry has waged an unprecedented assault on the democratic process, spending an estimated $1.4 million per day to influence Congress and hiring 70 former members of Congress and 940 former federal employees to lobby on their behalf (Connor, 2010).

As recent investigations have discovered, most large banks and hedge funds operated above the law, without regard for discovery or potential penalties. What penalties that have been ascribed have amounted to no more than 1% of their profits (Ferguson, 2012a). Despite their illegal activities, however, it is true that much of what the financiers did was legal. The laws that would have prevented mortgages, Community Development Corporations (CDCs), swaps, or risky financial speculation had been repealed. Bending to lobbying and other pressure, governments from Ronald Reagan to Bill Clinton formulated regulations that encouraged and even rewarded these strategies. And those who were caught point out that they were just "doing what everyone else was doing"; it was "business as usual." So the argument can be made that the crisis that has brought us such pain was, for the most part, not a product of a dysfunctional economic system, but was "merely" the capitalist system in action, the way the system works.

But it wasn't always this way. The U.S. had, for decades after World War II, an economy in which extreme financial risk was outlawed, and broad social equality (at least for whites) was a product of the way the system worked.

Contextualizing the Great Recession

Financial speculation is not new to the U.S. economy. The late 19th and early 20th centuries were littered with speculative crises (e.g., 1873, 1893, 1907, and 1914). The bank panic in 1907, for example, resulted from unsuccessful large-scale speculation in the stock market by the New York Knickerbocker Trust—and led to the establishment of the Federal Reserve System in 1913 to (attempt to) supervise the banks. Extensive financial speculation during the 1920s was a major contributor to the 1929 crash and the bank runs of the early 1930s. But the financialization that has taken hold of the U.S. economy since 1980 is singular in its intricate and arcane technologies and its global interconnectedness.

Intermittent periods of financialization, cycles of expansion, crisis and recession are recurring economic phenomena. And in mainstream academic and media accounts, these and other aspects of the U.S. economy typically appear as natural, perhaps inevitable, parts of an economy that constitutes a system unto itself. Just as descriptions of education that are bounded by school walls and education policies provide only a partial view of educational phenomena (Anyon, 1997; Anyon et al., 2009), so I argue here that economic matters abstracted from their political and social context miss important understandings. In order to contextualize reified views of the economy, I embed the economy in its social and political underpinnings. One way to theorize this embeddedness is to ascertain economic periods or "long waves" that seem to be associated with certain kinds of institutional arrangements and ideologies, their changes, and eventual decay (Diebolt, 2002). Political economists who utilize such an approach describe the institutions and cultures associated with periods of the economy as Social Structures of Accumulation (SSAs) (Kotz, 1987; Kotz, McDonough, and Reich, 1994; Tabb, 2007). When social structures of accumulation break down, crisis and stagnation occurs. I believe the crisis of 2008 may have inaugurated such a period of decay.

Institutions comprising an SSA include both domestic and international arrangements, broadly as well as narrowly conceived (Lippit, 2006). For example, domestic institutions may include the state of labor-management relations as well as individual unions; the character of industrial organization, and specific corporations; the role of money, banking, and finance, as well as individual banks and hedge funds; the role of the state in the economy; the line-up of political parties; the state of class, race, and gender relations; and the character of the dominant culture and ideology—that is, the habits, customs, and expectations that prevail in a particular society. The international institutions concern the trade, investment, monetary, financial, and political environment (ibid.; Kotz, McDonough, and Reich, 1994).

I describe the SSA of the two most recent periods, the post-World War II political economy and the "free market," neoliberal system, which followed.

The Keynesian Political Economy (1940–1980)

This social structure of accumulation was named after economic theorist and British Lord John Maynard Keynes, who was a major architect of the post-war Bretton Woods treaty of 1944 that laid out political and economic arrangements in and between nations of Europe and the U.S. In this SSA, the national economies, most particularly in the U.S., had "walls"—international trade was minimal and regulated, and federal economic policy could therefore have considerable traction within a nation's borders. Banking and other financial activities were closely regulated. A Securities Turnover Excise Tax—which an investor paid whenever a share of stock, bond, or other financial security was bought or sold (instituted in 1914 and doubled during the New Deal)—discouraged speculation and promoted investment (see Keynes, 1926, 1964; Minsky, 2008a). Unlike the "free market" theorists who preceded and who would follow him, Keynes argued that the market is inherently unstable, and does not adjust itself without intervention. Creation of demand (by households, businesses, and the government) and supply (of money for production and jobs) are among the mechanisms (interventions) that he believed must be utilized to adjust and stabilize the market. During the Keynesian SSA—for example, during the 1930s' New Deal, Harry Truman's Fair Deal, and the War on Poverty—public investment in the country's infrastructure (education, highways, research and development) was a major driver of the economy (Foster, 2008). Private non-residential investment in business and production was also high during the Keynesian SSA, stimulating the strong business growth of the period (ibid.).

A major economic goal of the federal government in the Keynesian political economy was to keep prices low and to maintain full employment (rather than to control interest rates and inflation, which have been the goals recently). Institutions like labor unions and labor-management relations were encouraged by enactment and implementation of supportive federal regulations.

Taxes on the wealthy were high: As I describe in more detail later, during the post-World War II decades the marginal (top) income tax rate for individuals with great wealth averaged 86% in the 1940s, 91% in the 1950s, 80% in the 1960s, and 70% in the 1970s. (The top marginal rate on income was lowered during the following decades, and since 2003 has been 35%.) Keynesian policies erected a social safety net (social security, unemployment insurance, welfare). The minimum wage was indexed to the median pay of highly unionized workers, so that it rose when unionized workers' pay rose (Ettlinger, 2006).

During this period, goals of education were discussed in terms of expanding democracy, rather than in business and accountability terms, as in more recent decades. The GI Bill increased opportunity for 16 million veterans and their families to attend college, receive job training, start businesses, and purchase their first homes (Madrick, 2009). Expansion of higher education, and civil rights and gender equity legislation of the 1960s and early '70s, increased access in line with the federal goals.

During the "Golden Years," as the Keynesian era is often called, inequality shrank from its height in 1929, just before the Depression. As the nation's economy was stimulated and regulated by federal policies, it grew substantially between 1945 and 1973. Working and middle income families received larger shares of the economic pie. Wages rose steadily and real median family income more than doubled from the late 1940s to the late '70s. (It rose less than 25% in the three decades following—with the increase largely accounted for by wives who entered the labor force (Leonhardt, 2008).) As I demonstrate in later chapters, real wages for working and middle income employees have actually stagnated or declined in most industries and sectors since the 1980s.

It is important to note, however, that most black American families did not share in the prosperity of the Golden Years. Nor, before the late 1960s, did the federal safety net reach them. Implementation of the 1930s' regulations had been left to states and localities, and southern politicians excluded agricultural laborers and domestic workers—the occupations of most southern blacks—from the minimum wage, social security, and welfare provisions. Moreover, as Ira Katznelson documents in *When Affirmative Action was White* (2005), returning black soldiers from World War II in both the North and South were often denied assistance of the GI Bill.

The Takedown of Keynesianism

In the mid-1970s, Keynesian policy in the U.S. met significant economic challenge. Stagflation (slow economic growth, high inflation, and high unemployment concurrently) had emerged in the early 1970s. Mainstream analysts attribute the demise of the Keynesian era to this long siege of stagflation of the 1970s (e.g., Krugman, 2009).

But some economists (including those in the SSA camp) suggest that there were additional causes of the decline in traction of Keynesian policy. For example, James Crotty (2005) points out that when globalization of industry developed in the late 1960s—as first apparel, shoe, television, then the auto and steel industries lost jobs to overseas competition—federal regulators in the U.S. were less able to manage the national economy, as it was becoming less contained within the nation's borders.

Crotty goes further to suggest that as the crisis (stagflation) continued and corporate profits dropped, business elites began to chafe under the expenses of the social compact that Keynesian policies had negotiated. The wage and benefit demands of "big labor," and the cost of "big government"—funded in part by high taxes on wealth—cut into profits. Federal policy had kept most wages and salaries high enough and prices low enough that the American consumer was able to purchase what U.S. industries produced. And businesses in the nationally bounded economy were indeed dependent on the American consumer's relative affluence. By the 1960s, corporations began to globalize in order to escape this dependence, the lower rates of profit, union power, and Keynesian policy constraints against financial speculation. The elites must also have felt threatened by the massive protests and social movements of the 1960s, which challenged both domestic and foreign policy of the U.S. David Harvey suggests that the takedown of Keynesianism was a bold attempt by corporate elites to restore the power they felt they had lost during the previous decades (2007).

When Ronald Reagan became President in 1981, the explicit assault on Keynesian practices began.

The Neoliberal, "Free Market" Political Economy (1981–?)

When, in August of his first year in office, President Ronald Reagan broke a national strike of 13,000 air traffic controllers and fired all but 2,000, he inaugurated a federal government publicly intent on freeing the market from the influence of unions, wage supports, and federal regulation of business.

Free market goals espoused by both Republican and Democratic administrations during the ensuing decades were to shrink government spending (e.g., privatize government services, and "end welfare as we know it," as Bill Clinton declared during his presidential campaign of 1993); balance the federal budget; roll back financial and other business regulations; free up international trade; and reduce taxes on wealth in attempts to stimulate the economy (rather than stimulating the economy by investing government funds directly, as in the previous period).

The belief system that accompanied these economic goals was termed neoliberalism, a renewal of Adam Smith's 19th century liberal ideal, in which "regulation was by competition and the market and not by the state, and in which each [person], thrown on his [or her] own resources, labored effectively for the enrichment of the society" (Galbraith, 1958/1998, p. 20). Individuals were free to make their way in the market through a surfeit of choices, and the market was free to, and capable of, adjusting and stabilizing itself without government or labor union interference.

In the decades since the Reagan revolution began, it has become clear that not all free market goals could be met—government spending has grown astronomically, and the federal deficit (over-budget yearly spending, adding to the national debt) in 2008 alone was $455 billion. (Even in Reagan's own administration, federal spending increased rapidly, on the military and Medicare, and interest payments on the soaring budget deficit (Madrick, 2009, p. 21).) It became standard government practice to intervene in the market by attempting to adjust interest rates, rather than creating jobs and other direct investment, as during the Keynesian era. And "free" trade became governed by complex international treaties and tens of thousands of pages of regulations.

Yet significant portions of the neoliberal, free market program were enacted. Taxes on corporations, for example, were sharply reduced. In the U.S., the share of the federal tax burden paid by corporations declined from 40% in the 1940s, to 26.5% in 1950, to 10.2% in 2000. In 2001, before the Great Recession, the corporate share of total federal taxes paid by corporations was down to 9.2% (Mishel, Bernstein, and Boushey, 2003).

State and local taxes paid by corporations also declined in the U.S. during the "free market" neoliberal period. In 1957, corporations provided 45% of local property tax revenues in the states, but by 1987 their share had plummeted to about 16% (Mishel, Bernstein, and Boushey, 2003). By 2002, the corporate share of total state and local taxes paid was only 2.9%, as states lowered their tax rates in what one analyst noted is the "disappearing state income tax" (Fisher, 2002).

Marginal tax rates on individuals were also sharply reduced from their levels in the Keynesian social structure of accumulation—from a high average of 91% during the 1950s to 35% since 2003 (Brookings Institute, 2008). Since the tax rates on the rich have plummeted, concentrated wealth and income accumulation by a few have climbed. The top 1% of income tax filers own 40% of all wealth in the U.S. and take home about a quarter of all income.

Middle-class taxpayers took up a good deal of the slack as taxes were slashed on corporations and wealthy individuals. Beginning with Reagan's administration, the effective tax rate of the middle-class (median income) family increased steadily: From 5.3% in 1948, to 24.63% in 1990. Payroll tax rates (FICA, or Federal Insurance Contributions Act for Social Security and Medicare, for example) paid by middle-class individuals have also risen dramatically: From 6.9% in 1950, to 31.1% in 2000 (Mishel, Bernstein, and Boushey, 2003).

In addition to tax goals, other items of the neoliberal agenda have been enacted as well: Former government functions—U.S. national security, armed forces, incarceration, postal service, welfare, and public education, among others—have been privatized to different degrees. And spending on the public sphere—such as education—has plummeted.

As indicated by the requisites of No Child Left Behind in 2001 and Race to the Top in 2009, K-12 public schooling also experienced a diminished sense of what counts as education, as goals of democratization through educational expansion after World War II gave way to technical goals of accountability through testing and the incorporation of business models like "total quality management" and privatization of services. During the late 1980s, business elites (led by corporate leaders of the Business Roundtable) developed a template for raised standards and high-stakes testing that was instantiated in the No Child Left Behind Act of 2001 (Emery, 2002) and continued in Race to the Top.

A final and remarkably important goal of the free market, neoliberal agenda was deregulation of financial institutions, which was implemented with the disastrous consequences I have already delineated. Analysts have described other consequences of "free market"/neoliberal action on American society: Stagnating wages (the share of U.S. national income going to wages and salaries reached its lowest recorded level in 2005), a vastly smaller middle class, diminished public sphere and safety net, and the increases in income and wealth inequality mentioned above, among others (Mishel, Bernstein, and Allegretto, 2006; Wolff, 2006, among many others).

What is not commonly remarked upon, but is centrally important in any sketch of "free market" policies, is that despite neoliberal theory that the market regulates itself, those decades—the 1980s, '90s, and early 2000s—were marked by almost continual crises of an economic nature: The Savings and Loan crisis of the early 1980s; the stock market crash of 1987; the crash in residential mortgages in 1994; the late 1990s Asian and Mexican crises; the 1998 Long-Term Capital Management hedge fund crisis, which the Federal Reserve feared might bring down the whole global finance system (Lowenstein, 2008); and finally the economic implosions of 2001 and 2008. Although the collapse of housing prices after the bubble of 2004–2005 is often cited in the media as having caused the 2008 crisis, as I have argued in this chapter, financial deregulation, risky speculation with other people's money, and the creation and use of complicated and abstruse, globally interconnected investment technologies, were underlying determinants of financial crisis (Stiglitz, 2008a; Krugman, 2009). And as Stiglitz reminds us, the extreme inequality of the system makes it fragile and prone to distress.

And neoliberal practice has proved catastrophic for most of us, while extremely profitable to only a few; it catapulted the U.S. (and the world) into a systemic crisis of truly cosmic proportions. I think it's abundantly clear that the capitalist class needs reigning in by federal regulation.

The economic crisis of 1929 was a systemic crisis, and the Keynesian form of capitalism that followed the Great Depression was structurally different from what preceded it, as I have pointed out above. It appears we have now experienced another systemic crisis, this time of the neoliberal form of capitalism. What will become of neoliberalism—what structural change to capitalism will take place— is not preordained, and, as in any crisis, there is opportunity, and different paths that can be taken. Yes, as many liberal/Left economists have argued, we certainly need to break up the big banks; yes, we should nationalize them and spread economic benefits more widely; and a financial transaction tax and increased taxes on the wealthy would put billions every year into U.S. coffers to be used to reconstruct the public sphere, fund education, create decent jobs and housing, etc. But for these—and perhaps more fundamental changes—we need a social movement.

In 2005, in the first edition of this volume, I argued that despite the conservative times we lived in and through (e.g., the Bush/Cheney years), social movements were a distinct possibility—as in the conservative 1950s when the civil rights movement developed national strength. And six years after my optimistic statement, there was Occupy Wall Street—whose language and resistance sparked a national conversation about financial political power and greed.

Despite the concentrated power and money I have described here, we have the numbers: The majority of families in the U.S. are working class (only about 20% of jobs are professional/executive positions). Most families are struggling. However brief the Occupy movement was, their 99% slogan and enthusiasm still reverberates widely. Now we have to change the practice. *We will need to utilize the strength and activism that lives in urban neighborhoods, and connect Occupy goals to the needs of those residents.* I come back to how we work for a better system in later chapters of this book.

Note

1 "Under a 33-to-1 leverage, a mere 3 percent decline in asset values wipes out a company. Had leverage stayed at 12 to 1, these firms wouldn't have grown as big or been as fragile" (Blinder, 2009).

PART II
Federal Policies that Maintain Poverty

2

THE ECONOMIC IS POLITICAL

Chapter One attempted to demonstrate that the Great Recession was a socially constructed product—a result of policies and actions by people in powerful positions over many years. In this and the next chapter I describe ways in which during *non*-recession years of the neoliberal period, times when the economy is not in crisis, policies that are part and parcel of the way the system has been set up also keep people, urban neighborhoods, and urban schools in poverty.

It is increasingly acknowledged that one of the most important causes of poorly funded, staffed, and resourced schools is the poverty of the families and neighborhoods in which the schools are located. What is rarely acknowledged, however, is the proactive role of the federal government in maintaining this poverty—and therefore poverty education.

All economies depend on government regulations in order to function. Capitalism would not be capitalism without Constitutional and other federal provisions that make legal the private ownership of property, the right of business to charge more for products than the cost of producing them, or the right of corporations to keep those profits rather than sharing them with workers or employees. The 14th Amendment to the Constitution, passed in 1867, has been recently interpreted by the Supreme Court to turn corporations into "persons" so they would be free from government "interference." Because economies are maintained by rules made by governments, economic institutions are inescapably political; they function according to determinative macroeconomic policies.

This chapter demonstrates that the poverty of U.S. families is considerably more widespread than commonly believed—and is catastrophic in low-income urban neighborhoods of color. I show that—contrary to the dominant rationales that posit "underclass" deficits as causal—the basic reason people are poor is that there are not enough jobs paying decent wages. In cities and impoverished suburbs, the harsh economic realities of poverty shape the lives of parents of school children, and therefore the lives of their children as well. Neighborhood poverty also impacts on the education students receive by contributing to low school funding levels, poorly paid teachers, and a lack of resources. Since the most common school reform strategies of the 21st century—high-stakes testing, school closure, charter schools, and privatization—do nothing to ameliorate the powerful effects of poverty on education, it is important to clarify the extent of poverty and how policy keeps families and students (and schools) poor.

I provide an overview of national poverty as a backdrop to the situation in urban America. The next chapter describes federal policies that maintain this poverty and the paucity of opportunity, and suggests alternatives to ameliorate the situation and thereby buttress the prospects of low-income families and schools.

Poverty

Poverty is, of course, typically a function of how much an adult makes a year in wages or other kinds of income. Wage trends, therefore, are fundamental to poverty levels.

In the three decades before the Great Recession, 70% of American employees saw their wages fall (in constant dollars—that is, adjusted for inflation). Even with the economic strength of the late 1990s, a majority of workers made less (in constant dollars) in 2000 than they had in 1973. New college graduates earned $1.10 less per hour in 1995 than their counterparts did in 1973. The earnings of the average American family did improve slightly over this period, but only through a dramatic increase in the number of hours worked and the share of families in which both parents worked (Lafer 2002; Mishel, Bernstein, and Boushey, 2003).

Some of the largest long-term wage declines were among entry-level workers (those with up to five years' work experience) with a high school education. Average wages for male entry-level high school graduates were 28% lower in 1997 than two decades earlier. The decline for comparable women was 18% (Economic Policy Institute, 2000).

The Great Recession exacerbated this trend of falling wages. In addition to creating massive unemployment and *under*employment, the Recession destroyed many of the remaining good jobs (those with decent pay and benefits). Jobs created since February 2010 pay, on average, substantially lower wages than jobs lost during the Recession. The biggest job losses during the Recession were those paying between $19.05 and $31.40 an hour. The largest gains since 2010 were of jobs paying $9.03 to $12.91 an hour—low-wage work.

> Three low-wage industries (food services, retail, and employment services) added 43% of net employment growth during that time. Better-paying industries (like construction; manufacturing; finance, insurance and real estate; and information) did not grow, or did not grow enough to make up

for recession losses … Other better-paying industries (like professional and technical services) saw solid growth, but not in their mid-wage occupations. And steep cuts in state and local government have hit mid- and higher-wage occupations the hardest.

(National Employment Law Project, 2012b; Zumbrun and Shobhana, 2011)

Low wages continue to predominate and are an important cause of poverty. (Low-wage workers are those whose hourly wage is less than the earnings necessary to lift a family above the official poverty line—in 2013, $23,550 for a family of four.)

The percentage of people who work full time, year round yet are poor is staggering. In 2000, *at the height of a booming economy*, almost a fifth of all men (19.5%), and almost a third of all women (33.1%) earned poverty-level wages working full time, year round. In the same year, over one in four black men (26.3%), over one in three black women (36.5%) and Hispanic men, (37.6%), and almost half of Hispanic women (49.3%) earned poverty wages working full time, year round (Mishel, Bernstein, and Schmitt 2001).

For the first edition of *Radical Possibilities* I analyzed figures provided by the Economic Policy Institute to calculate the overall percentage of people who work full time, year round, yet make *poverty-zone* wages. *I defined poverty zone as wages up to 125% of the official poverty threshold* needed to support a family of four at the poverty level. The analysis demonstrated that in 1999, *during a strong economy, almost half of people at work in the U.S. (41.3%) earned poverty-zone wages*—in 1999, $10.24/hour ($21,299/year) or less, working full time, year round (ibid., Table 2.10, p. 130). Two years later, in 2001, 38.4% earned poverty-zone wages working full time, year round (in 2001, 125% of the poverty line was a $10.88 hourly wage) (ibid., p. 134). These figures indicate that even in "good times" the U.S. pyramid of wages sits squarely on the shoulders of almost half of U.S. employees, who are the working poor—making only slightly more than poverty, although working full time, year round.

In 2009, after the Recession had officially ended, more than a quarter (25.7%) of the workforce were in jobs paying *actual poverty* wages (up to $21,654, or $10.55/hour for a family of four in that year). More than half (57.5%) of poverty-wage workers were women. More than half (56.8%) were white. Fourteen percent were black, and 23% were Latino.

Almost half of poverty-wage workers—44.3%—had some college, associates, or a bachelor's degree in 2009. In addition, an increasing percentage of college educated workers were jobless or underemployed—in jobs that did not require a college education. In 2011, 53% of college graduates, up from 41% in 2000, were jobless or underemployed (Fottrell, 2012; Weismann, 2012). These last statistics reveal the current inability of a college education to guarantee a good job. The creation of good jobs by government and business is required. I return to this issue later.

It is important to note that the figures above on workers who are poor or "almost" poor are based on official federal standards. Here are the latest official statistics as of this writing. The U.S. poverty rate was 15.0% in 2011, basically unchanged from 15.1% in 2010. The number of people the federal government counted as living in poverty in the U.S. was 46.2 million in 2011; in 2011, over one-third of black children (38.8%) and Hispanic children (34.1%) were living in poverty. The poverty rate for families with children headed by single mothers hit a high of 40.9% in 2011 (Shierholz and Gould, 2012).

These figures are tragically high. But federal calculations do not capture the fact that families with much higher incomes than the U.S. guidelines are in actuality quite poor. For example, according to federal guidelines, a single mother with two children with an income one dollar higher than $19,530 in 2013 is *not* considered officially poor. And a family of four with an income of over $23,550 is not considered poor. These cut-offs are, quite obviously, much too low.

As I demonstrate later, more realistic measures of poverty increase the percentages of who is considered poor (and near poor) substantially.

For example, the 2010 Census used a Supplemental Poverty Measure (SPM) in addition to the standard metric. By this new measure, a staggering *one in three people in the U.S. were poor or near poor*. Over 49 million Americans were below the poverty line and an additional 51 million were near poor—with incomes less than 50% above the poverty line. The SPM is intended to address the fact that the standard measure ignores the

> hundreds of billions of dollars the needy receive in food stamps, tax credits and other programs, and the similarly large sums paid in taxes, medical care and work expenses. The new method, called the Supplemental Poverty Measure, counts all those factors and adjusts for differences in the cost of living, which the official measure ignores.
>
> *(DeParle, Gebeloff, and Tavernise, 2011; see also Short, 2011; Citro and Michael, 1995).*

Many social scientists have come to believe that even this supplemental metric (with its threshold at 150% of official cutoffs) provides guidelines that are unrealistically low. These scholars argue that individuals and families with incomes up to 200% of government thresholds are poor. The official formula for figuring poverty—designed by federal employee Molly Orshansky in 1963 and used in the War on Poverty—utilized data collected in the 1950s. The formula Orshansky devised was based on the price of a minimal food budget (as determined by the Department of Agriculture). She multiplied the cost of food by three, to cover housing and health care costs. This figure, adjusted for family size, was the level below which families and individuals were designated poor.

Research in the 1950s showed that families spent about a third of their budget on food. Since that time, however, the costs of housing and health care have skyrocketed. Thus, most families today spend only about a fifth of their income on food, and considerably more on housing and health care.

A recent national assessment of working families concluded that *twice the official poverty line* is a more realistic measure of those who face critical and serious hardships in the U.S. The research discussed next documents that working families with income up to 200% of the poverty line experience practically as many hardships as families who are *officially* poor (Boushey, Brocht, Gundersen, and Bernstsein, 2001).

A calculation of the individuals who earned 200% of the poverty level or less in the strong economy of 2001 ($17.40/hour or $36,192/year) demonstrates a much larger percentage of poor employees than was commonly acknowledged: *84.3% of Hispanic workers, 80% of black workers, and 64.3% of white workers made wages at or under 200% of the official poverty line* (Mishel, Bernstein, and Schmitt 2001).

And thus a calculation of the *families* of those workers living with earnings up to 200% of the poverty line reveals that black and Latino families face the greatest financial hurdles. Over 50% of black and Latino families earned less than 200% of the poverty level, compared to only 20.3% of white families, even though white families make up the majority (50.5%) of families that fall below 200% of the poverty level (ibid.).

Families headed by a worker with less than a high school education were the most likely to fall below 200% (68.6%), but *over three-fourths of families who fell below the 200% cutoff were headed by a worker with a high school education or more.*

Another indication of the failure of higher education to secure good wages before the Recession is the fact that *over a third (33.6%) of families at or below 200% of the poverty line were headed by a worker with some college or a college degree* (ibid.). And an indictment of the failure of full-time work to provide a decent living is the fact that a full half (50%) of families falling below 200% of the poverty line had a full-time, year-round worker (ibid., p. 15).

The latest data concerning 200% of the poverty line are from 2010, and indicate that *over one third of people in the U.S. (over 100 million people) were living below twice the poverty line in that year* (Mishel, Bivens, Gould, and Shierholz, 2012).

Figure 2.1 demonstrates that the measure of 200% of the poverty rate more than doubles the rate of those considered poor from 15% to 34.4%. Over a third of the population in poverty is a figure typically associated with "undeveloped countries," not the U.S.—yet it characterizes us more accurately than do official census figures.

Costing out expenses of poor families demonstrates that families must have an average income of at least twice the current poverty level to cover basic expenses. "These family budgets include only the most essential living expenses and are based on modest assumptions about costs" (Levinson, 2012).

Even if one utilizes the standard, much less realistic or comprehensive federal guidelines, the results can be dramatic. For example, in Figure 2.2 we see that the percentage of the poor who are in deep poverty has increased dramatically over recent decades even by official measures.

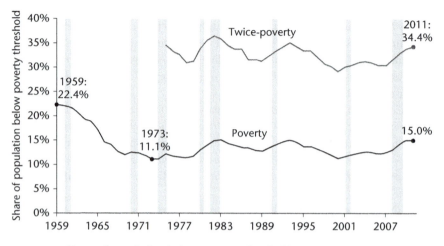

FIGURE 2.1 Share of population below poverty threshold

Source: Economic Policy Institute, SWA. http://stateofworkingamerica.org/explore/?subject=
poverty&demographic=0&x=67&y=16

Urban Poverty

Most metro area poverty today is urban poverty. Demographer Myron Orfield
analyzed the distribution of poverty populations in the 25 largest metropolitan
areas in the U.S. and found that about two-thirds of the U.S. poor live in central
cities and what I call "urbanized," financially distressed suburbs (Anyon, 2011a).
(Only about a quarter of the poor in metro areas is rural, with the rest scattered in
other suburbs.) The 2010 census revealed that a slight majority of the poor live
not in inner cities, but in inner-ring and other suburban areas—most of which are
fiscally stressed, and segregated. As has been the case since the mid-1960s, most of
the urban poor are black or Latino—native, or immigrant. Part III takes up the
issue of poverty in the suburbs.

The proportion of K-12 students who attend high poverty schools has
increased by 42% since 2000, with almost half of black and Latino students in such
schools (and 5% of whites) in 2009.

As we will see in later chapters, the concentration of African American and
Latino poor in low-income urban areas is due not only to a lack of jobs with
decent pay (and insufficient income to support a move out if desired), but to the
lack of federal and state implementation of anti-racial discrimination laws, the
lack of affordable housing outside of urban areas, and state-enabled local zoning
exclusions based on race and social class (income). Part III presents a detailed
discussion of this new metropolitan demographic, its causes, and the implications
it presents for urban education.

The statistics in this chapter relay in a fairly staid manner what is actually a
potentially inflammatory political situation. A humane reckoning of poverty

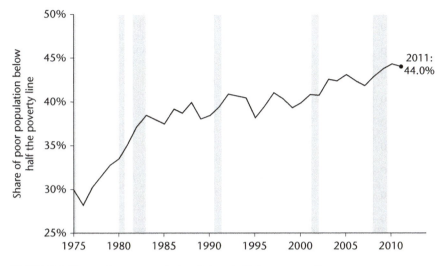

FIGURE 2.2 Share of poor population below half the poverty line

Source: Economic Policy Institute, SWA. http://stateofworkingamerica.org/chart/swa-poverty-figure-7g-share-poor-deep-poverty/

reveals that the vast majority of African Americans and Latinos who have jobs, and more than two-thirds of employed whites, do not earn enough to live on. This outrages me, as the experience must anger those who live it. But the situation is not immutable. Economies are indeed political, regulated by officials elected and appointed who formulate legislation, legal decisions, and other policy. These officials, and their mandates, can be changed—but only if all of us who are incensed by the policies' indecency stand together.

Before I close this section on poverty I want to offer two examples of existing federal policies that mitigate the extent of poverty in this country. The first and most dramatic example—an outgrowth of social movements in the 1930s—has vastly shrunk the percentage of one particular population that was overwhelmingly poor. Just as the U.S. cut poverty in half during the short-lived "War on Poverty" in the late 1960s (before that war was abandoned) by giving poor people funds, so *Social Security* payments have significantly lowered the poverty rate of elderly Americans (Figure 2.3).

The second example is the set of policies such as food stamps, the earned income tax credit, nutrition assistance, school lunch, and housing subsidies that target the poor. Research using the SPM, discussed above, offers a picture of how these policies make a difference in the lives of the working poor and poor families. However, the difference is very small. For example, the earned income tax credit, which makes the most difference, mitigates the incidence of official poverty by only 2%. The Earned Income Tax Credit (EITC), a federal tax credit for low- and moderate-income working families and individuals, was designed to encourage and reward

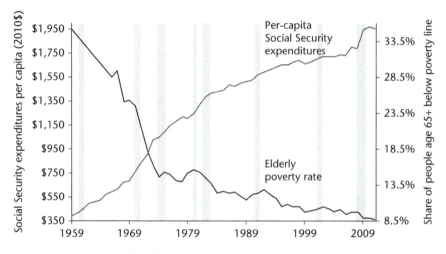

FIGURE 2.3 Per capita Social Security expenditures and the elderly poverty rate, 1959-2011

Source: Economic Policy Institute, SWA. Updated September 13, 2012. http://stateofwork-ingamerica.org/chart/swa-poverty-figure-7r-capita-social-security/

Notes: Authors' analysis of Current Population Survey Annual Social and Economic Supplement *Historical Poverty Tables* (Tables 2 and 3) and Social Security Administration (2009, Table 4a). No formal data exists for 1960–1965. The dotted lines denote a linear extrapolation between 1959 and 1966. Shaded areas denote recessions.

work. To claim the credit, a taxpayer must have earnings from a job. The EITC is "refundable," meaning that if it exceeds a low-wage worker's federal income tax liability, the Internal Revenue Service refunds the balance to the taxpayer.

The EITC's primary recipients are working parents with children. The credit rises with earned income until it reaches a maximum (which varies by the number of qualified children). "For 2013, the phase-outs begin at $17,530 for single filers and $22,870 for married filers, and the average size of the credit is expected to be $2,828 for a family with children and $280 for a family without children." By supplementing the earnings of low-paid workers, the EITC and The Child Tax Credit (CTC), a related credit that's designed to help offset the cost of child-rearing, lifted 9.4 million people, including 4.9 million children, out of officially designated poverty in 2011. Of these 4.9 million children, the EITC alone lifted 3.1 million of them out of poverty. Researchers have found even such meager supplements to poor families make a positive difference in their lives and in the children's school achievement (Marr, Charite, and Huang, 2013).

Jobs

The preceding section argued that people are poor because they cannot obtain jobs that pay enough to raise families from poverty. I provided information on how poor many full-time U.S. workers are, by various measures. Now I focus on the jobs that are (and are not) available.

Since the implosion of the financial system in 2007 and the lock on bank lending to businesses, we have heard a lot about the large numbers of jobless, unemployed, long-term unemployed, and underemployed in this country. The media are replete with stories about small businesses retrenching, closing, and laying off workers; consumers not buying goods; and, as I noted above, the fact that so many recent college graduates are jobless or underemployed in jobs not requiring college diplomas. One would not be remiss to assume that the severe lack of jobs in our country was a new phenomenon, brought on by the Recession.

The present section documents that this is far from the truth: As I reported in the first edition of *Radical Possibilities*, even during the "strong" economy of the 1990s, there were far fewer jobs than job seekers. The Great Recession has exacerbated this long-term trend.

For three decades, politicians, policy makers, and corporate spokespeople have been arguing that the U.S. must improve the education system for economic reasons—the mantra has been that most jobs require high skill levels and thus increasing education is necessary. This mantra is highly misleading. I argued in 2005 that most job openings in the next ten years will *not* require either sophisticated skills or a college degree. Seventy-seven percent of new and projected jobs will be low-paying. Only a quarter of the new and projected jobs are expected to pay over $26,000 a year.

The statement that increased education is necessary because of increasing job requirements is, if anything, less true now than it was in 2005. In 2012, the Bureau of Labor Statistics projected that of the ten occupational groups that will add the most jobs between 2010 and 2020, "*five do not even require a high-school education.* Three require high school, and one category requires a two-year associate degree" (Faux, 2012, p. 2).

Nine of the ten occupational groups that will add the most jobs in the next decade, that is, will require on-the-job training only, and will not require a college diploma. Most will be in areas like service and retail, food preparation and fast food restaurants, home health aides, telephone customer service representatives, laborers, clerks or cashiers—all of which typically pay poverty-zone wages (Bureau of Labor Statistics, 2012b).

An interesting point here is that most low-wage workers now work for large corporations, rather than small businesses, as used to be the case. Huge retail companies like Walmart and Gap, drug and food chains like Walgreens and A and P, and huge food dynasties like McDonalds hire most of the country's low-wage employees.

The typical job of the future is not in information technology, management, or high finance; it is in these low-wage retail and service positions. The *professional* occupations will also need more workers, but in much smaller numbers than the openings requiring less education.

One can see why over half of recent college graduates are jobless or in jobs that do not require a bachelors. The paucity of jobs for college educated workers challenges the educational reform focus on "college for all," and makes one wonder why we are not providing meaningful vocational (career and technical) education for the skilled work that does exist. A telling statistic here is the fact that "22 percent of those with an associate's degree in vocational/technical areas earn more than the median earnings of those with a BA ... and 25 percent of those with a BA earn less than those with an associate's degree" (Carnevale, Strohl, and Smith, 2009, p. 22).

I want to note that the assertion that jobs are plentiful—if only workers were qualified to fill them—has been a central tenet of federal policy for 20 years. In 1982, the Reagan administration eliminated the Comprehensive Employment and Training Administration (CETA), which by 1978 had created almost 2 million full-time jobs, and substituted a major federal job training program (Job Partnership Training Act) (Lafer, 2002, pp. 1–2). Since then, and continuing today, job training has been the centerpiece of federal and state efforts to solve both the unemployment problem and the poverty problem. For almost all of this time, however, the federal government has not collected data on job availability (vacancies). If they had, and if they had consulted studies that had been carried out, they would have found that all the evidence demonstrates that at any given time there are far more unemployed people than there are job openings (ibid., p. 23; see also Pigeon and Wray, 1999, among others). The federal government has spent $85 billion on job training since the Reagan years, claiming all the while that there are jobs for those who want them (ibid.).

In an exhaustive analysis, labor economist Gordon Lafer demonstrates that:

> over the period 1984 to 1996—at the height of an alleged labor shortage—the number of people in need of work exceeded the total number of job openings by an average of five to one. Moreover, *decent* jobs were even more scarce. In 1996, for example, during that 'strong' economy I've mentioned before, the country would have needed 14.4 million decent jobs in order for all low-income people to work their way out of poverty. However, there were at most 2.4 million such openings available to meet this need; of these, only one million were in full-time, non-managerial positions.
>
> *(Lafer, 2002, p. 3)*

Thus, "there simply are not enough decently paying jobs for the number of people who need them—no matter how well trained they are"—and therefore job training programs cannot hope to address more than a small fraction of either the unemployment or poverty problems (ibid.; see also Eisenhower Foundation, 1998; Jargowsky, 1998).

Lafer also demonstrated that throughout the 1984 to 1996 period, the total number of vacancies in jobs that paid above poverty wage was never more than one-seventh the number of people who needed those jobs, and "the gap between jobs needed and decently paying jobs available was never less than 16 million" (2002, pp. 34–35).

This suggests that we need to find ways to create good jobs—with decent pay (at least $18.50/hour in 2012), vacation, and benefits (Schmitt and Jones, 2012). In 2007, before the Recession, only 25% of jobs could be considered good jobs. The share of good jobs shrank by 2.8% by 2010, to 22.2% (Mishel, Bivens, Gould, and Shierholz, 2012).

In the last 20 years or so, corporate pronouncements and federal economic policies (regarding expansion of visas for foreign workers, for example) have often been premised on the assumption that there has been a U.S. shortage of highly skilled computer technicians. And employers report that scientific and technical positions are often hard to fill. Large corporations have argued that there are no skilled workers at home as a rationale for transferring computer-based and other operations to other countries. Although there are some shortages, the evidence suggests that there is no actual shortage of programmers or systems analysts, which have been a favorite target of outsourcing. "Rather, technology companies have hired lower-wage foreign programmers while thousands of more experienced (and more expensive) American programmers remained unemployed" (Lafer, 2002, p. 54; see also Lardner, 1998).

Even in occupations such as nursing where there have been shortages, most technical professions are quite small as a share of the overall workforce, and therefore the total number of such jobs going begging has never been a significant source of job openings. For example, *the combined total of STEM occupations—relatively high paying technical jobs in science, technology, engineering, and mathematics was only 6% of U.S. employment in 2011* (Cover, Jones, and Watson, 2011).

Furthermore, as computer technology has been adapted by business, "computer work" has been highly differentiated, with technical knowledge utilized by a relatively small group of well-paid specialists, and the vast majority of daily computer operators carrying out tasks in relatively low-wage occupations with few educational requirements (social workers, secretaries, credit card and computer call center operators, etc.).

Compounding the problem for entry-level workers, college-educated persons may be crowding them out. Research by Richard Murnane and Frank Levy shows that controlling for a person's mathematics or reading skills while a high school senior eliminates a substantial portion of the growth in the college-to-high-school wage premium in a later period (for women essentially all, and for men about one-third). *This suggests that it is basic high school-level skills that are increasingly in demand by employers, who are relying more and more on college completion as a screen to get the people who are more likely to have them* (Murnane and Levy, 1996, p. 29; see also Pigeon and Wray, 1999).

That employers hire college-educated workers for jobs that require high school skills (e.g., hiring college graduates as file clerks in law offices) helps to explain why a more highly educated workforce does not necessarily earn higher wages. As entry-level employees obtain more education, employers merely ratchet up the requirements (see Galbraith, 1998; Moss and Tilly, 2001). Indeed, if all—or even most—employees had college degrees, the vastly increased surplus would allow employers to pay even less than they do now.

African Americans and Latinos

As discouraging as the numbers on poverty and jobs are for the U.S. as a whole, they are much more discouraging for people of color. Rates of unemployment, underemployment, joblessness, and poverty are all much higher than—and sometimes double—the rates for whites. *And if the millions of African Americans who are incarcerated were counted in the poverty and unemployment figures, these rates would be even higher for this group* (Pettit, 2012).

Figure 2.4 compares official unemployment rates by race and ethnicity, from 1979–2011.

As I (among many others) have documented elsewhere, high unemployment and underemployment of adults in a family—like joblessness and poverty—are associated with decreased achievement of the family's school children (Anyon, 2005b). I return to this important issue later, when I report studies that show that even small increments of income and support for a low-income family can increase the children's school achievement.

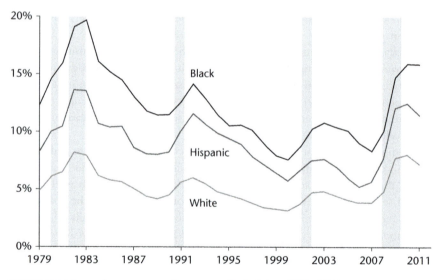

FIGURE 2.4 Unemployment rate, by race and ethnicity, 1979–2011

Source: Economic Policy Institute, SWA. http://stateofworkingamerica.org/chart/swa-jobs-figure-5i-unemployment-rate-race/

Note: Shaded areas denote recessions.

How to Create Good Jobs

After I delivered a talk in Florida several years ago on the lack of jobs in America—and argued that governments should be the "employers of last resort," a member of the audience rose and said, "But the government can't just create jobs!" I'm here to challenge that belief. Governments create jobs all the time—millions of them—including jobs for teachers, police officers, firefighters, soldiers, sailors, astronauts, doctors, scientists, antiterrorism agents, park rangers, diplomats, governors and congressmen.

In 2012, government at all levels—federal, state, and local—employed 22 million Americans, with the largest segment working in public education. And the federal government created jobs for millions of unemployed during the Great Depression—as an example, in the Works Progress Administration (WPA). This federal stimulus:

> employed 8.5 million people in the construction of 650,000 miles of roads, 125,000 public buildings, 75,000 bridges, 8,000 parks, and 800 airports. The WPA also administered the WPA Federal Art Project, the Theater Project, and the Writers' Project, which provided jobs for unemployed artists, actors, and writers.
>
> *(Merriam-Webster, No Date)*

People were paid with federal tax dollars to perform important tasks. World War II—probably the largest stimulus to the U.S. economy in the 20th century—created jobs for millions and ended unemployment, as the war effort got factories moving. In the 1970s, the federal government created the Comprehensive Employment and Training Administration (CETA) and almost 2 million full-time jobs, many for veterans returning from Vietnam. President Obama's stimulus in 2009, the American Recovery and Reinvestment Act, did not directly create jobs, but gave money to states to create jobs—paving roads, fixing bridges, teaching children and youth. This stimulus, relatively small as it was, did create and save a good number of jobs—including those of 400,000 teachers (Christman and Riordan, 2011; Folbre, 2011; *New York Times*, 2012).

The federal government could do much more. It could give money to local organizations to hire community people to do work that needs to be done in urban and rural neighborhoods—building low-income housing, making parks, and outfitting schools in poor areas with technology and air conditioning. Money could be given to businesses and organizations to hire people to do any number of things. There is no shortage of proposals (see Christman and Riordan, 2011; Folbre, 2011; Mishel, Bivens, and Eisenbrey, 2011).

A particularly interesting proposal was put forward by Representative Jan Schakowsky, Democrat of Illinois, in her Emergency Jobs to Restore the American Dream Act, which would provide funds to pay for over 2 million jobs in schools, health care, and community service. Schakowsky's proposal would be funded through the creation of "higher tax brackets for millionaires and billionaires, elimination of subsidies for major oil companies, and closing of corporate tax loopholes that encourage offshoring of American jobs" (http://schakowsky.house.gov/index.php?option=com_content&view=article&id=2975&Itemid=8).

The funds to put people to work teaching, building roads, and improving the infrastructure of communities will probably have to come from higher taxes on (and increased tax collections from) corporations and the rich. As I discuss in great detail in Part IV, we will most likely need sustained political struggle to shake free such funds. In order for injustice to create an outrage that can ultimately be channeled into public demands, knowledge of the facts is necessary, and an appreciation of the consequences must be clear. I hope this chapter clarifies the situation regarding poverty and jobs. It is also extremely important, and will be discussed at length later, that people who are poor come to see their situation as not at base a result of their own failure, but as resulting from systemic causes. That is, if governments created enough jobs, and if businesses paid higher wages, workers would not be poor.

And knowledge is crucial to an accurate understanding of what plagues urban education. We must know where the problem lies in order to identify workable solutions. We can only win the War on Poverty and poor schools if we know where the poverty originates. The next chapter describes one important source: federal policies that maintain low-wage work and unemployment in urban areas, and ways these can set up failure for the families and schools there.

3

FEDERAL POLICIES THAT KEEP PEOPLE POOR

Americans have long had faith in education to raise the economic prospects of the poor. And the federal government, primarily since the 1981–89 Presidency of Ronald Reagan, has relied on the policy assumption that increased education (e.g., college or job training) would put the poor to work, and thereby substantially reduce U.S. poverty. But workers of all races now have more education than ever before, and as the previous chapter demonstrates, wages have been falling across the board for more than two decades and poverty has grown. For an increasing number of Americans, but for African Americans and Latinos especially, job training, a two-year associate's degree—or even a bachelor's degree—does not ensure escape from poverty or even near-poverty wages. Indeed, despite increased education levels in the last few decades, *the share of workers earning poverty wages is about the same as in 1973.*

I believe it is important for educators, public policy analysts, and the public to take hold of the fact that current economic policies yield widespread low-wage work even among an increasingly educated workforce. This phenomenon seriously strains the credibility of school reform as a solution to the problems of the urban poor. Unless we make some changes in the way the political economy works, economic policy will continue to trump not only urban school reform, but the individual educational achievement of urban students as well.

Federal Policies that Maintain Low-Wage Work

Federal macroeconomic policies that conduce to widespread poverty-wage work in the U.S. include (among others) minimum wage legislation, anti-unionization laws, lack of job creation *except* of high-end scientific and technical investments, class-biased regulations of the Federal Reserve Bank, technology that replaces

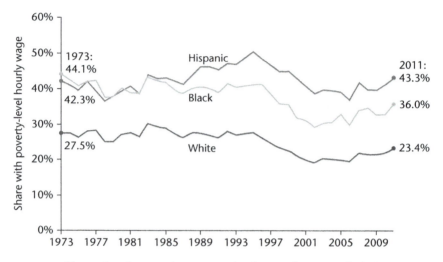

FIGURE 3.1 Share of workers earning poverty-level wages, by race and ethnicity, 1973–2011

Source: Economic Policy Institute, SWA. Updated May 14, 2012. http://stateofworkingamerica.org/chart/swa-wages-figure-4f-share-workers-earning/

Note: Authors' analysis of Current Population Survey Outgoing Rotation Group microdata.

workers, ineffective federal implementation of policies that outlaw racial discrimination in hiring, and free trade agreements that allow thousands of corporations to abandon U.S. workers for less-expensive locations in other countries, thus putting downward competitive pressure on wages in the U.S. (There are other, social—not strictly macroeconomic—policies that are important here, such as the lack of universal affordable childcare, which hampers parents' efforts to hold jobs.)

This chapter takes an in-depth look at two of the policies most directly responsible for poverty-wage work: minimum wage legislation and federal policies that prevent union organizing. The chapter also attempts a realistic assessment of the widespread belief that lack of education (rather than macroeconomic policy) is responsible for the low wages of workers, and that sufficient increases in education will ultimately reduce poverty.

Finally, the chapter presents a number of political-economic policies that would benefit workers as a class, and several additional strategies that would increase opportunities for black, Latino, and immigrant workers in particular, whose situation differs in important ways from that of whites.

Minimum Wage Policy

The minimum wage is a provision of the Fair Labor Standards Act (FLSA), passed in 1938. Its law was crafted by FDR and his wealthy colleagues as a direct result of the massive political demonstrations and social movement organizing during the Great Depression. The policy set a minimum wage and standards for overtime compensation. Minimum wage increases are legislated by Congress as amendments to the FLSA. Thus, minimum wage amounts are based solely on decisions made by Congressional legislators.

The federal minimum in 2012 was $7.25/hour. This amount yields a full-time, year-round salary of $13,930—well below the federal poverty line for a family of three ($19,090).

As Figure 3.2 shows, the minimum wage was $8.25 in 1967 (in 2011 dollars) and *a dollar less 44 years later.*

If the real value of the minimum wage had kept pace with the rising cost of living, it would be over $10.50/hour today (National Employment Law Project, 2012a). The paucity of the minimum wage was a major contributor to the growth in inequality after 1980, and to the increase in poverty-range wages of larger percentages of the workforce.

Statistics compiled in a proposal by the Economic Policy Institute (EPI) to gradually raise the minimum wage to $9.80/hour reveal the extent to which minimum wage work characterizes jobs in America. This proposal would raise the wages of 28.4 million workers—more than one in five people at work in the U.S. (22.3%). There are about 19.5 million workers whose wages would be directly affected. An additional 8.9 million workers, with wages just above the proposed

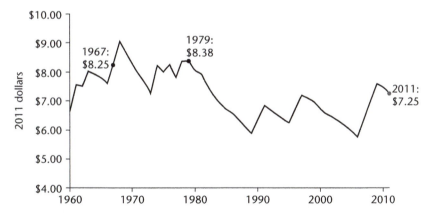

FIGURE 3.2 Real value of the minimum wage, 1960–2011

Source: Economic Policy Institute, SWA. Updated May 21, 2012. http://stateofworkingamerica. org/chart/swa-wages-figure-4-ae-real-minimum-wage/1213

Notes: Authors' analysis of U.S. Department of Labor Wage and Hour Division (2009). Documentation and methodology.
Underlying data are from U.S. Department of Labor Wage and Hour Division (2009), deflated using CPI-U-RS; see note to Table 4.39.

minimum, would also get a raise, "through spillover effects as employers adjust their overall pay scales" (Cooper, 2012, p. 2).

This raised minimum wage (to $9.80/hour) would also affect 21.5 million children—those who have a parent whose income would increase as a result of the proposed raise (21.5 million children is more than a quarter (28.2%) of the nation's children) (ibid.).

The perception that minimum-wage workers are teenagers working part time is not accurate. More than 88% of those who would benefit from a higher minimum wage are over the age of 20. And a majority (54%) of people who would be affected by the increase are full-time workers. Only 15% of those who would be affected work less than 20 hours a week (Hall, 2012).

Fifty-five percent of those affected by increasing the minimum wage to $9.80/hour are white. Yet large percentages of black and Latino workers would also be affected. And over three-quarters of those affected by the proposed increase to $9.80/hour have completed high school or more, including 42.3% who have completed some college, have an associate's degree, a bachelor's degree, or more.

As seen in Figure 3.3, over three-quarters of those affected by the proposed increase to $9.80/hour have completed high school or more, including 42.3% who have completed some college, have an associate's degree, a bachelor's degree, or more. Here we have more evidence that increased education does not prevent low-wage work.

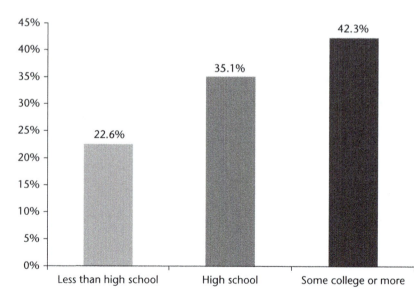

FIGURE 3.3 Educational attainment of those affected by increasing the Federal Minimum Wage to $9.80 (by July 1, 2014)

Source: Economic Policy Institute, SWA. www.epi.org/publication/ib341-raising-federal-minimum-wage/

To reiterate an important development: the majority (66%) of America's lowest-paid workers are employed by large corporations (those with over 100 employees), not small businesses. The three largest low-wage employers in the U.S. are Wal-Mart, Yum! Brands (the owner of Pizza Hut, Taco Bell, and Kentucky Fried Chicken), and McDonald's. These and most of the other large corporations that pay poverty wages are in good financial health. A 2012 report found that "[t]he 50 largest employers of low-wage workers have largely recovered from the recession and most are in strong financial positions.... They returned $174.8 billion to shareholders in dividends or share buybacks over the past five years" (Reilly, 2012).

Despite their affluence, these corporations pay their workers poverty-level wages. Or perhaps their affluence is in part *due to* how little they pay their employees. Consider just one company—Caterpillar. This corporation, "despite earning a record $4.9 billion profit [in 2011] and projecting even better results for 2012 ... is insisting on a six-year wage freeze and a pension freeze for most of the 780 production workers at its factory here" (Greenhouse, 2013, p. 4). Yet this company made a profit of *$39,000 per employee* in 2011 and $45,000 per employee in 2012 (Greenhouse, 2012a, 2013).

Interviews with executives in other companies reveal that they pay their workers the minimum "because they can"—they know that replacement workers are easy to find (Leonhardt, 2003).

The fact that there is a pool of unemployed labor in reserve keeps all employees' wages down. As Federal Reserve Chairman Alan Greenspan acknowledged, a large number of unemployed or underemployed workers leads to a "heightened sense of job insecurity and, as a consequence, subdued wage gains" (cited in Pollin, 1998, p. 20).

Contrary to the claims of those who oppose raising the minimum wage (that an increase will force employers to fire workers, or hire fewer of those affected by the increase), studies of both the 1990–91 and 1996–97 minimum wage increases failed to find any systematic, significant job losses associated with the increases, and found no evidence of negative employment effects on small businesses (Card and Krueger, 1997; Economic Policy Institute 2004a; Lester and Jacobs, 2010; Schmitt and Rosnick, 2011).

A classic, widely cited study on the relationship between minimum wage raises and job loss was carried out by Card and Krueger in the early 1990s. They utilized data from a series of minimum wage increases, including the 1992 increase in New Jersey, the 1988 rise in California, and the 1990–91 increases in the federal minimum wage. In each case they found that increases in the minimum wage led to increases in pay, but no loss in jobs (Card and Krueger, 1997).

Eighteen states (plus the District of Columbia) have minimums above the federal level of $7.25/hour. In all but three cases, the difference is less than a dollar an hour (see the United States Department of Labor, USDL, Minimum Wage Laws in the States, January 1, 2013, www.dol.gov/whd/minwage/america.htm). Many cities have enacted "living wage laws" in recent years as well, establishing a slightly higher minimum wage for employers that receive contracts or subsidies from the local government.

Concerted grassroots struggle has been necessary to raise the minimum wage in localities and states that have done so. Some of these campaigns are portrayed in Chapter Ten. It is important to note, however, that even an increase to $9.80 an hour (as described in the proposal above) would only bring a full-time year-round worker to a salary of $20,384 a year—which is still a poverty wage; it is only $854 a year higher than the official poverty level cut-off for a family of three ($19,530) in 2013.

One of the main lessons of the minimum wage is that this poverty wage is a result of a political decision. It is a decision made by Congress; and it is a crucial determinant of who lives in poverty. And thus being poor while working is very much a result of a federal policy.

An important consequence of widespread poverty wages paid by businesses is that when companies do not pay wages on which workers can support themselves, taxpayers are asked to ante up dollars for public assistance (welfare, food stamps, housing subsidies, etc.). This process effectively subsidizes business with taxpayer money. Unfortunately, many taxpayers who complain typically blame workers rather than the companies that underpay them.

Union Membership

I have been discussing the rise of poverty wage jobs and the decades-long decline of income. Wages have fallen from 53% of GDP in 1970 to 44% today—a shift of nearly $1.5 trillion away from wage income. Profits, dividends, and capital gains have been growing at the expense of workers: "J.P. Morgan chief investment officer Michael Cembalest calculated that reductions in wages and benefits were responsible for about 75 percent of the increase in corporate profits between 2000 and 2007" (Meyerson, 2013).

Lowered wages over time are the results of many factors, important among them the decisions of politically and economically powerful individuals and groups, mostly at the federal level. In sum, the following decisions (policies and actions) have lowered wages: deregulation of finance and the financialization of the economy, which moved money from public and private investment in business to asset gambling and the profits of a few wealthy investors; the shrinking of investment in businesses, inducing employers to lay off workers; the deregulation of large industries like trucking, airlines, and telecommunications, which, since companies were free to do so, lowered workers' wages in those industries; the shift to low-paying industries as a consequence of globalized trade pacts like the North American Free Trade Agreement (NAFTA) and the General Agreement on Tariffs and Trade (GATT), which encouraged deindustrialization here and industrialization abroad, where it is cheaper, thus reducing employment in the U.S.; taxation and other laws that encourage corporations to move industry abroad, where they have access to cheaper workers, meaning that U.S. workers must then compete with those making smaller wages in other countries; policies like congressionally set, poverty-level minimum wages that keep full-time workers poor; and last but not at all least, declining unionization, which decreases the bargaining power of workers.

I focus here on the decline of unionization. As union power has declined, so has their power to demand higher pay. The share of private-sector employees who are unionized has declined from 23% in 1979 to less than 8% in 2012. However, a much larger share, 40.7%, of *public-sector* employees (e.g., employed by local, state, or federal governments) are represented by unions. Overall, the number of workers covered by union representation is 16.3 million. The average weekly earnings of union workers in 2011 was $938, compared to an average of $729 for non-union workers (Schmitt and Jones, 2012). Employees in education, training, and library occupations have the highest unionization rate, at 36.8%, while the lowest rate occurred in sales and related occupations (3%). Black workers were more likely to be union members than were white, Asian, or Hispanic workers. Among states, New York continues to have the highest union membership rate (24.1%) and North Carolina the lowest (2.9%) (Bureau of Labor Statistics, 2012a).

As I have indicated, unionized workers earn higher wages than comparable non-union workers; in addition, they are 18.3% more likely to have health insurance, and 22.5% more likely to have pension coverage. Large union premiums (extra dollars per hour accruing to those in a union) exist for blacks and Latinos, who gain premiums of 17.3% and 23.1% of pay, respectively, much higher than the 10.9% union premium for whites (ibid.; see also Schmitt, 2008).

These extra dollars per hour as a consequence of being in a union mean that unions raise the wages of minorities more than of whites, thus helping to close racial/ethnic wage gaps. Hispanic and African American men tend to reap the greatest wage advantage from unionism, though minority women have substantially higher union premiums than their white counterparts (ibid.).

An important cause of the decline of unions in the workforce is federal policy since the early 1980s that allows businesses to fire and otherwise penalize workers for attempting to organize unions. In a study presented as testimony before the National Labor Relations Board in 2011, Kate Bronfenbrenner and Dorian Warren documented extensive business owner practices aimed at preventing the organization of unions by employees.

> Our findings show that serious violations occurred … from discharging, harassing, and threatening [union] leaders … to using surveillance, interrogation, and threats to try to dissuade workers from attending union meetings or speaking with organizing committee members … all the way to retaliating against the most outspoken union activists…. Employers increasingly use fear and violence.
>
> *(Bronfenbrenner and Warren, 2011)*

Despite corporate harassment, men and women do join unions. And as I pointed out above, there is a premium for belonging to a union that is high, especially for workers of color. One could argue, as does labor economist Gordon Lafer, that for non-college-educated workers, unionization can be much more important than further education:

> For nonunion high school dropouts, the advantage of finishing school is an increase of $2.25 per hour, while organizing one's workplace will benefit the worker more than twice as much. Similarly, high school graduates contemplating getting some college training short of a bachelors would actually do three times better to organize than go back to school.
>
> *(2002, p. 78)*

There is a particularly serious implication here for urban high school students who will not, under present policy conditions, have the funds to complete college. Rather than obtain further higher education, they could become involved in the political contention necessary to organize a union at their place of work. There is a lesson in this for educators, too, as it challenges our notion of the power of further education to boost income for low-income minority students. This challenge is explored in detail in the next section.

Education and Income

I want to return to the issue of education and income. As I have indicated, macroeconomic policies—as well as federal education policies—are based on the assumption that increased education of the workforce will alleviate poverty by putting better educated people into better jobs. We have already seen that the preponderance of low-wage jobs, and the concomitant lack of good jobs, undermines this assumption quite a bit. But doesn't a college education guarantee a high-level salary? Can education be used as a remedy for poverty and low-wage work? Or must we change federal policies in the economic sphere in order to solve the problem of poverty and poverty-wage work?

A person's education is, of course, an important determinant of their income. However, it plays less of a role than we typically assume. Indeed, the evidence on the relation between education and earnings below suggests that education explains about only a *third* of income levels. Therefore, it cannot serve either as an explanation for Americans' falling income, or as a workable strategy for correcting this trend.

There is no question that in most cases individuals with more education earn higher salaries than those with less. Of full-time workers aged 25 and over, the median weekly earning (with half above and half below) for high school graduates in 2011 was $638, while the median weekly earning for those with a bachelor's degree was $1,053 (Bureau of Labor Statistics, 2013).

However, medians can be misleading. Many factors can mitigate and even reverse the wage effects of education. For example, women earn less than men, even when they work the same number of hours—a gap that persists across all levels of educational attainment. In fact, women with a bachelor's degree earn about as much as men with some college education but no degree. On average, to earn as much as men with a bachelor's degree, women must obtain a doctoral degree. Similar gaps also exist by race and ethnicity. African-Americans and Latinos earn less than their white counterparts, even among the most highly-educated workers. African-Americans and Latinos with master's degrees don't exceed the median lifetime earnings of whites with bachelor's degrees.

(Carnevale, Rose, and Cheah, 2011, p. 7)

In these cases it is the absence of federal (and in some instances state) policies that is the problem. There are no effective, enforced, comparable worth laws to equalize the pay for men and women who do the same kind of work, and the lack of enforcement of federal anti-discrimination law allows employers to assign women to low-wage jobs without government reprisal. One study found that effective pay equity policies would enable up to 40% of poor working women to leave public assistance (Lafer, 2002).

In addition, discrimination on the basis of race often renders education irrelevant. For example, in the nation's largest labor market, California, a study of entry-level workers found that black and Latino youth had improved significantly on every measure of skill, in absolute terms, as well as relative to white workers. Yet their wages were falling further behind those of whites. The effects of race outweighed those of education, with minority workers at every level of education losing ground to similarly prepared whites. Whenever trials have been carried out in which identically qualified black and white candidates applied for the same job, a "pattern of discriminatory hiring has been revealed across a wide range of entry-level occupations.... It is clear than more vigorous enforcement of anti-discrimination laws is a prerequisite to enabling minority workers to realize any payoff to skills" (Lafer, 2002, p. 84; see also Galbraith, 1998; Wolff, 2003).

Educational attainment, then, is mitigated by institutional factors such as unionization, gender, and race. Since these institutional factors cut across all levels of education, the ultimate wage which any person earns is determined by the interaction of these (and other) factors (Howell, Houston, and Milberg, 1999). A telling statistic regarding the weakening effect of education on income is that *by 1996*, one out of every six college graduates was in a job that paid *less* than the average salary of high school graduates (Monthly Labor Review, 1998, as in Lafer, 2002, p. 47). Thus, while education and wages are indeed positively related, this relationship is often compromised and can even be reversed by other determinants.

Indeed, over the past 30 years, the real wages (adjusted for inflation) of high school graduates fell by 11.3%, while those of college graduates rose only by 5.7%. Most (60%) of the change in the college premium over these years was due to a worsening situation for high school graduates rather than to increasing wages for college graduates. For male workers the trend is bleak. Since 1973, the gap between wages of college- and high-school-educated male workers has increased by $4.06 an hour; nearly two-thirds (70%) of this change is due to the bottom falling out of the high school market, rather than rises in the wages of college workers (Gottschalk, 1997; Wolff, 2003). Thus, it is difficult to see how the rising college premium can be interpreted as a growing demand for higher education.

Figure 3.4 shows how the relative demand for college graduates has shrunk over the period 1940–2005.

Additional evidence that the college wage premium is less valuable now is the increasing percentage of college graduates who are making poverty wages. Decades ago, at the beginning of the 1940s, between 1.4% and 1.6% of employed heads of households earned around the minimum wage (that is, 50% below the federal minimum wage, to 50% above it). The vast majority of employed heads of households made more than this in that decade. The percentage of workers making around the minimum wage has increased over the years so that by 1990 between 8.8% and 11% of those with a *bachelor's degree* made around the minimum wage. This means that *before the Great Recession, about one out of ten workers with a four-year college degree was making poverty wages* (Levin-Waldman, 1999).

In the 20 years between 1979 and 1999, the number of college graduates in the labor force grew from 17.9 million to 38.9 million—an increase of over 100%.

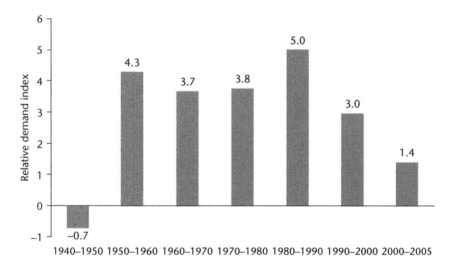

FIGURE 3.4 Growth in relative demand for college graduates, 1940–2005

Source: Economic Policy Institute, SWA. www.epi.org/publication/ib341-raising-federal-minimum-wage/. Updated June 14, 2012. http://stateofworkingamerica.org/chart/swa-wages-table-ai-growth-relative-demand/

Note: Authors' analysis of Goldin and Katz (2008, Table 1). Documentation and methodology.

But—and this is before the Great Recession—they were not in great demand. Rather, a significant share of them was unable to find jobs in occupations that make use of their degrees. By 1990, almost 20% of graduates—almost 6 million (5.7 million) college-educated workers—were not able to find college-level work. This total included "75,000 college graduates working as street vendors or door-to-door salespeople, 166,000 as truck and bus drivers, 83,000 as maids, housemen, janitors, or cleaners, and 688,000 who were unemployed" (Lafer, 2002, p. 61). These figures are derived from workers' experiences in the 1990s. The Department of Labor predicted in 2000 that in the first ten years of the 21st century, although the retirement of college-educated baby boomers would create more openings in college jobs, the number of new college graduates would continue to grow more rapidly than the number of jobs that require a bachelor's degree. They were correct; and the college diploma has become increasingly less valuable, as more and more people obtain the four-year degree.

Figure 3.5 demonstrates that there were more people with college and advanced degrees in 2011 than will be needed in 2020.

As the number of college graduates increases beyond what the economy needs, people with bachelor's degrees are forced to take jobs that (formerly, at least) did not require one. And as employers have the pick of more and more college graduates, they pay lower salaries than they would have to if there were fewer college graduates available.

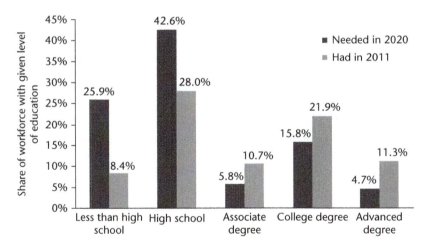

FIGURE 3.5 Education needed in 2020 workforce and education levels of the 2011 workforce

Source: Economic Policy Institute, SWA. Updated May 21, 2012. http://stateofworkingamerica. org/chart/swa-wages-figure-4a-education-needed-2020/

Notes: Figure is based on authors' analysis of Thiess (2012) for Table 4.46 and education attainment data from Table 4.17. Documentation and methodology. Totals do not sum to 100% because some categories were omitted.

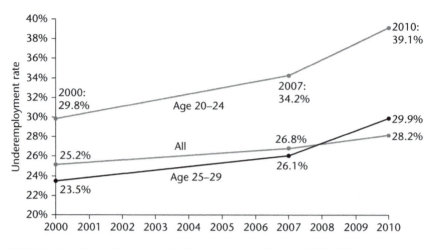

FIGURE 3.6 Underemployment of college graduates, by age, 2000–10

Source: Economic Policy Institute, SWA. Updated June 14, 2012. http://stateofworkingamerica. org/chart/swa-wages-figure-4ak-underemployment-college/equire a college education

Notes: Figure is based on authors' analysis of Fogg and Harrington (2011), Table 1. Documentation and methodology. Underemployment is defined as college graduates working in occupations that do not require a college degree to perform the work. "Underemployment" occurs when a college graduate works in an occupation that does not require a bachelor's degree.

Notice that even before the Recession, almost one in four college graduates was underemployed. As I reported in the last chapter, by 2012 the percentage of recent college graduates who were underemployed or jobless was 53%.

Levels of education in the U.S. have been increasing steadily; yet as we have seen, incomes have been falling for the last 30 years. The average education of American workers was 9.2 years in 1940; it is now over 13 years. The percentage of American workers with a high school diploma has also increased over the past three decades. This is true for men, women, and all racial and economic groups. Even the education levels of welfare recipients have improved significantly. Before the Great Recession, the share of welfare recipients who had high school diplomas increased from 42% in 1979 to almost two-thirds (70%) in 1999 (Loprest, 1999; U.S. General Accounting Office, 2001).

It is important to note that even though college levels have risen across the board, they are still considerably lower for African Americans, Latinos, and low-income students of all colors.

College attainment figures vary by social class: Although 48% of low-income students *who complete high school* now enroll in a two- or four-year college degree upon graduation, only 7% obtain a bachelor's degree by age 26, compared to 60% of upper-income students. A study by Martha Bailey, an economics professor at the University of Michigan, *revealed that the difference in college-graduation rates between the rich and poor has widened by more than 50% since the 1990s—despite two decades of "college for all" policy* (Bailey and Dynarski, 2011).

High-scoring, low-income youth complete college at a lower rate than low-scoring, upper-income youth.

The lack of financial assistance, and a reluctance to take on huge loans that they fear they will not be able to repay, is a crucial reason why low-income students do not finish college (Fossey and Bateman, 1998; National Center for Public Policy and Higher Education, 2002; Gladieux, 2004). By 2010, a record one in five households owed student debt and the average debt was $26,000 (Fry, 2012).

Whether computed as a share of household income or assets, the relative burden of student loan debt is greatest for households in the bottom fifth of the income spectrum, even though members of such households are less likely than those in other groups to attend college in the first place.

No evidence exists for the belief that deteriorating education—whether measured as fewer years of school, falling achievement levels, or demographics of the workforce—are the cause of the falling wages of U.S. workers. Rather, as I have argued here and throughout this book, the evidence points to macroeconomic policy and resulting employer practice as more to blame for the worsening position of U.S. workers than any failures of education. This is an important issue for education and educational reformers, as it implies that even academically successful school reform can only rarely trump macroeconomic conditions and policies. I return to this issue in later chapters.

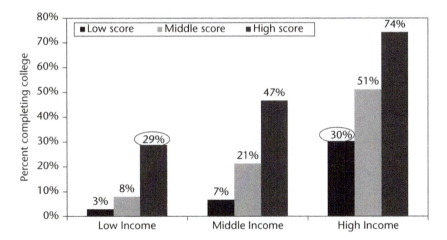

FIGURE 3.7 Incomes matter more than test scores for college completion: college completion by income status and 8th grade test scores

Source: Economic Policy Institute, SWA. Fox, Connolly, and Snyder (2005).

Note: Low income is defined as bottom 25%, middle income is middle 50%, and high income is top 25%.

Despite the abundance of evidence to the contrary, some argue that the U.S. has a growing *unmet need* for college graduates (Autor, 2010; Rampell, 2012).

It is important to note that when these analysts argue that the economy needs more people with college degrees, they are lumping all college graduates together, combining people who have four-year college degrees with those who have advanced or professional degrees. They argue that "good jobs" require college. But as I have shown, college graduates (those with bachelor's degrees only) have not fared well in the labor market for at least ten years—real wages are no higher than ten years ago. And most jobs do not require a college degree. But people with *advanced degrees* have seen their wages grow strongly. The difference is the advanced degree.

It is misleading to argue that having more people go to college is the answer to growing wage inequality or middle-class wage stagnation; "*getting onto the better wage track requires either getting an advanced or professional degree (not just a college degree) or joining a clear subset of college graduates* [who are doing well]" (Mishel, 2012). The meaning of this is that there may indeed be a need for doctoral degrees in some areas (e.g., hard sciences), but not of bachelor's degrees in general (see also Mishel, 2011). I want to point out that there are good jobs going begging that require only technical education or on-the-job training:

> The empirical evidence to date certainly provides some support for the notion that middle-paying or middle-skill jobs declined in magnitude (and in pay levels) more than others, especially during the 1990s. At the same time, it is clear that many well-paid middle-skill jobs, requiring some post-secondary schooling or training but less than a four-year college degree, remain in the U.S. labor market. These jobs remain good jobs for workers with appropriate levels of skill and previous training, even if they do not have college diplomas, and many of them cannot easily be outsourced or replaced by machines.
>
> *(Holzer, 2011, p. 9)*

A good example is skilled auto mechanics, of which there is a shortage in the New York City area, where I live.

U.S. politicians and mainstream economists often argue that we must reform education in order to be competitive in the global economy. Yet in highly developed industrial/technical economies like ours, it is investments in high-end technology and scientific research that make significant contributions to national competitiveness (e.g., the development of the computer and more recent digital advancements). In countries where most of the people are *not literate* is where advances in education of the general population are important for economic competitiveness.

I would offer two lessons from the discussion in this chapter of income, education, and the declining power of a college degree to provide good jobs. First, for better education to provide better jobs, there have to *be* better jobs. Our financial-ized, globalized economy has not been producing these in sufficient number for several decades. Second, for many students, especially females and students of color, economic and other social policies will, if current practices are not altered, trump educational attainment.

We cannot expect education to compensate for ravages wrought by macroeco-nomic policy. The primacy of federal economic regulations in maintaining poor wages suggests that it is not prudent to rely on the reform of education to increase the economic opportunities of women, or blacks and Latinos from poor families. A change in macroeconomic policies is also crucial.

Fortunately, federal policies that make the economy more responsive to the needs of working-class employees are not without precedent in the U.S. As I pointed out in Chapter One, during the decades following World War II, federal price and wage guidelines kept prices stable and wages up. During those years, the minimum wage was kept at 50% of the median industrial wage. When unionized, well-paid workers did better, minimum wage workers did better, too (Galbraith, 1998). The antipathy of recent U.S. economic elites to wage and price controls is so strong that—as an example—the U.S. is the only major developed nation without price or profit controls on even that most important commodity, medicine (Weiner, 2001).

The Federal Reserve Bank was created in 1913. Its statutory goals are set out in the Employment Act of 1946, and amended by the Humphreys-Hawkins Full Employment and Balanced Growth Act of 1978. Both laws are very clear: The twin goals of economic policy are to maintain a high level of employment and production, as well as to maintain reasonable price stability. In recent decades, Chairmen Burns, Volker, and Greenspan have concentrated on the stability of prices (Thorbecke, 2000, p. 2).

They have, for the most part, ignored the mandate to maintain low unemploy-ment—despite the low employment of the late 1990s, which was a function of the booming economy itself. Low unemployment, if it is sustained over several years, generally helps the poor first, and helps the poor the most, as more of them are able to obtain work (Economic Policy Institute, 2004a). We observed this in the late 1990s, in the uptick of wages in the retail sector, and in the (albeit slight) rise of employment in many central city neighborhoods.

To reinstate the other half of the federal reserve mandate, we need to imple-ment policies that produce low unemployment: Policies like maintaining low interest rates, increasing government spending on infrastructure and human capi-tal development, and creating demand-side pressure—a need for workers. In addi-tion to the support of full employment policies, we should reinstate price and wage guidelines. The wages corporations pay need to be regulated like they used to be, so that wages in the retail and other low-wage sectors are indexed to union standards, like the minimum wage used to be.

Macroeconomic policies that would be important for workers include the creation of decent jobs by the federal government for those who need and want them; the passage of significantly higher minimum wage laws with health insurance and other benefits; the elimination for the working poor of regressive tax policies that fall most heavily on them (payroll taxes, for example, as detailed in the next chapter); and the enactment of policies that protect union organizing.

Moreover, the body of worker protection law that already exists does not extend to the new, large group of working poor, many of whom are immigrants. Laws covering workplace health and safety, protection from discrimination, family and medical leave, wage and hour enforcement, unemployment compensation, workmen's compensation, and business-closing notice, all bypass low-wage workers in low-wage jobs employed by small businesses. Some eligibility requirements for employment and labor statutes, such as minimum hours, disqualify many low-wage workers. "In other words, workers who are the most vulnerable to the dictates of employers are left without assistance from the government" (Shulman, 2002, pp. 1–3). Many of these most vulnerable workers are African American, Latino, and immigrant residents of urban areas.

African American Workers

Following the Civil Rights Movement, during the 1970s, many African Americans made substantial economic progress. With mass migration to cities came increased years of education and rising wages in industry; and civil rights laws and affirmative action conjoined to increase opportunities (Smith and Welch, 1989). Indeed, by the late 1970s, wages of black and white college graduates were nearly equal, and the wages of black women surpassed those of white women (Freeman, 1976). The numbers of black managers and professionals—especially in government agencies—increased significantly (Moss and Tilly, 2001).

During the 1980s, the wage gap between employed working- and middle-class blacks and whites began to increase. Black women were less likely to find work than in the 1970s and early '80s (Bound and Dresser, 1999, cited in Moss and Tilly, 2001). During this decade there was also a downward movement out of middle-wage employment for blacks into very-low-wage employment for many, and relatively higher-wage employment for a few (Mishel, Bernstein, and Boushey, 2003; see also Bound and Dresser, 1999).

And in the early 1990s, in part because of the recessions of 1990 and 1991, young black workers suffered further wage and employment setbacks, even though blacks were obtaining higher levels of education than ever, and had been closing the gap with whites in both educational attainment and test scores (Moss and Tilly, 2001; see also Jencks, 1991; Bound and Freeman, 1992). During the 1990s wages diverged widely between young black and white male college graduates (Bound and Freeman, 1992). Latinos also experienced economic regression in the 1990s (Moss and Tilly, 2001; see also Corcoran, Heflin, and Reyes, 1999).

By 1990 there was a large group living in concentrated poverty in America's inner cities. This inner city concentrated poverty was particularly prevalent among black urban populations. In that year there were more people living in concentrated poverty in America's cities than at any time since the 1960s. Prolonged unemployment, underemployment, and detachment from the labor market were prevalent (see Anyon, 1997; Wilson, 1997).

What accounts for the deteriorated position of blacks and Latinos in the labor market when they had been obtaining higher levels of education? The common explanation is that they do not have the skills required by the information/technology economy. The increase in earnings inequality of the last two decades of the 20th century is often laid to an upward shift in skill demands. Thus, it is said that because blacks and Latinos have less- or lower-quality education, they are not hired by employers. A corollary to this argument is that the "digital divide" is producing a growing racial divide.

To test these assumptions, Philip Moss and Chris Tilly (2001) assessed employers' desires for workers' "hard skills" (literacy, numeracy, computer familiarity, cognitive abilities)—which are said to be the basis of the digital divide—and "soft skills," which refer to interaction (ability to interact with customers, coworkers, and supervisors, including friendliness, teamwork, ability to fit in, and appropriate affect, language use, grooming, and attire), as well as motivation (which refers to enthusiasm, positive work attitudes, commitment, dependability, integrity, and willingness to learn).

Managers in various economic sectors interviewed by Moss and Tilly expressed increased demands for soft skills more frequently than for any hard skill but for computer literacy. Except for employers in manufacturing firms where workers needed to program computers or read printouts, "all other employers emphasized the soft skills of interaction with customers and motivation for work as just as important as basic reading and arithmetic skills" (or, to use these researchers' phrase, "attitude trumps technical facility" in a large numbers of jobs) (Moss and Tilly, 2001, p. 61). Indeed, another researcher, Peter Cappelli, has concluded that the alleged "skill shortages" decried by employers in the first half of the 1990s referred mainly to issues of worker motivation (1996, in Moss and Tilly, 2001). Osterman (1995), as well, found that in a large representative sample, managers report behavioral traits as one of the two most important job criteria in about 82% of cases, and the top criterion in about half.

What Moss and Tilly also discovered, however, is that managers' definition of, and evaluation of, applicants' soft skills is highly subjective and is context bound. Moreover, employers typically conflate the two, aggregating appearance, ways of talking and self-presentation, with possession of the hard skills. In interviews, managers mixed and entangled comments on inner-city blacks' and Latinos' hard skills (education, intelligence) with evaluation of soft skills (use of language, dress, and attitudes) (Moss and Tilly, 2001, pp. 44, 99).

Unfortunately, most employers do not screen applicants for entry-level jobs through formal measures; rather, they rely on the pre-employment interview. Thus, the increased desire by managers for "soft skills" may make it harder for non-white applicants because it may increase racial discrimination by employers. Moss and Tilly conclude,

> This tells us that skill- or location-based policies that fail to address race are likely to fall short of the mark. Providing added training programs for black and Latino job seekers will not easily dissolve the suspicion that many employers harbor. And employers' unease may block access by workers of color to the critically important training that takes place on the job. Similarly, new transportation systems such as vanpools to crack inner city isolation will have limited effects if suburban businesspeople remain chary of the urban minority workforce. Policies to dissipate stereotypes, *and to constrain employers' ability to act on them, are necessary complements*
>
> *(2001, p. 254, italics added)*

The lack of enforcement of federal laws against discrimination in hiring is an important reason, then, that—despite more years of education—a smaller percentage of African American men are working now than in recent decades. Only 52% of young (aged 16 to 24) non-institutionalized, out of school black males with high school degrees or less were employed in 2002, compared to 62% 20 years ago. In contrast, the labor force activity of comparable white and Latino males has been steady over the last two decades, and employment among young black women has increased.

Employment for young black men even declined fairly continuously between 1989 and 1997, despite the strong economic recovery that occurred after 1992. Labor force *attachment* (which includes searching for work) for young black men suffered a sharp 14 percentage point decline over the 1980–2000 period. This contrasts sharply with the experience of young, less-educated Latino men, who essentially achieved employment parity with their white counterparts during these decades (Offner and Holzer, 2002; see also Mishel, Bernstein, and Boushey, 2003).

It is important to understand that the weakening attachment of young, less-educated black males to the labor force occurred despite the higher educational attainment of the group: A much larger percentage of the group held high school degrees at the end of the period than at the beginning (see Freeman, 1991; Cherry and Rodgers, 2000).

Discrimination in hiring because of the emphasis on soft skills may be one reason fewer young African American men are working. It is also the case, however, that a high incarceration rate among members of this group contribute to their declining employment. In 2000, 10% of black males aged 20–24 were incarcerated and among high school dropouts, over *one-third* were incarcerated (Mauer, 2003b, p. 4). Research by Holzer and Stoll documented that many employers are reluctant to hire individuals with criminal records. Since substantial numbers of the prisoners released every day in the U.S. return to low-income urban neighborhoods, their joblessness contributes to the low rates of employment in young black males (Holzer and Stoll, 2001; see also Mauer, 2003b). Indeed, as Pettit (2012) has documented, if one counted the black and Latino men who are incarcerated, joblessness and poverty figures (as well as high school dropout figures) for these groups would be much higher than their current official rates.

The reluctance of employers to hire young black males and workers of color in general—this widespread, illegal discrimination in hiring—has important implications for federal policies to assist them. It suggests that policies that might reduce *overall* unemployment in the U.S. in the hopes of employing significant numbers of black workers may not assist African American males. During the nearly "full" employment economy of the late 1990s, for example, the employment rate of young black women who did not finish high school rose by 14 points. However, the percentage of those young black women who were employed went from 23% to 37%—still very low (Bernstein and Baker, 2002). So policies that create jobs—with the federal government as employer of last resort—are indicated.

Moreover, it is crucial that we establish programs to ease the formerly incarcerated into jobs, education, and civic life. Each year, approximately 700,000 prisoners are released from state and federal prisons (Guerino, Harrison, and Sabol, 2011). Nearly two-thirds of the nation's prisoners are African American or Latino. In many states, men and women returning to civilian status are barred for life from receiving even temporary welfare benefits. Without access to jobs and without welfare, there is little they can do to obtain money legally.

Former prisoners also lose access to student loans for higher education. In 2001–2002, 48,000 applicants were denied aid for further education under this provision. And in some states they are barred from living in public housing (in which many of them grew up). In 48 states and the District of Columbia, voting rights of convicted felons are restricted. As a result of these laws, almost 5 million (4.7) persons are currently unable to vote, and an estimated 13% of black men are barred from the voting booth (disenfranchisement figures for women are not available). As Marc Mauer notes, the consequence of these policies can be huge:

> Consider the 2000 presidential election in Florida, which was decided by just 537 votes. In that state, an estimated 600,000 former felons were excluded from the ballot box under state law, even though they had completed their sentences. We will never know what impact their votes might

have had, but the fact that the narrow margin of victory in Florida put George W. Bush in the White House clearly suggests that a small fraction of that group could have changed the outcome.

(Mauer, 2003a, pp. 16–17; see also Mauer, 2003b)

As we have seen in this and the previous chapter, most jobs in the U.S. economy do not require college degrees, and a large share of these pay little more than subsistence wages. I also reported that about 80% of black and Latino persons who are at work fill these unrewarding, sometimes degrading, slots. Urban students know these jobs are their future if they join the mainstream workforce. Many minority students, rather rationally it seems to me, reject meaningless work, and take up other, often illegal, activities. If they do not have the funds to see them through to college completion, urban school reform could not have offered them more.

As educators who care deeply about these students, we must come to grips with the fact that no amount of school reform as presently conceived will make the economy accept minority high school graduates in a more humane manner. Even the latest equity-seeking reform—small, democratic, and personally nurturing high schools where advanced courses are offered to make students college-ready—lacks meaning and consequence when students and their families cannot obtain support for the college years.

We need, therefore, to change the way the macroeconomy receives these students. Federal policies that mandate a living wage for entry-level work, that create urban jobs with advancement possibilities, and that penalize employers who prevent labor organizing or discriminate on the basis of color, would yield a vibrant set of economic opportunities that could give substance and meaning to the potentiality of school reform.

Another policy—to provide public funding for qualified low-income students to complete college—would certainly reward and motivate achievement efforts of urban students and, I suspect, teachers as well. Where there is a way, there is will. Unless the labor market is equalized for low-income students, or until they have sufficient college support, public macroeconomic policies will continue to trump educational achievement—and probably educational effort, as well.

Federal policies that are not considered here but that absolutely contribute to the ability of people to enter and sustain employment when jobs are available include health care and childcare. Without sufficient health care, minor sickness can turn into major illness and an impediment to work. Indeed, increasing percentages of jobs are part time now, and therefore do not offer health care (the retail and wholesale sector has cut a million full-time jobs since 2006, while adding more than 500,000 part-time jobs; in 2011, half of retail workers in New York City were part time (Greenhouse, 2012b)).

And for parents of young children, universal subsidized childcare as national policy would make employment possible for those who cannot afford expensive nursery schools. Many other capitalist countries provide both national health care and subsidized support systems for families with young children (Polokow, 2007). The lack of such policies in this country contributes to the maintenance of poverty and low income in the U.S. population.

There is another kind of federal policy that will be discussed at length here, one that maintains the poverty of people as well as school systems—tax policies that cull the income of the working poor but not of vast corporations—and these are described in the following chapter.

4

INCOME, WEALTH, AND TAXES

Money matters. Family income shapes what parents can offer children, and thus affects children's life chances. I demonstrated in Chapter Three how federal policies regarding minimum wage and union organizing maintain poverty incomes for millions of Americans. This chapter reveals that rules set by Congress also protect great wealth and the extremes of inequality that characterize the U.S. We will see that inequality of income and wealth are directly related to U.S. tax regulations. Regressive payroll and state taxes, historically low taxes charged to those of high income, unethical but legal—as well as illegal—tax dodges for the wealthy, and laws that allow corporations with billions of dollars in profits to pay little or no tax and in some cases to obtain tax rebates, all support income and wealth inequality.

Tax regulations thus affect the amount of money available in government coffers for public services like urban education. The dollars available for such spending are directly related to the federal rules about who pays how much tax. The less tax money available for public expenditures, the fewer the services, and the lower their quality. If we are concerned with fully investing in urban schools, job creation, and other policies that would create a more just society, we need to find moneys to pay for these investments. This chapter demonstrates that one viable source of income for the public sphere is the vast untaxed income of very rich individuals and corporations. First, let me document the extent of inequality in the U.S.

Inequality

In 2007, before the onset of the Great Recession, the U.S. was in fact a more unequal society in terms of income distribution than many countries in the world, including China and Iran (CIA Factbook, 2012; see also Stiglitz, 2013a). Even in the "strong" U.S. economy of the late 1990s, income inequality was at its highest level since the Census began tracking these data in 1947 (Economic Policy Institute, 1999). By 1999, the income gap between rich and poor was so wide that the richest 2.7 million Americans had as many after-tax dollars to spend as the bottom 100 million Americans (about $620 billion). That ratio more than doubled since 1977, when the richest group had as much as the bottom 49 million (Johnston, 1999). The income disparity grew so much that four out of five households, or about 217 million people, were taking home a thinner slice of the economic pie in 1999 than in 1977 (ibid.; see also Johnston, 1999).

As I reported in the introduction, the Great Recession has increased income inequality even more—as the rich received the lion's share of income produced in 2009–10, with the very wealthiest getting the most.

Figure 4.1 reveals that income growth for households in the two bottom portions of the top 1% was significantly lower than growth for those at the very top of the income distribution. These data are from income reported by the very wealthy to the IRS, and thus may be underestimates, as many keep income abroad, in corporations they control (Shaw and Stone, 2011).

Pre- and post-Recession figures typically cited actually understate the income of the richest 1%, because they exclude income from stocks, which grew rapidly in the 1990s and again in the first decade of the 21st century. By 1998, almost half (48.2%) of all households owned stock directly or indirectly (e.g., through

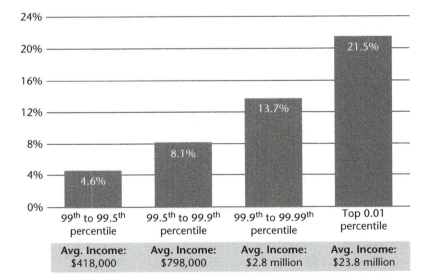

FIGURE 4.1 Percentage growth in income for households with the top 1%, 2009–10

Source: Center on Budget and Policy Priorities. www.cbpp.org/cms/?fa=view&id=3697

retirement plans). But only 36.3% of all households owned stock worth $5,000 or more. And the top wealthiest 1% of households owned 42% of all stocks; in 1998 almost 90% of all stock was owned by the wealthiest 20% of American households (Wolff, 2002; Mishel, Bernstein, and Boushey, 2003). In 2010, the wealthiest 20% owned slightly more, 91.7% (Wolff, 2013).

By 2010, stock ownership had declined to 46.9% of households owning any stock at all—even indirectly through mutual funds and retirement plans. Less than one-third (31.1%) owned more than $10,000 in stocks. The median African American and Latino family owned no stock at all (Economic Policy Institute, 2012).

Before the Great Recession, wealth (as opposed to income) inequality in the U.S. was at a 70-year high (in 1998), with the top 1% of wealth holders control-ling 33% of total wealth. In 2012, the most affluent controlled more than in 1998—40% of wealth, in addition to taking in almost 25% of all income (Stiglitz, 2013a). The decades-long trend toward increasing inequality was exacerbated by the Recession.

It should be pointed out that many of the wealthy did lose money in the Great Recession. From 2007–10, the average wealth of the top 1% dropped 15.6% (while wealth at the median plummeted 47.1% (http://stateofworkingamerica. org/files/book/factsheets/wealth.pdf).) A survey of the top 25 hedge fund man-agers shows that "their profits plummeted from $22.5 billion in 2007 to $11.6 billion in 2008—but then more than doubled to $25.3 billion in 2009, hence surpassing the previous 2007 peak" (Saez, 2010).

The inequality reported in this chapter has also been caused by trends I have already discussed at length: Falling wages for most workers, decline in union power, retracted worth of the minimum wage, increasing numbers of poverty-wage jobs, underemployment, etc. Our country's stark inequality is expressed in particularly extreme form in the minority-white wealth gap, which widened during the Great Recession. In 1998, the median black household had a net worth of about $10,000—about 12% of the corresponding figure for whites (Mishel, Bernstein, and Boushey 2003; see also Oliver and Shapiro, 1997). In 1998, 27% of black families reported zero or negative net worth, compared to 14% of white families (Wolff, 2002). The gap in income between African American and white households was almost identical in 1967 and 1989, despite two decades of civil rights reform (Wolff, 2002).

In 2010, African American families at the median made $39,715, down from about $44,000 in 2000. As a percentage of white median family income, blacks made 61% in 2010, down from 63.5% in 2000. *In 2010, the median wealth, or net worth, for black families was $4,900, compared to median wealth for whites of $97,000.* Blacks are nearly twice as likely as whites to have zero or negative net worth—33.9% compared to 18.6% (Economic Policy Institute, 2013).

In 2010, median wealth was $1,300 for Latino households, compared to the median wealth for white households of $97,000. Black and Latino households are nearly twice as likely as whites to have zero or negative net worth. A total of

18.6% of white households, 33.9% of black households, and 35.8% of Latino households have no wealth, or have liabilities exceeding their assets (ibid.).

Concentration of Wealth

The concentration of wealth into relatively few hands in the U.S. is not a new phenomenon. It has a long, instructive past. This history demonstrates that tax rates on the rich directly affect inequality, and that the wealthy, until the early 1960s and President John F. Kennedy's administration, were taxed at much higher rates than in decades since. The historical record also reveals that the only periods during which the concentration of wealth has been halted or *reversed* are years following sustained political contestation—i.e., mass social movements.

In Philadelphia in the decade before the revolution, the wealthiest 4% of city residents owned 56% of all assets in the city (Phillips, 2002, p. 6). Tax lists in Boston in the 1770s show that the top 5% of Boston's taxpayers controlled 49% of the city's taxable assets (Nash, 1979).

The southern colonies, however, were the wealthiest in North America because of slave ownership (Phillips, 2002). By 1774, wealth in the South per free person was 137 British pounds, compared to 46 pounds in the middle colonies and 38 in New England. Half of southern wealth was in slaves—some $600,000, valued at about $120 million by 1780 (ibid.).

In 1800, there was a large gap between rich and poor in large U.S. cities. The share of assets owned by the top 10% in New York, for example, rose from 54% in 1789 to 61% in 1795. During the mid-19th century, concentration of income in some cities increased further. In Boston the share of the top 1% climbed from 33% in 1833 to 37% in 1848. In Baltimore, Brooklyn, Milwaukee, and New Orleans the top 1% held between 39% and 44% of the wealth in the mid-19th century (ibid.).

Below the Mason-Dixon line in the 1850s, slave prices were 300% to 400% above 1800 levels, and the South was at its highest post-colonial share of U.S. wealth—roughly 30%. Kevin Phillips reports that on the eve of the Civil War, "Dixie's four million slaves were worth between two and four billion dollars" (ibid., p. 32). Defeat of the South in the Civil War realigned national wealth and income. The share of U.S. assets held by the antebellum south of 1860 (about 30%) fell in 1870 to 12%.

In the North, income during the latter half of the 19th century became more concentrated as major industrialists and financiers, such as Carnegie, Rockefeller, and J.P. Morgan, amassed personal fortunes. In 1863, the upper 1% of Manhattan residents (1,600 families) owned 61% of the city's wealth, up from 40% in 1845. One analysis in 1890 revealed that over half of the assets in the U.S. were held by 1% of U.S. families (up from almost a third of assets right after the Civil War). In Massachusetts, where the top 8% owned 83% of the wealth in 1859–61, they had 90% by 1879–81.

Labor, Socialist, and other protests against the "Robber Barons" and massive wealth in the decades surrounding 1900—and the Progressive legislation that resulted during the 1930s—slowed down the amassing of the great U.S. fortunes, and temporarily halted the increase in the gap between rich and poor. Policies that halted the increase included the 16th and 17th Amendments to the U.S. Constitution, which (respectively) authorized a federal income tax, and required direct election of U.S. Senators instead of their selection by legislators—often on the basis of their connection to wealthy industrialists and other sources of wealth. The top rate of the income tax passed in 1913 was 77%—authorized in order to pay for World War I.

During the Progressive Era, some anti-trust legislation was also passed, but was weakened during the "Roaring Twenties" by the Supreme Court. In addition, four tax cuts between 1921 and 1928 lowered the top individual income tax rate from 77% to 25% in 1929. In part as a result of these tax cuts, by the end of the 1920s, the top 1% had increased their share of wealth to between 37% and 44% of overall U.S. wealth, depending on the calculation.

In the 1930s, a period of mass protest against the resurgence of excess wealth during the 1920s and the widespread poverty and unemployment of the Depression, tax increases were levied on the rich. Wealth deconcentrated once again. In 1935, during Roosevelt's second term, a Wealth Tax was passed. Several new regulations separated banks and investment companies (the connection that had built the J.P. Morgan fortune), made the Federal Reserve Bank more responsive, and prohibited public utility holding companies. Tax and revenue acts between 1935 and 1943 shrank the share of wealth of the top income bracket from 44% in 1929 to 28% in 1944.

By the late 1950s, however, the rich had returned. Tax avoidance was on the rise, made possible by increasing numbers of loopholes in the IRS code; and the share of wealth owned by the top 1% climbed back up to 30% by 1958. Its climb has continued since then, as the federal government has almost continually cut tax rates on the rich, as detailed in the following section.

Income Tax Rates

As suggested in the preceding sketch of the history of wealth concentration, the level of federal taxation is directly tied to the level of concentration of income and wealth and thus also to social inequality. A history of the income tax in America reveals this relationship clearly.

America's first experience with an income tax was in 1861, when the Union needed extra revenue to fight the Civil War. Based on an individual's ability to pay, a 3% tax on yearly income over $800 was imposed (Lewis, Allison, and the Center for Public Integrity, 2001). Taxes were withheld from corporations' dividends and from government employees' salaries. After the Civil War, in 1872, most taxes were repealed, including the income tax itself. Taxes on liquor and tobacco were the main source of government revenue by 1868 and made up nearly 90% of government income from then until 1913, when the income tax became a permanent feature of American life *via* the 16th Amendment to the Constitution (ibid.). By 1918, there were 55 income brackets, a maximum individual tax rate of 77%, and a corporate rate of 12%. Still, only the wealthiest 5% of the population paid income tax. After World War I, however, a series of four tax cuts during the 1920s lowered the top individual income tax rate from 77% to 25% (Phillips, 2002).

During the Great Depression, Franklin Roosevelt and Congress raised the top individual tax brackets, implemented inheritance taxes, and eliminated personal holding companies through which some of the rich had deducted the expenses of their estates, stables, etc. A number of other taxes were implemented as well, including taxes on capital stock and dividend receipts. The Social Security Act of 1935 imposed a wage tax—half paid by employers, half by employees—for a system of federally funded retirement benefits (ibid.). By 1936, the maximum individual tax rate had jumped back up, to 79%, and the concentration of wealth had plummeted.

During World War II, Congress dramatically expanded the reach of the income tax. The number of taxpayers grew from 4 million to 43 million between 1939 and 1945. From 1940 to 1944, tax rates were raised from 4% to 19% for the bottom tax bracket, while the marginal (top) rate for the wealthy was increased to 88% (Lewis, Allison, and the Center for Public Integrity, 2001, p. 11). As noted above, this high tax rate decreased wealth concentration by half by 1944 (Phillips, 2002).

During the post-World War II years of broadly shared prosperity in the U.S., income taxes on the rich were high. In 1948, the effective tax rate of the richest 1% of families was 76.9%. During the 1950s, it was 85.5%. But Democrat John F. Kennedy brought tax rates for the rich down in 1963 to 77%; and then the effective tax rate of the top 1% was reduced further, in 1965 (ibid.).

In the 1980s, Ronald Reagan's administration cut the top income tax bracket from 70% to 28%. By 1989 the portion of the nation's wealth held by the top 1% had jumped to 39%, nearly twice where it was during the New Deal—and almost where it had been in 1929 (ibid.). Since then, tax rates on the rich have plummeted further, and concentrated wealth and income have climbed again. Phillips describes the "Reagan Revolution":

> During the 1980s, conservative governments cut taxes, conservatized the judiciary, deregulated the economy, passed punitive labor policy, freed trade for corporations to go abroad, and increased the federal role in bailing out shaky banks, savings and loans, and Latin American debtors.
>
> *(2002, p. 93)*

As a consequence, there was a shift from the broad-based prosperity of the post-World War II decades to the prosperity of the financial elite (see also Galbraith, 1998).

However, beginning with Reagan's administration, the effective tax rate of the *middle-class* (median income) family increased steadily: From 5.3% in 1948 to 24.63% in 1990 (Phillips, 2002). Payroll taxes (FICA, or Federal Insurance Contributions Act for Social Security and Medicare, for example) paid by middle-class individuals have also risen dramatically: From 6.9% in 1950 to 31.1% in 2000 (ibid.).

Taxes and the Very Rich

In 2011, multi-billionaire Warren Buffet famously announced that his effective tax rate was lower than his secretary's, whose effective rate was 30% (effective rates include payroll taxes).

Research reveals that Buffett's situation is typical. The Citizens for Tax Justice found in 2011 that taxpayers with $10 million or more in investment income in 2012 paid an average of 17.2% of their income in federal income taxes and payroll taxes—which means Buffett's effective federal tax rate of around 17.4% is not unusual for investors with his income (Citizens for Tax Justice, 2011b).

Indeed, the IRS confirmed this disparity, reporting that the average effective tax rate (after deductions and credits) of the 400 highest-income taxpayers in 2008 was only 18.1%, lower than most middle-income rates (Internal Revenue Service, 2011).

Tax havens, multiple deductions only available to those with great wealth, and a lower tax rate of 15% on dividends and long-term capital gains (which are the primary source of income for the wealthy) constitute the main reasons why many of the affluent pay at lower rates than middle-class families.

It is sometimes argued that the rich give to others philanthropically, so they should not have to pay taxes. However, a Forbes study in 2007 revealed that, with the exception of Bill Gates and Warren Buffett, whose giving is quite large, the average rate of giving by the wealthy is a mere 1% of their income. An IRS study reported that the wealthiest Americans—those making over $500,000 annually, which is less than 1% of all tax filers—gave away a slightly larger portion, 3.4% of their income in 2008 (Congressional Budget Office, 2010).

In either case, the proportion of income donated is far smaller than would be paid in legally owed taxes. And the more money one has, the more taxes are deducted for each "gift." The amount of tax savings depends on the donor's marginal, or highest, bracket. For taxpayers in the top bracket, a $10,000 gift would reduce taxes by $3,500, while those in the 25% bracket would save $2,500 in taxes (Rosen, 2011).

This section has described ways in which rich individuals and families have been paying less and less over the decades, and the middle class has been paying more. As we see in the next section, however, many of the large U.S. corporations pay nothing.

Corporate Taxes

In 2012, the U.S. had the highest corporate tax rate in the world, at 35%. However, due to both legal and illegal machinations, corporations rarely pay that rate—as this section documents. Despite the higher statutory rate, corporate income tax revenues are lower in the U.S. than in most European countries.

> According to data from the Organization for Economic Cooperation and Development, total federal and state corporate income tax revenues in the United States in 2000, measured as a share of the economy, were about one-quarter less than the average for other OECD member countries. Thirty-five years ago, the opposite was true—corporations in the United States bore a heavier burden than their European counterparts.
>
> *(Friedman, 2003)*

This section reveals how far the corporate share of federal and state revenues has shrunk.

The share of the total U.S. federal tax burden paid by corporations declined from 40% of the total in the 1940s to 26.5% in 1950, and to 10.2% in 2000. In 2001, the corporate share of total federal taxes paid by corporations was down to 9.2%. And *The Wall St. Journal* reported in 2011 that the corporate share of the total revenue collected by the federal government in that year was an even lower 7.9% (Paletta, 2012).

A look at the share of federal *income* taxes—as opposed to total federal taxes—paid reveals that the share of income taxes corporations pay has also plummeted over the decades, while the share paid by individuals has risen. Corporate income taxes were more than half (59.6%) of all federal income taxes paid in 1943, and by 2008 had plummeted to 20.9% (author's calculations based on White House Data, Office of Management and the Budget House, www.whitehouse.gov/omb/budget/Historicals).

During the 1940s, corporate income taxes averaged 4.9% of the GDP. During the 1950s, they averaged 4.7% of GDP. They have declined further, to where in the 1990s, corporate tax receipts averaged 1.9% of GDP; in 2003, they were a slightly lower 1.3% of GDP (U.S. General Accounting Office, 2004, p. 5; see also Fisher, 2002). In 2009, corporate contributions were about the same as in 2003.

Corporations have been contributing less and less to the U.S. Gross National Product in part because more of their operations and sales take place in other countries. Forty-seven percent of sales of the largest corporations were produced and sold outside of the U.S., up from 45.8% in 2007 and 43.6% in 2006 (Silverblatt, 2009).

The corporate share of GDP has declined also because they take advantage of off-shore strategies to hide income. In 2008, the Government Accountability Office reported that 83 of the 100 largest publicly traded corporations in the U.S. had subsidiaries in jurisdictions listed as tax havens (Shaxson, 2012).

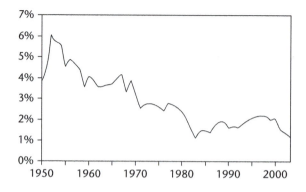

FIGURE 4.2 Corporate income tax receipts as a share of GDP, 1950–2003

Source: Center on Budget and Policy Priorities. www.cbpp.org/cms/index.cfm?fa=view&id=1321

State and local taxes paid by corporations have also declined. *In 1957, corporations provided 45% of all local property tax revenues in the states*, but by 1987 their share had plummeted to about 16%. *By 2002, the corporate share of total state and local taxes paid was only 2.9%* (Mishel, Bernstein, and Boushey, 2003). Research has shown that the decline in the effective state-local corporate income tax rate is due to changes in state tax policies, not to shifts in economic activity toward lower-tax states (Fisher, 2002; Fox and Luna, 2010).

Probably the most egregious aspect of the corporate tax situation is the fact mentioned earlier: Most of the largest corporations pay little or no federal income tax at all, and some obtain tax rebates. In the first edition of *Radical Possibilities* I cited a study by the U.S. General Accounting Office which revealed that 60% of the largest and most profitable corporations pay no federal income tax at all (U.S. General Accounting Office, 2004). I also discussed a study by the well-regarded organization, Citizens for Tax Justice, showing that low audit rates since Reagan's administration, tax breaks, and "congressional indifference to abusive offshore corporate tax shelters," cost the American taxpayers over $170 billion annually (2002b, p. 1). Three examples from this 2002 study follow (details are available on the Citizens for Tax Justice website, http://ctj.org).

Microsoft enjoyed more than $12 billion in total tax breaks between 1996 and 2000. In fact, Microsoft actually paid no tax at all in 1999, despite $12.3 billion in reported U.S. profits. Microsoft's tax rate between 2000 and 2002 was only 1.8% on $21.9 billion in pre-tax U.S. profits.

General Electric, one of America's most profitable corporations, reported $50.8 billion in U.S. profits between 1996 and 2000, but paid only 11.5% of that in federal income taxes. That low tax rate reflected almost $12 billion in corporate tax welfare for General Electric.

IBM reported $5.7 billion in U.S. profits in 2000, but paid only 3.4% of that in federal income taxes. In 1997, IBM reported $3.1 billion in U.S. profits, and instead of paying taxes, got a tax rebate. Between 1996 and 2000, IBM enjoyed a total of $4.7 billion in corporate tax welfare.

Later studies confirm this trend toward lower corporate tax payments, noting that *corporate profits are higher than they were before the recession, but tax rates are lower* (Eavis, 2013). As *The Wall St. Journal* reported,

> Corporate tax receipts as a share of profits are at their lowest level in at least 40 years. Total corporate federal taxes paid fell to 12.1% of profits earned from activities within the U.S. in fiscal 2011 … according to the Congressional Budget Office. That's the lowest level since at least 1972…. Corporate income-tax receipts typically fall during recessions, and they declined sharply after the 2008 financial crisis, which wiped out big swaths of profits across the huge financial sector. But U.S. profits have rebounded sharply in recent quarters, while tax receipts have stayed low.
>
> *(Paletta, 2012, p. 1; see also Eavis, 2013)*

In November of 2011, the Institute on Taxation and Economic Policy and Citizens for Tax Justice issued a study of the federal income taxes paid, or not paid, by 280 profitable Fortune 500 corporations between 2008 and 2010 (Citizens for Tax Justice, 2011c). As the authors of the report noted, the federal tax code states that corporations are supposed to pay 35% of their profits in income taxes. The vast majority of these profitable corporations paid considerably less. And some paid nothing at all and received rebates.

> Over the three years covered by our study, the average effective tax rate for all 280 companies was only 18.5%. For the past two years, 2009 and 2010, the effective tax rate for all 280 companies averaged only 17.3%, less than half of the statutory 35% rate.
>
> *(ibid., p. 1)*

Thirty corporations, whose pre-tax U.S. profits totaled $160 billion, paid less than nothing in aggregate federal income taxes over the entire 2008–10 period. These companies included Pepco Holdings, General Electric, DuPont, Verizon, Boeing, Wells Fargo, and Honeywell. The government paid out over $31 billion of taxpayers' money to these and other companies in the form of tax rebates. A June 2011 report by the same group found that 12 of the largest corporations pay effective tax rate of negative 1.4% on $175 billion in profits, and take in $63.7 billion in tax subsidies—Exxon Mobil, FedEx, Wells Fargo, Yahoo, Boeing, and Verizon are in this group (Citizens for Tax Justice, 2011a).

It seems fair to say that corporate America does not contribute to U.S. federal, state, or local public expenses commensurate with its ability to pay. By the estimates provided above (some are much higher) this tax avoidance by corporations deprives the federal government alone of at the very least $200 billion a year with which to provide for the public good, including services like education.

Taxes, the Deficit, and Social Spending

We often hear complaints from politicians, officials, and policy wonks that "we have no money" for better schools, higher teacher salaries, preservation of Medicare, Medicaid, Social Security, efforts to eliminate poverty, create jobs, etc. Pundits in Congress and elsewhere argue that the U.S. debt (the deficit) is too large; if we spend money, they say, we should be spending it to repay the banks and others who have lent the government money. The very rich invest money wherever it seems to provide safe interest—like U.S. Treasury bills, which are interest-bearing loans to the federal government. Foreign investors own most of the U.S. national debt, but over 40% is owned by Americans—mostly the very wealthy (Reich, 2011b).

When Bill Clinton was President in the 1990s, Congress raised tax rates on the affluent, and the economy boomed. Tax revenues were strong, and there was no deficit. In the early 2000s, George Bush cut taxes on the wealthy and spent $3 trillion on the war in Iraq and Afganistan (Stiglitz, 2008b); then, the Great Recession reduced tax revenue, and the government provided billions to the largest banks. All these factors combined to produce a deficit of over $1 trillion.

Yet I, along with others on the political left, argue that there are plenty of funds to pay for deficit reduction *and* social programs—but the money is in the hands of the wealthy and the large corporations rather than in government accounts. A simple answer? Tax the rich and end the wars. Indeed, numerous studies provide ways to raise much-needed money by collecting taxes that should have been paid, and by instituting a small financial transaction tax on Wall Street. A consensus among the estimates produced by these studies includes the following:

The IRS estimates that about 17% of individual and small business taxes owed is not paid each year, leaving an underpayment of $450 billion a year. Tax avoidance by large corporations is between $200 billion and $500 billion yearly. Corporate tax haven losses range from $337 billion to $500 billion yearly. A tiny financial transaction tax on Wall Street financial activities would yield up to $500 billion each year (Buchheit, 2012; for similar proposals to raise money by taxing the rich see Baker, Pollin, McArthur, and Sherman, 2009; Hacker and Pierson, 2010; Anderson and Cavanaugh 2011; Bernstein, 2011; Leonhardt, 2011; Bartlett, 2012; Huang and Marr, 2012, among others).

The income gathered by these means would more than pay off the deficit in a 12-month period. If we combined these efforts with a repeal of the Bush-era tax cuts for the wealthy, and a more progressive tax code, as we saw in a previous section characterized earlier decades of our history, we would have plenty of money to pay down the deficit, build and better equip poor schools, pay teachers equitably, create good jobs, alleviate poverty, and buttress the social sphere overall. I provide other mechanisms for creating financial equity later in this chapter.

Conservatives often argue that cutting taxes, especially for those with wealth, stimulates the economy and thereby produces jobs. However, research consistently shows that cutting taxes does not stimulate the economy. Periods of higher taxation are associated with stronger economic growth, and periods of tax cuts with less economic growth—compare, most recently, the 1990s Clinton-era tax raise and the strong economy of the late 1990s with the 2001 and 2003 Bush-era tax cuts and the ensuing weak economy. *Indeed, a study by the non-partisan Congressional Research Service employing data since 1945 found that cutting tax rates on the rich does not grow the economy—it just increases income inequality* (Fieldhouse, 2011; Fieldhouse and Pollack, 2011; Hungerford, 2012; Porter, 2012).

So why has the federal government failed to collect taxes from large profitable corporations, impose higher taxes on the rich, and institute a financial transaction tax on Wall Street trading activity? One reason such laws have not been forthcoming may be that rules concerning taxes and money are made by Congress—and members of Congress are almost always wealthy: In 2012, over half were in the top 1%. Typically, other members of Congress are in the 91st–95th percentiles. Much of this wealth is in the form of investments in the large banks and other profitable corporations that would be subject to collection efforts and higher taxes (Center for Responsive Politics, 2011).

Tax Policy and the Working Poor

The largest businesses may experience corporate welfare, and individuals at the top of the income scale may find loopholes to avoid taxes, but—like the middle class—the working poor pay taxes that take a real bite out of pay. Despite years of tax-cutting, poor families in many states still face a substantial burden when they file personal income taxes. I reported in the first edition of this book that at the turn of the 21st century, in almost half of states that levy income taxes—19 out of 42 states—two-parent families of four with incomes below the federal poverty line owed income tax. In 17 of those states, single-parent families of three who are poor also pay income taxes. Moreover, about half of 23 states that do not tax the poor still tax families with incomes just above the poverty line, even though as we saw in previous chapters, such families typically have great difficulty making ends meet. In some states, families at poverty-level incomes are charged income tax bills of several hundred dollars (Johnson, et al., 2002). This situation continues in 2012, most egregiously in the South, and many states have raised fees (e.g., for vehicle registration, etc.) that take larger percentages of pay from low-income workers than others (Newman and Rourke, 2011).

It's often claimed by conservatives that the richest Americans pay a disproportionate share of taxes while those in the bottom half pay nothing. This is a disingenuous claim. Indeed,

Virtually every person in America pays some type of tax. Everyone who works pays federal payroll taxes. Everyone who buys gasoline pays federal and state gas taxes. People who shop in stores pay the sales taxes that most state and local governments impose. State and local property taxes affect everyone who owns or rents a home. (Even renters pay property taxes because landlords pass some of the tax on to them in the form of higher rents.) Most states also have income taxes, most of which are not particularly progressive.

(Lowrey, 2012; see also Citizens for Tax Justice, 2012)

The payroll Social Security tax, for example, is extremely regressive—low-income workers pay proportionally more than rich ones. Social Security tax is paid on money earned up to a threshold of 6.2% of income—or a limit of $113,700 in 2013. Income earned above that amount is not taxed for Social Security, although people who earn above that amount collect top rates of Social Security later on. Wealthy earners pay only the tiny 1.45% Medicare portion of the payroll tax on their earnings. As federal income tax has been cut, a larger and larger portion of federal revenues has been coming from payroll taxes. At the end of World War II, the payroll tax provided 2% of federal revenues; in 2002 it provided 37%, and in 2011 about the same (36%). The rise in the proportion of payroll taxes is a consequence of the fact that major tax cuts of the past 30 years have been heavily tilted toward the rich, and federal payroll taxes have been

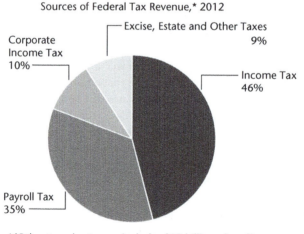

Sources of Federal Tax Revenue,* 2012

Excise, Estate and Other Taxes 9%

Corporate Income Tax 10%

Income Tax 46%

Payroll Tax 35%

* 'Other taxes' category includes $82 billion of profits on assets held by the Federal Reserve.

FIGURE 4.3 Federal policy basics: where do federal tax revenues come from?

Source: Center on Budget and Policy Priorities. August 20, 2012. www.cbpp.org/cms/?fa= view&id=3822

increased to compensate. The payroll tax rose substantially in the 1980s, during the years Reagan was cutting income taxes on the rich.

The tax break provided by the EITC for low-income workers and their families is dwarfed by the federal tax breaks provided for middle-class and affluent homeowners. Homeowners are allowed five different federal tax breaks that cost the government billions of dollars a year. The best-known of these allows interest paid on mortgages for principal residences and vacation homes to be deducted on federal income tax returns. Two-thirds of the benefits go to families with high incomes.

Government regulations allow homeowners to deduct the interest on loans spent to buy, build, or improve a home, for mortgages up to $1 million. The tax break is extremely regressive. According to research by Poterba and Sinai (2008), the tax savings for households earning more than $250,000 is ten times the tax savings for households earning between $40,000 and $75,000 a year.

The National Housing Institute calculated that the mortgage interest deduction cost the Treasury slightly more than $58 billion in 1995. (In comparison, the entire 1995 budget for the Department of Housing and Urban Development was $26 billion that year (Zepezauer and Naiman, 1996).) By 2011, analysts figured that the mortgage deduction cost the Treasury about $100 billion a year (Gitis and Brannon, 2011).

Corrective Policies

Inequality, the concentration of huge amounts of income and wealth of America in a few hands, and the inequities of who is taxed for what are not the products of a laissez-faire economic system. They are the products of the same governments that have set minimum wage laws, appointed conservative judges, deregulated prices and wages, enacted punitive labor policies, passed trade laws that push employers to other countries, and appointed officials who do not enforce anti-discrimination laws.

This section describes policies that would shrink the concentration of wealth in the U.S. A wealth tax is one policy that would correct some of the financial inequities and would provide moneys to revitalize urban neighborhoods and schools. Wealth taxation is part of many systems in Europe. According to simulations produced by well-known economist Edward Wolff, even a very modest wealth tax like the Swiss system, with marginal tax rates ranging from 0.05% to 0.30% of wealth (with household effects, pensions, and annuities excluded) could have raised $38 billion in 1989. In the process, only 3% of families would have seen their federal tax bill rise by more than 10% (Wolff, 2002). Imposing the Swedish wealth tax, at 1.5% initially, rising to a high of 3.0%, would have added an additional $328.7 billion to U.S. public coffers in 1989.

Wolff updated these simulations to 1998, using the modest Swiss wealth tax system where the top bracket (the 0.30% range) begins at $1.66 million. If enacted in the U.S., this wealth tax would have created $52 billion in extra tax revenue in 1998 (and a slightly more modest tax would have produced $55 billion in 2001). The 1998 figure represents 1.0% of total family income and 7.1% of the total income tax revenue. This compares with actual U.S. personal income tax proceeds in 1998 of $737.5 billion, or 13.8% of total income. Only 16.7% of families would have seen their tax bill rise by more than $100, and only 8.5% by more than $300 (ibid.).

A 2011 analysis proposed that we levy a 2% annual wealth tax on households in the top one-half of 1%—those owning at least $7.2 million. "On very conservative assumptions, this tax would yield at least 70 billion dollars a year.... This means that, over the coming decade, a wealth tax on the super-rich would yield at least half the $1.5 trillion dollar deficit-reduction target" set by Congress in 2011 (Ackerman and Alstott, 2011, p. 1).

The most recent analyses (as of late 2012) estimate that if a 2% wealth tax was applied to everyone who had a net worth in excess of $5 million, the government would take in about $700 billion a year—a sum that would certainly be useful to shore up social service and pay down debt (see Krasting, 2012).

There is one more type of federal policy to be mentioned here that contributes significantly to inequality: The elevation of a U.S. financial governing body that is not elected—the Federal Reserve Board. This group of 13 appointed bankers has official authority over the money supply of the nation (Johnson, 2010). An example of how this can become important has been offered by James Galbraith, economist son of mid-20th century economist John Kenneth Galbraith.

James Galbraith argued that decades of high interest rates contributed heavily to the dramatic increases in the income of the richest 10% of Americans since 1980. The Federal Reserve Board continually raised interest rates during the 1970s and 1980s, and as a result working-class and middle-class Americans began paying more and more interest on their credit cards, mortgages, and other debts (including the national debt). Some of this interest payment went to the relatively affluent—like many professionals—through well-performing pension funds. But most of the interest went to the wealthiest 10% of Americans—because they are the ones who hold major stock in the banks owning the credit cards, mortgages, and other debts. And by the mid-2000s, average American credit card, mortgage, and other debt was at an all-time high. Galbraith (1998) demonstrates that these interest payments became a major component of the incomes of the wealthiest Americans throughout the 1980s and of the increases in inequality during that decade.

Indeed, Galbraith demonstrates that the interest payments Americans paid on their debts became a huge transfer program—*a transfer of money from working class and middle class to the rich*. This transfer of money through interest payments to the very wealthy is almost equal to the entire amount that the government pays out to those receiving Social Security, Medicare, Supplemental Security Income (SSI), unemployment insurance, welfare, and veterans' benefits combined. In 1995, government transfer payments for Social Security and Medicare constituted about 17.5% of income in the U.S., while interest payments by the middle class and poor to the wealthy constituted 13% of income, only 4% less (ibid.).

During the years of high interest, while Americans were paying these vast sums to wealthy stockholders, many Americans lost their jobs: Unemployment had been 3.9% in 1969 after a period of low interest rates, and it was 11% in 1982 after almost a decade of higher interest rates. Federal Reserve policy that kept interest rates relatively high is thus one more macroeconomic policy that contributed to increased inequality.

When governments tax their wealthy citizens at rates of 77% and 80%, as the U.S. did for many decades of the 20th century, the concentration of resources in a few pockets shrinks considerably, and there is more money for spending on public needs. In the U.S., high taxes on the rich paid many social expenses in the decades after World War II. Since the mid-1960s, the rich have paid smaller and smaller percentages of their wealth in taxes, and relative social spending has slowed. Today, as I have noted, wealth is as highly concentrated as it was in 1929 before the Stock Market Crash; and for millions of Americans, the social safety net has been shredded. The more of society's resources the rich accumulate, the less available for investment in education, infrastructure, and other public goods; and the less there is to provide resources for those who are in need.

Poverty in America may be "good for business," as Alan Greenspan implied when he remarked that large numbers of unemployed people keep wages down, but poverty also follows this decline, and has tragic consequences for those who suffer through it (Greenspan's remark, in Pollin, 1998, p. 20).

Poverty and extremes of inequality have direct effects on urban students and schools. A detailed look at some of these consequences is the subject of the next chapter.

5

NEW HOPE FOR URBAN STUDENTS

Macroeconomic policies that set the minimum wage below poverty levels, that train inner-city hopefuls for jobs that do not exist, that do not extract from the wealthy a fair share of social expenses, and that rarely enforce laws that would decrease substantially the economic discrimination of people of color, all support persistent poverty and near-poverty among minority urban populations. This economic and social distress can prevent children from opportunities to develop their full potential. Holding two low-wage jobs to make ends meet can sap the energy of a parent and make it more difficult for her to negotiate the public systems in which her children are enmeshed. Being poor in a rich country can lead to ill-placed shame, pervasive despair, and anger. Living in poverty is to experience daily crises of food, a place to live, and ways to keep your children safe. All this can be debilitating, and can certainly dampen the enthusiasm, effort, and expectations with which urban children and their families approach K-12 education.

Moreover, the low social status and perceived lack of clout often ascribed to those who are poor and black or Latino may prevent staff in institutions like schools, government agencies, and hospitals from offering respect and proper treatment. It often leads to a lack of accountability on the part of the public institutions themselves—a situation that is rarely, if ever, allowed to occur in affluent suburbs.

While poverty does not prevent educational achievement, it certainly limits one's chances to obtain it. As I report below, many studies confirm the potential of impoverished circumstances to prevent the acquisition of the kinds of knowledge middle-class institutions like schools require of students. Of countervailing power, however, is an increasingly robust body of research demonstrating that when parents obtain better jobs or more income and increased family supports, the educational achievement of the children typically improves significantly. These findings empirically support the argument that for the urban poor, even with the right educational reforms in place, school achievement may have to await a family's economic access.

The following two sections of this chapter describe the consequences of poverty for urban education and children, and the final section provides hopeful results of efforts to provide economic and social supports to low-income families.

The Urban Political Economy

It is prudent to remember that federal policies are not only implicated in personal and familial poverty, but make significant contributions to the erosion of the property tax base in urban neighborhoods as well. In *Ghetto Schooling* (Anyon, 1997), I examined 20th-century federal policies that provided strong encouragement for business enterprises to move from urban locations to suburbia. Such policies included the following, among others: Federal guidelines that forbad bank loans for housing rehabilitation or purchase in city neighborhoods ("redlining," beginning in the 1930s), with the resulting deterioration of housing stock and discouragement of business investment in cities; in the late 1940s and '50s, policies that gave substantial tax deductions to businesses that moved from the city rather than renovate; investment tax credits beginning in 1962 that allowed manufacturers to take credit for new industrial plants and equipment but not renovation of existing ones; relocation tax breaks to large corporations; and, during the suburbanization of the post-World War II periods, federal (as well as state) subsidies and land grants to developers and municipalities to build highways, sewer and electric lines, homes and office buildings in the suburbs there but not in the city (ibid.).

By the mid-1960s, many inner cities had lost to the suburbs not only most of their middle-class residents, but most of their supermarkets, banks, doctor's offices, department stores, hospitals, pharmacies, theatres, and movies. Liquor stores and undertakers remained. Indeed, in old industrial cities like Newark, Baltimore, Boston, Chicago, Cleveland, Detroit, Milwaukee, Philadelphia, Pittsburg, St. Louis, and Trenton, Boards of Education had begun complaining in the mid-1930s of a dearth of business "ratables" with which to fund education. The city property tax base (which provided the major funding for education) continued to deteriorate following the Great Depression, and remains low—despite the redevelopment of many "downtowns," and the gentrification of some neighborhoods, from which low-income people are pushed out by higher rents. Indeed, many cities have extremely valuable downtown property (think of the financial centers in New York, Chicago, San Francisco, and Atlanta) but city, state, and federal corporate tax rates on this property are about the lowest on record. As a result, wealthy corporations in these downtowns contribute little toward urban education and other city services.

Contrary to the assumptions of education policy, analysts who argue that "money doesn't matter" and contradicting federal legislation (e.g., the No Child Left Behind Act) that assumes it does not, low urban property tax receipts and insufficient additional school financing have devastating effects on public education. The lack of a property base to pay for services in cities affects school districts by impoverishing them. Despite 30-something years of educational finance litigation, the moneys available to large urban school systems have not increased enough to offset the disadvantages wrought by the ravages of the macroeconomy.

The Education Trust, an independent Washington, D.C.-based group monitors funding available to city districts, and in a 2001 study demonstrated cities' continued lack of financial resources—despite the strong economy of the time. "The Funding Gap: Low-Income and Minority Students Receive Fewer Dollars" (The Education Trust, 2001) reports that in most states, school districts that educate the largest number of poor and minority students have fewer state and local dollars to spend per student than districts with the least number of poor and minority students. They found that districts that educate the largest number of poor students receive an average $966 less per student than low-poverty districts.

These individual gaps in funding sum to significant gaps per school. In New York, for example, the state with the largest discrepancy, there is a difference of $2,152 per student between state and local revenues available in high poverty districts and revenues available in low poverty districts.

> This gap translates into a difference of $860,800 between two elementary schools of 400 students each, enough to compete with elite suburban schools for the most qualified teachers and to provide the kinds of additional instructional time and other resources that research and data show can make a difference.
>
> *(ibid., 2)*

The per-student funding gaps translate into the following school-wide gaps per year in a typical elementary school of 400 students with classrooms of 25 students: In Illinois, $824,000; in Montana, $614,000; in Pennsylvania, $499,200; and in Michigan, $441,200.

The Education Trust's latest study (2012) of education funding finds the same kinds of disparities, and reveals that they have increased—we are still spending less on schools with concentrations of low-income children of color. Nationally, the districts that serve the largest concentrations of students of color receive an average of $1,100 less per student in state and local funds than the districts that do not serve predominately minority students.

These funding gaps magnify the effects of family poverty in urban neighborhoods.

Urban Children and Social Class

I have already presented adult poverty figures at the official threshold, and the alarming increase in numbers when a more realistic assessment is made. The same disparities exist between federal and alternative counts of poor children.

In 2010, after the Great Recession had officially ended, the percentages of children in poverty and near poverty had increased substantially over former years. In 2010, 44% of children under 18 (31.9 million) lived in low-income families and 21% (15.5 million) lived in poor families, according to official count. (In this and the following paragraphs, poverty is defined using the U.S. Census Bureau's official measure. Children in families with income less than 100% of the poverty threshold are considered poor. Children in families with income less than 200% of the poverty threshold are considered *low income*.)

The percentage of children living in low-income families (i.e., both poor and near poor) has been on the rise—increasing from 40% in 2005 to *44% in 2010*. During this time period, the overall number of children of all ages increased by nearly 2% while the numbers who were low-income and poor increased by 11% and 17%, respectively (Addy and Wight, 2012).

Black, American Indian, and Hispanic children comprise a disproportionate share of low-income children. Together, they represent 38% of all children but more than one-half (54%) of low-income children. They are also more than twice as likely to live in a low-income family as white and Asian children.

- 31% of white children (12.1 million) live in low-income families.
- 64% of black children (6.5 million) live in low-income families.
- 31% of Asian children (1.0 million) live in low-income families.
- 63% of American Indian children (0.4 million) live in low-income families.
- 43% of children of some other race (1.3 million) live in low-income families.
- 61% of children of immigrant parents (8.1 million) live in low-income families.
- 41% of children of native born parents (22.4 million) live in low-income families.

Although a majority of children in rural areas are in low-income families, there are many more low-income children in urban areas:

- 42% of children in urban areas (24.0 million) live in low-income families.
- 51% of children in rural areas (5.7 million) live in low-income families (ibid.).

We have long known that social class, or socio-economic status (SES), is highly correlated with educational achievement: Generally, the higher the resource background of the child's family, the higher the achievement (see Coleman, 1993; Lee and Burkam, 2002, among others). Demographer and independent scholar David Rusk, for example, measured the correlation between SES and educational success by identifying school percentages of low-income students. He found that in communities across the U.S., a full 65% to 85% of school variation in standardized test scores is explained by variations in the school's percentage of low-income students (Rusk, 1999; see also Kahlenberg, 2003; National Center for Educational

Statistics, 2003). The rest of this chapter addresses the power of poverty and low SES to affect school achievement.

An Important Caveat

As a professor in a doctoral program in urban education, I work with students to develop deep critiques of scholarship that we read, including my own (Anyon, 2011b). In the fall semester of 2012, as I was rewriting *Radical Possibilities*, several members of my class argued that this chapter in the 2005 version presented a deficit view of urban students. In that text I described research studies that found "lower cognitive development" in young children of lower SES (regardless of race). But since I was discussing urban schools, the implication was that the children with low cognitive development were African American or Latino. I presented this research to lay the foundation for the argument that followed—that since poverty caused lower cognitive development, providing poor families with financial and other supports would assist in developing children's full potential.

Later that evening I read the chapter over, and was startled to find that I agreed with the assessment of "deficit thinking." The very use of the phrase "lower cognitive development" to describe young children implied deficits. But I taught elementary school in extremely poor, urban, African American neighborhoods for seven years, "way back in the day," and I *know* how bright, creative, linguistically adept, and resilient these youngsters are. So I rethought, and have rewritten, the following section of this chapter with an eye toward being clearer about achievement and poverty: Poverty doesn't stunt children's cognitive growth so much as it prevents opportunities for educational achievement.

The measures on which low-income children fall short are those calibrated on middle- and upper-middle-class (white) language usage, experience, and knowledge. Therefore, deficits on these scales are deficits in what is standard for the middle and upper-middle classes. The vibrancy and fluency of language use, and the extensive knowledge of and insight into the world that urban children have acquired are not typically captured by these tests.

Yet school expects students to have, and evaluates students on the basis of, this middle and upper-middle class *cultural capital*—a patently unfair situation, since (as Pierre Bourdieu would remind us) schools do not distribute this cultural capital to those who do not have it. Importantly, the standardized scales identify the kinds of knowledge all students need to know in order to enter into and succeed in a white middle-class economy. Thus, as Lisa Delpit has said, while we must respect and celebrate other ways of knowing and speaking, it is important also to teach low-income students of color the "codes of power" (Delpit, 2006).

Given the obsession with high-stakes standardized tests today, we need to continually remind ourselves that these tests do *not* measure everything—and as I noted above, they miss much of value that working-class and poor students of all races acquire as they develop. The problems poor children may have with these tests and in school are typically produced by the constant crises of living in poverty—not by skin color or other genetic differences among races or social groups. As I have been at pains to explain throughout my career, the following factors, among others, can lower academic achievement for poor students: Lack of primary medical care, resulting in frequent health problems, lack of glasses, and school absences; frequent or long-term parent unemployment and subsequent family crises; apartment or house losses that require too frequent moves to new schools; life in neighborhoods of high crime and the stress this can cause, among others.

The confluence of these and other hardships in poverty neighborhoods and families has been found to have consistently negative effects on children's performance on standardized tests. Longitudinal studies demonstrate that family income consistently predicts children's academic performance, even when other family characteristics are taken into account (see, among others, McLoyd, Jayaratne, Ceballo, and Borquez, 1994; Bolger and Patterson, 1995; Duncan and Brooks-Gunn, 1997; Korenman and Miller, 1997; Houser, Brown, and Prosser, 1998; McLoyd, 1998a, 1998b; Dahl and Lochner, 2008).

In fact, Sean F. Reardon and Kendra Bischoff discovered in 2011 that the *income-based gap* in test scores of children born since the 1950s has increased by a wide margin.

> Among children born around 1950, test scores of low-income children lagged behind those of their better-off peers by a little over half a standard deviation, about 60 points on an SAT-type test. Fifty years later, this gap was twice as large.
>
> *(cited in Duncan and Murname, 2011, p. 5)*

They found that during this period racial gaps in test scores diminished considerably. Indeed, the test scores of low- and high-income children parallel those of the highly skewed income distribution itself, with income-based gaps in test scores now twice as large as test score gaps between African Americans and whites (ibid.; see also Duncan and Murnane, 2011).

Explanations offered for the larger differences in scores of poor and affluent children are the large increases in inequality between the groups, and the more intense efforts of affluent parents to ensure educational supports for their children through frequent tutoring for standardized exams, multiple academic enrichments and lessons, and in general much larger outlays by middle- and upper-middle-class parents on educational supports than in decades past (Lundberg and Rose, 2004; Kornrich and Furstenburg, 2012).

Taken together, studies of poverty, SES, and educational achievement—which demonstrate that poverty often produces conditions suppressing the experiences that support school achievement—suggest that programs to raise the incomes of poor families would in turn enhance the achievement of children and improve their chances of success in education and later, in the economy.

Income Supports and Educational Achievement

There is strong evidence to suggest that income supports improve educational achievement. In March, 2001, for example, the Manpower Development Research Corporation (MDRC) published a synthesis of research on how welfare and work policies affect the children of single mothers (Morris et al., 2001). This synthesis reviewed data from evaluations of five programs that provided income supplements to poverty-wage workers (Florida's Family Transition Program; the Minnesota Family Investment Program; the National Evaluation of Welfare-to-Work Strategies; the New Hope program; and the Self-Sufficiency Project). These programs offered supports of differing kinds to poverty-wage workers—income supplements, earnings disregards [rules that allow working welfare recipients to keep more of their income when they go to work], subsidized health care, employment services, counseling, supervised after-school activities for children and youth, and informal get-togethers with project staff.

MDRC's review of the studies found that even relatively small income supplements to working parents—(amounting to about $4,000 per year) improved children's elementary school achievement by about 10% to 15% of the average variation in the control groups. These improvements were seen on test scores as well as ratings by parents and/or teachers. The earning supplements had "consistently positive impacts on children's [school] achievement" (ibid., p. 63). The positive effects were small, but were statistically significant (see also Morris, Duncan, and Clark-Kauffman, 2005; and Dahl and Lochner, 2008).

The earning supplements provided by these programs did not bring the families out of poverty. The improvements in children's school achievement and behavior from even these relatively meager cash supplements for working families suggest that if we were to increase family resources substantially, we could probably improve educational and social outcomes for children substantially.

A rigorous evaluation of New Hope, a work support program in Milwaukee, also documented gains in achievement and reductions in antisocial behavior that were particularly strong for boys (Duncan, Huston, and Weisner, 2007; Duncan, Ludwig, and Magnuson, 2010).

Duncan, Morris, and Rodrigues (2010) analyzed ten anti-poverty experiments and found a consistent pattern of better school results for children in programs that provided more income. Each $1,000 increase (in 2005 dollars) in annual income continued for two to five years led to statistically significant increases in young children's school performance on test scores. Chetty, Friedman, and Rockoff (2011) compared data for grades 3–8 from a large urban school district with corresponding families' federal tax records. They found that even with conservative estimates, small amounts of additional income leads to significant increases in students' achievement test scores.

Additionally, a study by Duncan and Magnuson (2011, p. 27) found that an additional $3,000 (in 2005 dollars) provided to a working parent during a child's early years "appears to boost children's achievement by roughly one-fifth of a standard deviation … so 20 percent of a standard deviation amounts to about two months' advantage in school."

Gordon Berlin, the president of MDRC (one of the nation's leading research organizations, well-regarded for its careful evaluation of anti-poverty and welfare-to-work programs) has summarized the results of studies of income and education. Berlin (2007) noted:

> [There is] a remarkably strong body of research—much of it based on large-scale, well-implemented, experimental research designs—showing that supplementing the earnings of parents helps raise families out of poverty and improves the school performance of young children. This point is so important—and to many so surprising—that I want to state it again: We have reliable evidence involving thousands of families in multiple studies demonstrating that "making work pay" causes improvements in young children's school performance.

The fact that school achievement improves as family resources increase makes sense: Parents with sufficient time and money are more likely to be able to nurture their children's school achievement with educational supports—computers linked to the internet, tutoring, lessons, sports and arts programs, and educationally useful visits to museums and concerts. These parents will typically transmit positive expectations of college acceptance and labor market preparation. And they will have, or be able to procure, the funds for these. There is firm logic in the attention of parents to developing the capacities and cultural capital of their children: The social class resources purchased by affluence are certainly the educational "basics." They are demanded by curriculum and pedagogy, and rewarded by colleges and the labor market.

I believe that in the long run we would do better to enhance the access of the urban poor to economic resources so they, too, can afford the time, money, and inclination to prepare their children for school success. As it is, we depend on school reform to create the economic resources and capital that school success already requires; we depend on public schools to create equitable opportunities for urban graduates in a society that hoards economic resources from the minority poor. We are putting the cart before the horse.

Rather, we should—alongside equity-seeking educational reform—provide the financial base of support to urban families and communities that will in itself lay the basis for more school learning and better resourced schools, as in more affluent neighborhoods and towns. *The educational success of affluent districts demonstrates to me that economic strength is the engine of systemic school reform.*

In this and previous chapters I have delineated federal policies that undermine systemic school reform by maintaining large poverty populations in city neighborhoods. I have provided evidence that this poverty works against the achievement of urban students, and thus dwarfs the effects of curricular, peda-gogic, and administrative changes. I have also briefly reprised the political econ-omy of urban history and reminded us of federal decisions over the years that depleted the tax and other political economic resource sources of city govern-ments (and therefore districts) long ago. Importantly, however, we have also seen that even modest financial and other supports for poor families allow the children higher school achievement.

Before we can delve into ways to re-order federal policy priorities, I want to examine the effects of metropolitan dynamics on urban populations and schools. For metro-area arrangements exacerbate the inequitable consequences of federal policies. We will see, however, that regional coalitions of community-based groups challenging the federal and regional rules of the game have been making gains in the re-distribution of resources in a number of U.S. metro areas. These groups provide an example of what can be accomplished when we unite groups of people around a common goal and organize for more just public policies.

PART III

Metro Area Inequities

6

METRO AREAS AND THE REGIONAL GEOGRAPHY OF POVERTY

Job and Public Transit Mismatches

The U.S. is a nation of regions. Over 80% of Americans live in one of 366 metropolitan areas. Almost half the population lives in the 25 largest regions. While states are defined by geographic and political boundaries, metro areas are shaped by regional markets—for investment, jobs, and housing. Metro areas account for over 80% of national output, driving the economic performance of the nation as a whole. Each metro area is anchored by at least one city.

The Boston metropolitan area, for example, includes the city itself in a region encompassing five counties, 129 municipalities, and almost 3.2 million people. The metropolitan economy constitutes about two-thirds of the state economy. The City of Boston has less than 10% of the state's population, but provides 16% of its employment, produces 24% of its goods and services, 21% of total earned income, and 18% of state tax revenues. It is the largest city and the economic and cultural hub of the New England region and its 13.2 million people.

The first attempt to delineate regions of the U.S. was in the 1850 census— which reported educational statistics for five geographical divisions: New England states, middle states, southern states, southwestern states, and northwestern states. At the end of the 19th century, New York, Chicago, and many other cities moved to annex or consolidate adjacent territory to include land that could be developed. The formation of Greater New York from New York City, Brooklyn, the towns of Queens, Bronx, and Staten Island in 1898 was one of the first successful experiments in metropolitan consolidation (Dreier, Swanstrom, and Mollenkopf, 2001, p. 177).

The 2010 census revealed that, for the first time, within the nation's 100 largest metropolitan areas, a majority of whites, Hispanics, blacks and Asians live in the suburbs. The same is true of the foreign-born and poor, a majority of whom live in the metropolitan areas' suburbs rather than in the central cities.

Regional Spatial Mismatches

If we were to make a list of the strategies typically called upon to improve education in impoverished urban communities, policies intended to improve curriculum, assessment, and pedagogy would all appear. Policies that would place jobs in urban communities would *not* appear. And transportation policies that established bus and train routes from cities to outlying suburbs where entry-level jobs exist would also be left off our list.

Yet the availability of jobs in neighborhoods, or transportation to places of work elsewhere, are fundamental to the well being of urban residents—and therefore to their communities and schools—just as in more affluent communities.

This chapter demonstrates that the location of businesses and public transit routes in a metropolitan area are crucial determinants of where poverty is concentrated in the region—and important therefore to where in the metro area both private and public funds are available for families and for public schools. Inserting urban neighborhoods back into regional economies by locating metro area relevant business there, and providing bus and rail lines so low-income urban residents (most of whom lack auto transport) can reach outlying suburban job centers, are fundamentally important to the amelioration of urban poverty and the support of city schooling. It is in this sense that metro area job location and public transportation policies become covert education policies—and thus worthy of the support and active advocacy of those concerned about urban educational reform.

The arrangements and policies by which employment and public transit (and affordable housing and municipal tax receipts, discussed in the next chapter) are dispersed throughout the cities and towns of a metropolitan area not only have direct effects on resources available for individuals and schools in metro area neighborhoods. They support and in some cases exacerbate the deleterious effects of the federal polices described in previous chapters. The reform of metro area inequities needs to be among the solutions we seek to urban poverty and poverty schools. Indeed, this and the next chapter argue that *foundational education reforms would be regional transportation, housing, and municipal tax reform.*

While metropolitan areas exhibit problems of sprawl, traffic gridlock, long commutes, and environmental degradation, the problems of concern here are those that work to maintain individual and institutional poverty in central cities and segregated, urbanized suburbs: Spatial mismatches within regions of jobs and public transportation networks. These are determinative in important ways of the poverty of urban families, and (as a result) of their neighborhoods and schools, as well.

Jobs

For the last quarter-century, a spatial mismatch of entry-level jobs and prospective workers has characterized metropolitan regions: Most workers with low to moderate education levels live in central cities and low-income inner-ring urban suburbs, and most jobs for which they qualify are located in outlying suburbs. Two-thirds of all new jobs have located in these suburbs. Entry-level jobs such as routine manufacturing, retail, call centers, and data-entry have declined in central cities while growing on the urban fringe (Weitz and Crawford, 2012). High-density job clusters have emerged outside of the central business district, often along freeways and highways, creating multi-nucleated regions (Belzer and Srivastava, 2011).

A study of 92 metropolitan areas found only 17 places where city job growth outpaced suburban job growth during the 1990s. The bulk of the cities did gain jobs but at a slower pace than their suburban neighbors. For example, from 1994 to 1997, the central business districts in Ohio's seven major cities had a net increase of only 636 jobs. Their suburbs, by contrast, gained 186,410 new jobs (Katz, 2000, p. 8).

Employment steadily decentralized between 1998 and 2006: 95 out of 98 metro areas saw a decrease in the share of jobs located within three miles of downtown. The number of jobs in the top 98 metro areas increased overall during this time period, but the outer-most parts of these metro areas saw employment increases of 17%, compared to a gain of less than 1% in the urban core. Southern metro areas were particularly emblematic of the outward shift of job share to the suburban outer ring (Kneebone, 2009).

Exclusionary zoning (state or local regulations regarding land lot size, for example, taken up in more detail in the next chapter) limit the construction of affordable housing in the job-rich suburbs, and thereby prevent people who need the jobs from moving closer to them.

Few very low-income city residents have cars or public transportation available to travel to these out-lying jobs (Congressional Hearings on Reauthorization of Transportation Bill 1998). Thus, their transportation costs are high.

Indeed, housing and transportation are the two largest expenses for most households in the 28 metropolitan areas studied by the Center for Housing Policy in 2006. For households of all income levels, 27% of income goes on housing alone and another one-fifth goes to transportation costs. Together these items account for almost 48% of household income. Working families with incomes between $20,000 and $50,000 spend a similar percentage of income on housing; *however, their transportation costs consume almost 30% of their income* (Lipman, 2006).

Moreover, family location far from suburban employers means that they are not part of personal networks that apprise job seekers and employers of each other. Studies have found that most entry-level jobs are located through friends and relatives, not through want ads. In a study carried out in the Chicago region, for example, more than 40% of Chicago firms reported that they did not advertise their entry-level openings in newspapers. Rather, they relied on informal means, such as referrals from present workers, which they felt ensured a better-quality worker (Holzer, 1996, p. 82; see also Moss and Tilly, 2001). Yet, as William Julius Wilson (1997) has argued for this same city, residents of low-income neighborhoods are not only physically distant from those networks, they are less likely than others to have friends who are employed.

The spatial mismatch between jobs and people has a racial character. Two-thirds of all whites (including 55% of *poor* whites) now live in suburbs outside central cities where more than 80% of new job creation has occurred (including most low-skilled job creation). And many poor whites live in economically mixed, more middle-class areas. But African American and Latinos, as noted earlier, typically live in inner cities or segregated, fiscally distressed urbanized suburbs that have only sketchy public transit and few job opportunities (Stoll, 2005).

Understanding the association between employment decentralization and the suburbanization of poverty is important because of the continued growth of the suburban poor. During the first year of the Recession that began in 2007, suburbs added more than twice as many poor people as did their cities. The suburban poor face unique disadvantages. These include concentration in inner-ring, disadvantaged, and jobs-poor suburbs; overreliance on public transportation, which often provides inferior access to and within suburban areas; and spatial mismatch between where the suburban poor live and the locations of important social services, which are very few in low-income suburban areas.

The spatial mismatch between entry-level jobs and the minority poor suggests that *employment decentralization is a driver of the suburbanization of poverty* (Stoll, 2010; Liu and Painter, 2012).

There are a number of policies the implementation of which would connect urban job seekers with employment in regional economies: Training programs that make explicit connections between workers in urban centers and suburban employers; transportation reforms that provide public bus or train routes between the city and outlying job centers; the placement of businesses already successful in the regional market within central city and inner-ring suburban neighborhoods; mobility programs that move families who want to relocate to higher income, less-segregated areas; and affordable housing in more affluent areas so entry-level workers could reside closer to job centers.

As one example, innovative job training programs in a number of metropolitan areas have sought to link inner-city job seekers with suburban jobs through collaborations between community-based organizations, businesses, and educational institutions. One of the most successful is Project Quest in San Antonio, Texas. Two community organizations that are part of the Industrial Areas Foundation network—Communities Organized for Public Service (COPS) based in Catholic congregations in Mexican American neighborhoods, and Metro Alliance, based in Protestant churches in African American neighborhoods—joined together to create Project Quest. In the early 1990s, they learned that the San Antonio area had added about 19,000 jobs in health care, office work, education, and mechanical repair—with most of them long distances from urban neighborhoods. With the assistance of several local corporations, Project Quest identified occupations and sectors with growth potential and career ladders, and worked with businesses to design curriculum to train prospective employees. They put community pressure on elected politicians to provide $6 million in local, state, and federal funds. Between its inception in 1993 and the end of 1995, Project Quest placed more than 800 trainees in a "comprehensive, expensive package of supports, including child care, transportation assistance, medical care, tutoring, modest cash assistance for incidentals, and tuition to community colleges" (Dreier, Swanstrom, and Mollenkopf, 2001, p. 199). For these programs to succeed, however, transportation between cities and outlying jobs is essential.

Transportation

An ethnographic report in the *The New Yorker* magazine by MacArthur Award winner Katherine Boo (2003) describes efforts of two African American women living in a low-income neighborhood in Oklahoma City to obtain jobs and commute to work without a car. The only source of jobs for people in this low-income neighborhood was a distant shopping mall. The city provided no direct transit lines between the two places, so the women were forced to ride busses up to five hours a day to get to the mall and back. At one point for one of the women, the only available job at the mall was a night shift that ended at 9:00 pm; but the city busses on the routes she needed stopped running at 7:00 pm. In 1998, testimony before Congress in preparation for amendments of the Federal Transit Act documented the following: Even in metropolitan areas with excellent public transit systems, less than half the jobs are accessible by public transit; 94% of very low-income families do not own cars; most workers with annual incomes below $10,000 do not commute to work by car; many of the 2 million Americans who were scheduled to have their TANF (Temporary Assistance for Needy Families) grants terminated in 2002 were unable to get to jobs they could otherwise hold because there was no transportation available (Federal Transit Act of 1998, Congressional Findings).

In 1956, federal politicians promoted the Interstate Highway and Defense Act, which would depend on tax dollars, by arguing that it would defend Americans against the Soviet Union (Rusk, 2000, p. 79). This Act established the Highway Trust Fund, which built 41,000 miles of highways around cities and out to the developing suburbs and beyond. By the end of the 1990s, the Highway Trust Fund was spending gas taxes and other state and federal funds in the amount of $20 billion a year. Between 1975 and the mid-1990s, the U.S. spent $1.15 trillion on roads and highways, but only $187 billion for mass transit and $13 billion for intercity train transit [Amtrak]) (Dreier, Swanstrom, and Mollenkopf, 2001, p. 105). While more and more entry-level jobs have located in outlying areas, mass transit lines were never built to connect them to cities—travel by automobile has been the only route (see Jackson, 1995, 2000).

Indeed, in many states, cities and metro areas pay more in transportation taxes than they get back in services. In Colorado, for instance, the Denver metro area is allocated only 69 cents in revenues for each dollar of tax revenue it contributes. In the state of Washington, Seattle metro area raises 51% of the state's total revenues but is provided only 39% in return. Moreover, metropolitan areas now control only about 10 cents of every tax dollar they generate for transportation spending (Katz, Puentes, and Bernstein, 2003, p. 4).

In 1990, a number of transportation reform advocates created a national coalition to advocate for a new course in U.S. transportation policy. This coalition, the Surface Transportation Policy Project (STPP) was an alliance of environmentalists, social equity activists, transit supporters, community groups, and others. The coalition hoped to influence federal transportation law that was to be re-authorized in 1991; they wanted to increase funding for links between inner cities and suburban job centers. STPP crafted and successfully advocated for the new law—titled the Intermodal Surface Transportation Efficiency Act of 1991 (ISTEA)—which increased funding for public transit, and gave states and regions the discretion to transfer even more of their highway dollars to routes between inner city and outlying job centers. ISTEA also included requirements for public involvement in regional transportation planning (Chen and Jakowitsch, 2000, p. 4). However, only four states and the District of Columbia (California, Massachusetts, New York, and Oregon) transferred more than one-third of available funds to public transit allowable under ISTEA (Katz, Puentes, and Bernstein, 2003, p. 5).

In 1998, the Clinton administration was successful in obtaining passage of a transportation bill that for the first time provided the possibility of federal subsidies to metro areas to support the development of new bus routes, vanpools, shuttles, and mass transit connections between low-income urban and rural locations and suburban employment centers (potential funding for programs such as Bridges to Work, Access to Jobs, and Reverse Commute) (U.S. Department of Transportation, 1998). Localities had to compete for grants from $42 billion in federal funds allocated and, beginning in 1999, match them 50-50 with local funds. To date, only a few states or municipalities have taken advantage of opportunities for federal funds under this Act to build transit connections between inner cities and far-flung suburban job centers; most of those that did obtain grants built pedestrian-friendly walkways, or light rail systems for suburban commuters. In 2003, during reauthorization hearings for transportation funding, the Senate cut 16% of the "reverse commute" program in order to provide more money for suburban commuter rails. The transportation bill was the first to establish a regional approach to public transportation that would benefit urban job seekers (Puentes, 2003).

In a number of states, grassroots groups have organized around transportation issues. In North Carolina, a coalition called Democracy South worked with local media:

> to unmask an illicit quid-pro-quo system in which major state campaign contributors (mostly developers and contractors) were rewarded with a seat on the state Department of Transportation's powerful Board of

Transportation—the body responsible for highway routing, construction priorities, and other factors that affect where transportation money is spent.
(Chen and Jakowitsch, 2000, p. 4)

In East St. Louis, Illinois, the Emerson Park Development Corporation convinced its regional transit authority to reroute a new rail transit line so that it came to their neighborhood. This generated economic development opportunities and better accessibility to outlying jobs for community residents (5). In Chicago, the Lake Street El Coalition—a collaboration of civil rights, community development, and environmental groups—prevented the Chicago Transit Authority from closing the transit station in low-income Lake Tree. The coalition convinced the authority to reinvest in the station. This would encourage businesses to open near the stop and provide an anchor for neighborhood economic development (5). (Developers more typically build apartments and stores around commuter train stations in affluent suburbs (Holusha, 2003).)

Without available transportation, residents of low-income neighborhoods cannot reach distant job centers and, since there are fewer entry-level jobs in the cities and inner-ring suburbs, many urban residents who could otherwise earn incomes and support families remain unemployed and in poverty. And their neighborhoods, as a result, lack the services and amenities of more affluent places.

Connecting Urban Neighborhoods to Regional Economies

Large and small factories used to dot the downtowns of most large cities. Today, most neighborhoods in the central cities and urbanized low-income suburbs have bodegas, "deli's" and other small businesses—and relatively few jobs, compared to the number that are needed. One method of increasing the number of jobs in economically depressed urban areas is to reconnect neighborhood economies to regional markets and firms by locating businesses that are successful parts of the larger regional economies in inner-city neighborhoods. For example, Boston is home to a world-class health care cluster that abuts the inner city. There are opportunities to link inner-city companies to this cluster as well as to develop focused programs for training and the development of job opportunities for inner-city residents.

Large supermarket chains that open stores in inner-city neighborhoods can connect those areas to the regional economy; and they can generate average grocery sales per square foot of up to 40% higher than the regional average—in some cities the grocers average twice the regional average of sales (Porter, 1995). Pathmark stores in high-poverty Bedford Stuyvesant (in Brooklyn, New York) and Newark's central ward, were two of the highest sales generators in the 144-store chain (Porter, 1995b). Neighborhood community-based organizations can share ownership of the stores: New Community Corporation, in Newark, New Jersey, has a majority equity stake in a Pathmark supermarket in Newark's central ward with sales per square foot twice the national average.

Porter cites many examples of community-based corporations that are successfully collaborating with businesses. For example, in Boston, the Dorchester Bay Economic Development Corporation was responsible for rehabilitating a building for use by America's Food Basket supermarket. The supermarket operates successfully there and has helped revitalize the (Uphams Corner) shopping district in which it is located. Also in Boston, the Super Stop and Shop located at the South Bay Center in Boston's inner city was *the* highest grossing store in the entire 186-store chain.

Porter estimates that fulfilling the unmet inner-city retail demands could create 300,000 new jobs in these communities. In Harlem, New York, alone, unmet retail demand could create up to 8,000 jobs. If employers paid local workers a living wage, these chains could make a dent in inner-city poverty.

Basing retail chains in inner-city neighborhoods creates jobs; and recruitment and training of local workers should be tied specifically to those opportunities. Studies have shown that generic education and training programs—that is, those not connected to specific jobs—generally do not succeed (see Freeman and Gottschalk, 1998; Bartik, 2001, among others). Training programs are most effective when they are offered at no cost to prospective employers as part of a locational incentive package. For example, Rosabeth Moss Kanter points out that customized training programs have been instrumental in bringing major job generators to former economically depressed areas of the South. The BMW automobile plant in Spartanburg, South Carolina, and the Mercedes Benz plant in Vance, Alabama, are examples. For individuals participating in the training programs attached to these companies, the job placement rates are as high as 99% (2000, p. 161).

In addition, if we are going to support bringing large businesses into urban business centers, then we must also insure that local, neighborhood entrepreneurs get access to the same tax write-offs—say, for renovation and expansion—that the large chains obtain. Otherwise, inner-city neighborhoods will become dominated by large corporations and local stores will be forced to close.

If one cannot find a job near one's home, or obtain travel to a job that is available elsewhere, one is quite effectively rendered jobless and poor. The spatial mismatches delineated in this chapter between urban populations, jobs in outlying areas, and public transit routes are thus important causes of the poverty in urban neighborhoods, and thus in urban schools.

The next chapter demonstrates how these employment and transportation inequities are compounded by the maldistribution of affordable housing and municipal resources. These regional inequities exacerbate macroeconomic policies by concentrating affordable housing in areas where there are few if any jobs, and by channeling funds for investment to towns that are already affluent.

7

HOUSING REFORM AS EDUCATION REFORM

One of the most egregious social phenomena, one that undermines urban school reform continually, is the housing concentration of low-income students into central cities and urbanized suburban neighborhoods and towns in metropolitan areas across the country. This housing segregation produces the educational segregation of urban blacks and Latinos into schools where the vast majority of students are poor. Such schools are notoriously under-resourced and lack academic opportunities.

Yet housing policies that could lead to the de-concentration of urban minorities from low-income schools are not in the panoply of strategies we typically entertain as solutions to urban school reform. Again and again we attempt to integrate school children by busing, magnet programs, and other court-ordered plans. Yet the underlying cause of school segregation is housing segregation itself. One of the tasks of this chapter is to lay the foundation for the idea that *one of the most important education reforms may be housing policy reform.*

The historical balkanization of U.S. metro areas into discrete, and unequally resourced municipalities that rely on property tax for education, is an important reason for the under-financing of schools in most urban areas. This metropolitan balkanization exacerbates the problems for urban districts that result from federal macroeconomic and tax policies. Some states already spread tax dollars from more affluent suburbs to cities to increase educational funding in cities, and this is an important step. This state-wide educational funding, in fact, is an extant quasi-regional model that could be used for other kinds of revenue sharing among metro area municipalities. But let me start with the issue of affordable housing for poor families.

Housing

Today there are about 2.3 million public housing residents. Although many of them work, they are among the nation's poorest citizens, with an average annual household income of $13,414 (Dreier, 2010). "Without public housing—for which they pay about 30 percent of their incomes—they would be living in substandard slums, paying half or more of their incomes to keep a roof over their heads, or ending up homeless" (ibid., p. 1; see also Goetz, 2010).

There is a critical shortage of affordable housing throughout metropolitan regions, even in central cities, where most low-income housing has been placed. There are more than 500,000 families on public housing waiting lists; in many cities the wait is two to five years, and often longer. According to recent data, the number of units renting for $500 or less fell by 1 million from 2007 to 2010, and during that same time period, the number of units renting at $1,250 or more grew by 2 million units (Brave, 2012).

Congress has failed to provide adequate funding to maintain and repair low-income housing—much of it built many decades ago—and in the past 15 years alone about 200,000 units have been torn down. Only about 50,000 of those units have been, or are planned to be, replaced. After years of neglect, the nation's remaining public housing projects now need $20 to $30 billion of critical repairs. Current subsidies aren't enough to pay for decades of deferred maintenance.

Gentrification, encouraged by developers and federal projects like Hope VI, has contributed to the diminution of low-income housing. Hope VI, for example, despite its stated intention to create mixed-income neighborhoods in areas where housing projects are located, has actually increased gentrification in poor neighborhoods. Hope VI destroys public housing and builds new homes in its place which are supposed to include less costly units. The poor families displaced from the original projects are also supposed to be offered this affordable housing once the rebuilding has been completed. But to date, low-income units have been insufficient to house those families displaced. Home values in neighborhoods where the projects are based have also skyrocketed in most places, pricing out families who lived there. According to data generated by the U.S. Department of Housing and Urban Development (HUD) itself, in the year 2001, Hope VI redevelopment awards "resulted in the displacement of an estimated 6,046 families—95% of whom were people of color, and 79% of whom were African American families" (Popkin et al., 2004, p. 39; Goetz, 2010).

As in the spatial mismatch of jobs, the problem of affordable housing in metropolitan areas has a clear racial dimension (see Powell, 2000; Powell and Graham, 2002). By one estimate, three out of four poor whites live in middle- or mixed-class, often suburban, neighborhoods, thereby coming in contact with opportunities for better housing, jobs, and education. By contrast (and as noted in the last chapter) most poor Latinos and blacks live in low-income inner-city or suburban neighborhoods where substantial numbers of residents are poor, housing and education is poor, and jobs are lacking.

David Rusk argued in 1999 that a major reason overall why white poverty rates (less than 8% that year) are so much lower than Latino and black poverty rates (then 24% and 28%) is this "mainstreaming" of most poor white households in more middle-class communities. He argued that opening up middle-class areas to low-income minorities would lead to lower poverty rates among blacks and Hispanics as well, as they would be nearer better schools and job opportunities.

Although early 20th-century government housing built for low-income people was often racially mixed, federal housing policies since the 1950s have promoted economic and racial segregation by locating public housing in areas of already concentrated poverty (Rusk, 1999; Powell and Graham, 2002). Between 2000 and 2005, for example, poverty was a key determinant of a neighborhood's receipt of low-income family units, with a 10% increase in a neighborhood's poverty rate in 2000 associated with an 87% increase in the odds of receiving family units during the following five years. More heavily Latino neighborhoods, as well as those with existing low-income housing developments, also were more likely to receive family units. A primary outcome of low-income housing was to concentrate the poor and minority in neighborhoods that feed into segregated and underperforming schools—conditions that reproduce conditions of poverty and disadvantage (Orfield, 2009).

Effects of Residential Segregation on Education

The confluence of policies and practices that confine low-income people of color to housing in poor urban neighborhoods and low-income minority suburbs also produces segregated, low-income schools—neighborhood elementary schools as well as high schools, since most city black and Latino high school students attend large, comprehensive high schools where the enrollments are almost all low-income students of color. The following characteristics of low-income schools in segregated neighborhoods are extremely well documented: Insufficient school funding; few, if any, advanced courses; too few qualified teachers; undemanding pedagogy; buildings in disrepair and unprepared for technology; too few classroom computers and computer-prepared teachers; large classes; and all-too-often, unchallenging academic content. All of this contributes to fewer opportunities to learn, lower graduation rates, ultimately very low college graduation rates, and fewer labor market possibilities (see Anyon, 1995 and 1997; Lipman, 2011, among many others).

Substandard housing also has health consequences that can interfere with educational achievement of residents. Lead poisoning, for example, is a continuing problem in cities with old, unrenovated housing stock and surrounding ground soil contaminated by years of industrialization and traffic.

The U.S. Public Health Services estimates that one child in six suffers from lead poisoning, with a total of 3–4 million children affected nationwide. In most old cities, the vast majority of the housing stock in which low-income families live was built before 1955 and, therefore, contains paint with a high proportion of lead (see http://detroitleaddata.cus.wayne.edu/problem-about.asp).

Lead ingested from even a few paint chips, or breathed in as air containing dust in nearby contaminated soil is enough to cause permanent brain damage in very young children. This damage has been linked to:

1. An inability to learn because brain tissues constructed of lead do not bind properly to form the neural learning connections;
2. Attention deficit disorders because lead damaged brain tissues have a tendency to misfire and disrupt normal concentration;
3. Violence because the careful balance of brain structures in the prefrontal cortex that inhibits impulsivity and violence is disrupted; and
4. Later drug use because untreated sufferers find illegal drugs help to medicate the agitation caused by lead damaged brain cells.

(Martin, No Date)

Tests in cities around the country have shown links between even moderate levels of lead and low educational achievement. In Detroit, data showed that about 60% of Detroit public school students who performed below their grade level on 2008 standardized tests had elevated lead levels. Students in special education classes had higher lead levels than other students. Research in North Carolina and Connecticut linked lead exposure to lower reading scores; the lead levels of African American children were higher, and helped explain the black–white achievement gap in reading tests. Similar results have been found in Massachusetts and Connecticut. Chicago third graders were tested in 2003 and 2006. At three-quarters of Chicago's 464 elementary schools, the students' average blood lead level was high enough to be considered poisoned, according to standards set by the Centers for Disease Control and Prevention (Cottrell, 2012; Lam, 2009; Amato, Moore, and Magzamen, 2012).

Thus, federal housing policies that concentrate low-income residents in urban neighborhoods contribute to effects on education that prove in many cases to be overwhelming barriers to high-quality schools and educational achievement.

There are several kinds of housing policies that would desegregate urban residential areas: Mobility programs that re-locate urban families who want to move to less-segregated and/or higher income areas in the region; construction of more affordable housing not only in central cities, but in medium- and high-income areas of the region; enforcement of federal policies that render illegal the widespread discrimination in housing rental and sales; and—perhaps of greatest consequence—the de-financialization of housing.

Mobility Programs and Educational Achievement

Experience in the 1990s in Albuquerque, New Mexico, demonstrated that the integration of the poor into working-class and middle-class neighborhoods can work to the benefit of poor children. Albuquerque, then the nation's 25th largest district, was one of only five metro-wide school systems. Its zoning policy required that housing projects and rental subsidies be widely scattered throughout the city. Thus, there was an unusually high number of public housing children living in middle-class neighborhoods and attending middle-class neighborhood schools.

David Rusk and researchers at the Urban Institute studied the test results of pupils from public housing families in the Albuquerque public schools. They found that for every percentage point decrease in poverty among a public housing project child's classmates, that child's test scores improved 0.22 of a percentile. In other words, attending a middle-class neighborhood school with 20% poor children rather than a high-poverty neighborhood school with 80% poor children meant a 13% point improvement in an average public housing child's test scores. They also looked at the schools' average test performance and results were even more positive. For every percentile increase in the *school's* average test scores, the public housing child's scores improved 0.53 of a percentile point. Attending a school whose students ranked on average in the 80th percentile in the national tests as opposed to a school whose students were in the 20th percentile meant a *32 percentile improvement* in the average public housing child's test scores (Rusk, 1999; see also Schwartz, 2010; Kahlenberg, 2012).

The positive educational results in Albuquerque of mixing children of different social classes points up the importance of housing policies for education. In most urban regions, where a child is housed largely determines the quality of his or her school experience. The child's school performance is often deeply influenced by the socio-economic status of the child's family and classmates. Thus, one of *the most effective education reforms for improving poor children's school performance would be housing policies that integrate poor families into middle-class neighborhoods and middle-class schools.*

Indeed, there is now substantial evidence that families who move to less-segregated and/or higher-income areas from their inner-city homes typically improve educational outcomes for their children and economic opportunities for themselves. The oldest of these mobility projects is the Gatraux program in Chicago. As a result of a victorious lawsuit charging the Chicago housing authority with segregation in public housing, the court ordered the housing authority to move families who wanted to move to less-segregated areas of the city and suburbs. The Gautraux program moved over 7,000 families to higher-income areas of the Chicago metropolitan region between 1976 and 1998. By 1984, the program was in such demand that on the day that families could enroll in that year, almost 10,000 called in (Rubinowitz and Rosenbaum, 2002).

The vast majority (88%) of the Gautreaux movers to the suburbs attended schools with standardized test scores at the national average or above (Briggs,

Ferryman, Popkin, and Rendon, 2008) and had significantly higher test scores in reading than the schools of those in the city (Rosenbaum, 1991).

Although at first a disproportionate number who moved were placed in classes for the learning disabled by their suburban schools, the students were ultimately significantly more likely than their urban counterparts to be in college high school tracks, to attend four-year colleges, and were more likely subsequently to be employed in jobs with higher pay and benefits than children who stayed in the city. Benefits have continued for the children who moved, as they have grown to adulthood (see, e.g., Mendenhall, DeLuca, and Duncan, 2006; DeLuca, Duncan, Keels, and Mendenhall, 2010).

The success of the federal Gatraux program can be attributed to the fact that many of the inner-city residents were moved to places that were less segregated, less poor, and had demonstrably better schools. Gatraux led to over 50 mobility programs, including the federal "Moving To Opportunity" program (MTO), begun by HUD in 1994.

The more recent Hope VI, as well as "Choice Neighborhoods" and "Promise Neighborhoods," advertise mixed-income housing in poor areas. None of these has been as successful as the Gatraux program in improving the lives of low-income residents, because the programs did not move the families to areas with significantly lower poverty, and did not provide the families with better schools (Briggs, Ferryman, Popkin, and Rendon, 2008).

Evidence is also developing that the programs such as Choice Neighborhoods and Living Cities that promised economic opportunity from mixed-income housing in low-income neighborhoods have actually dispersed poor people away from their neighborhoods, as did Hope VI, and have moved middle-class and upper-middle-class families in, as gentrification has washed over formerly low-income inner-city neighborhoods (Duncan and Brooks-Gunn, 1997; Venkatesh, 2004; Duncan and Zuberi, 2006; Sanbonmatsu, Kling, Duncan, and Brooks-Gunn, 2011).

Moreover, none of the programs—not even Gatraux—led to significant upward economic mobility for those who moved as adults. The jobs the parents found in the suburbs to which they moved continued to be low-wage ones (Popkin, Levy, and Buron, 2009).

The failure of programs that depend on moving residents, or building new housing, without *economic* reform, supports the argument that economic opportunity—e.g., the creation of decent jobs—must accompany other reforms we employ, whether they are housing or educational.

There is a further caveat I want to mention about housing and neighborhood opportunities. Discussions I have had with audiences and students about housing issues I raised in the first edition of *Radical Possibilities* have led me to believe more strongly in the importance of the right that students should have to a quality education in their own community; they should not have to "sit by white children" to get a good education (Dumas, 2007), even though that is where the better funding is; nor should they have to be moved to foreign neighborhoods. We have a societal responsibility to make all neighborhoods livable and all schools workable.

But the zoning of affordable housing requirements for developers and home builders *throughout* the metro area, including in affluent areas, seems to me a proper way to provide opportunities for families with limited incomes to rent or buy in areas where jobs and good schools are to be found.

Fair Share Affordable Housing

Discrimination against individuals of color who want to rent or buy a home is illegal. The 1968 Civil Rights Act outlawed racial discrimination in both publicly assisted and private housing. Indications are that this Act, its legislative strengthening in 1989, and mechanisms such as fair housing laws have reduced some forms of housing discrimination against black and Latino prospective home buyers. However, recent national studies point to severe continuing problems. These assessments analyzed indicators of discrimination across the U.S.: One study in 23 housing markets, and the other of 331 municipalities. The reports identify three problems that have increased dramatically since 1989: Geographic steering of prospective home buyers to some neighborhoods and not others, difficulty in obtaining financing information from realtors, and discrimination in the sub prime lending market (Bradford and Associates, Inc., 2002, p. 1; see also Squires, 2003; Dawkins, 2004). These studies suggest that much racial exclusion in metropolitan housing markets still exists.

While racial discrimination in housing is illegal, *discrimination on the basis of social class is not.* Federal, state, and local laws generally do not bar communities from housing discrimination on the basis of income.

> Local governments are largely free to regulate land use and building requirements in ways that add to the cost of housing and exclude potential residents based on their income. Moreover private housing providers are generally free to discriminate against purchasers or renters based on their income.
>
> *(Rubinowitz and Rosenbaum, 2002, pp. 4–5)*

Class-based exclusionary zoning is clearly an area that needs policy and behavioral change. Only a few states have managed to provide places for low-income families to live outside the central city and its inner ring of distressed, low-income suburbs—in most cases by legislating what are called Fair Share Housing laws. These laws mandate that all municipalities in a region build their fair share of low-income and moderate-income housing.

The Massachusetts Fair Share Housing program, for example, reduces barriers to affordable housing in all cities of the state and allows an appeals board to override local zoning codes when less than 10% of a community's housing stock is for low- or moderate-income. After ten years, more than 25,000 units of housing had been built as a result of this legislation (Orfield, 2002). In New Jersey, litigation against so-called "snob-zoning" led to a State Supreme Court ruling in 1975 ("The Mount Laurel Decision") that required that each community construct a fair share of the metro area's need for affordable housing. Despite some affluent towns' reluctance—that led to state legislative compromises weakening the original decision—over 60,000 units have been built statewide (Massey, 2012).

Indeed, Massey and his colleagues found highly positive outcomes for both township and residents who moved into affordable housing built in the relatively affluent area of Laurel Township, New Jersey. Results of the assessment of the consequences of 140 units for low-income families in the development showed no negative effects for the area, and unequivocally positive effects for the low-income families who bought there.

> Trends in home values, crime rates and taxes were the same in Mount Laurel as in similar townships nearby. Even in neighborhoods immediately adjacent to the Ethel Laurel Homes (ELH) project, we found no effect on crime, property values or taxes.... Our comparison of matched residents and non-residents revealed a dramatic reduction in exposure to neighborhood disorder and violence as a result of moving into the development, which in turn yielded a significantly lower frequency of negative life events and improved mental health. Owing in part to these improvements, along with other advantages associated with suburban residence, ELH residents displayed higher rates of employment, larger share of income from work, greater total incomes, and lower rates of welfare dependency.
>
> As for the children living in ELH, school quality also improved dramatically relative to the comparison group [of students whose families had applied but not bought and who remained in low income urban neighborhoods], while exposure to school disorder and violence declined steeply. ELH children also reported greater access to a quiet place to study, more time spent studying and more educationally engaged parents. Although we found no significant direct effect of ELH residence on the grades earned by students, we did find significant indirect effects through hours studied, school quality and school disorder, which on net improved grades.
>
> *(Massey, 2012, p. 3; see also Albright, Derickson, and Massey, 2011;*
> *Casciano and Massey, 2012a, 2012b)*

Thus, an equitable distribution of affordable housing throughout a metropolitan area could have important effects on students from low-income homes. An equitable distribution of incomes would deconcentrate poor students from central cities and poor suburbs, and place them with their more affluent peers where, as research discussed here demonstrates, poor students have the opportunity to achieve at higher levels. Indeed, a spread of poor families in municipalities throughout a region would also help to deconcentrate affluence, and contribute to a diminution of the extreme financial inequities that characterize U.S. metro areas.

De-financialization of Housing

Perhaps the most basic reason that decent housing for poor families is so hard to come by is the reliance on banking and corporate profit-making to provide homes for the nation's families. Financial policies and programs that finance the cost of housing by providing loans (mortgages) or grants (subsidies or tax exemptions) for the purchase, rental, construction, or improvement of housing "have as their avowed goal *not* adequate housing but development of the financial sector and expansion of the terrain for capital" (Rolnik, 2012, p. 1).

During the run-up to the Great Recession, housing finance was a central pillar of the financial market and the source of huge profits to the large banks and hedge funds. Thus, housing has left its post-World War II (Keynesian Era) status as a social good to be provided for all, and has been transformed into a commodity and a strategy for wealth accumulation by investors.

Like the right to education, adequate housing was recognized as a human right in 1948, upon the adoption of the Universal Declaration of Human Rights (http://housingisahumanright.org). But the neoliberal "free market" paradigm of housing provision forsakes this more humanistic Keynesian view that the public sphere—including housing—necessitated government investment and support. The period between 1937 and 1973 gave rise to both the birth and apex of Keynesian public housing (KPH) in the U.S. Major acts in 1937, 1949, and 1968 (along with many smaller programs and experiments) paved the way for an expansion of the public housing stock, though never reaching the level of provision of Western Europe (ibid.).

The current privatization of housing leaves provision for the poor a financial burden to be avoided by those who fund home construction and sale—rather than a social responsibility in which the federal, regional, state, and local governments share the costs (Brenner, Marcuse, and Mayer, 2012).

Metro Area

Metro Area Finance Inequities

During the boom decades of the 1980s and '90s, the condition of cities and city schools actually worsened—with a higher percentage of students on free lunch and a higher percentage of poverty census tracks; the schools grew poorer and more segregated; growth in cities' tax capacity lagged behind their metropolitan averages; and tax capacity became more unequal between city and suburb (Orfield, 2002; Frankenburg and Orfield, 2012).

One cause of their financial difficulties was that a city's revenue-raising capabilities have been based primarily on what taxes the state legislature permits it to collect. For the most part, mayors and city councils can set tax rates only within narrow, legislatively prescribed limits (ibid.). For example, in New York, the state never granted the five large cities (home to early 20th-century European immigrants and then people of color) the power to raise education taxes—as the suburbs and small cities and towns do. The large cities have been dependent on regular tax assessments, state allotments, and federal largesse.

The federal government provides funds to both cities and suburbs for a variety of purposes. However, these monies typically have different mandates in the two kinds of places: Wealth generation in the suburbs, and services and income in the cities. A spatial analysis of federal funds in metropolitan Chicago, for example, found that although there was more money spent per capita in cities than in the newer suburbs, the funds in cities went primarily to income support, and in suburbs to wealth creation. Wealth-building programs add to a municipality's future capacity to produce income. For example, home ownership subsidies add to flow of housing services in the long run. Similarly, federal subsidies for local infrastructure allow an area to produce public services in the future. These programs are investments in the area's capital stock. On the other hand, those federal programs that subsidize current consumption in urban areas through income support have few, if any, long-term consequences on finances (Persky and Kurban, 2001).

Politically, cities do not have sufficient numbers of residents to wield the clout in state legislatures necessary to obtain tax policies that would benefit them (Swanstrom and Sauerzopf, 1993, in Pastor, Dreier, Grigsby, and Lopez-Garza, 2000, p. 193). U.S. cities have never had much power in state legislatures, primarily because former rural elites held chairships of powerful state and Congressional committees (which are now typically held by suburban representatives) (Anyon, 1997). And the share of the cities' vote in national elections has declined in recent decades. During World War II, 32 major cities cast 27% of the national vote for U.S. President. By 1992, their share had declined to 14%. A study of 12 large cities found that they cast 21.8% of the national vote in 1948 but only 6.3% in 2000 (Dreier, Swanstrom and Mollenkopf, 2001, p. 35). As metro area suburbs have grown in population since the 2000 Census, metro area cities' share of the voting population has shrunk further.

An additional cause of most cities' low tax base is that they have lost manufacturing companies. As I have noted, a hundred years ago, most manufacturing was located in cities, and was a major source of local revenue. But in all cities with a population over 100,000, industry began moving out to the suburbs beginning in the 1920s (Anyon, 1997). This trend has continued. High-end office space is a major source of revenue for municipalities.

However, most of the high-end office space is located in wealthy suburbs. The affluent 7% of the population in the 25 regions that Myron Orfield identified has more than four times the office space per household than any other group of suburbs *or* the central cities. They have a disproportionate share of the high-quality office space, too, as 60–70% of their office space is rated "A" or "B." Central cities have 51% of office space, but most of it is old, and including wealthy financial centers only 52% of it is rated A or B. At-risk older segregated suburbs *together* have only 7% of metropolitan office space, with about half (53.5%) rated highly (Orfield 2002, p. 36).

When federal and state aid is added to the revenues of large cities, their financial capacity on average is actually 12% higher than that of their suburban counterparts. However, this is more than offset by the cities' higher costs. Poverty dramatically raises the cost of providing local public services. And higher density in cities also outweighs the greater comparative revenue capacity in 28 of 30 metropolitan areas studied by Orfield (2002). State aid (not including education aid) does increase most central cities' revenue capacity (in 21 of 27 cities studied)—but by an average of only 32% (ibid.).

An additional source of financial inequality among municipalities in regions is racial segregation of low-income minorities in cities and financially distressed suburbs. Tax base inequality among municipalities in metro regions is highly correlated with racial segregation: The more segregated an area, the more unequal the tax base (ibid.). Thus, there is a very strong tendency for more segregated metropolitan areas to show greater than average degrees of inequality in tax capacities among municipalities.

Another factor increasing metropolitan inequality in financial capacity is the fact that, as noted earlier—the geographic separation of the affluent has increased since the 1970s, meaning that their tax dollars are less available for cities' use. In 1970, the typical affluent person lived in a neighborhood that was only 39% affluent. By 1990, that had increased to 52% affluent. Many families with more money have chosen to flee the cities and older suburbs (Jackson, 2000; Reardon and Bischoff, 2011).

Educational Finance Inequities

Regional financial inequities have serious consequences for urban education since schools are financed by municipal and state funds. Federal education spending— even in urban schools—has never amounted to more than 10% of district spending; the last year for which we have figures is 2009, when the national average was 9.6% (http://nces.ed.gov/pubs2011/expenditures/tables/table_01.asp?referrer=edfin).

In most districts, the amount of money that local residents and businesses pay is typically a major determinant of the amount that is spent on schools. And all regions have municipalities that are affluent. I would argue, therefore, that sufficient tax resources exist in metro areas—were they distributed equitably—to fund quality schools for the vast majority of the students. But federal and state policies, regional zoning, and various "gentlemen's agreements" that segregate low-income families in fiscally stressed urban areas condemn them, in essence, to under-funded education.

The racial discrepancies in school funding identified by The Education Trust (2001) and reported previously are actually exacerbated by a majority of states, as they send a disproportionate amount of state money to their *lowest-minority* districts. For example, of 47 states studied, 22 send substantially *less* money (that is, a difference of $100 or more) per student to districts educating the greatest numbers of minority students. New York, for example, sends an additional $1,339 per student in state revenue to the districts educating the fewest minority students as compared to those districts educating the greatest number. When this is added to the disparity in local revenue, New York's highest-minority school districts have $2,034 less per student than the districts educating the fewest minority students. In Kansas, differences in locally raised revenue leave the highest-minority districts with $204 less than the lowest minority districts, but when you add state revenue the funding gap jumps to $1,403 per student (Baker and Welner, 2010; Baker, Sciarra, and Farrie, 2010; The Education Trust, 2005).

Legal challenges to state funding inequities can and have made a difference (for an overview, see Orfield, 2007). The *Abbott v Burke* victories in New Jersey, for instance, resulted in that state targeting its high-poverty districts more heavily than any other state (rank of 1 at 252% more). This is true even though New Jersey ranks toward the bottom on the percentage of state revenues making up its overall education funding (40%). Other states that target state funds heavily toward poorer districts include Connecticut, Massachusetts, Wyoming, Pennsylvania, Rhode Island, and Virginia (in descending order).

Policies to Alleviate Educational and Other Regional Fiscal Inequities

One method of reducing fiscal disparities between municipalities in metropolitan environments not implied by the suggestions above is to implement regional revenue sharing. "Vertical" intergovernmental revenue sharing is widespread: Before the Great Recession, federal and state governments in the U.S. provided more than one-third of all local government revenues. Of $721 billion in local government revenues (fiscal 1994), direct federal grants-in-aid totaled about $30 billion; state aid (including pass-through federal funds) totaled about $212 billion (Bureau of the Census, 1997, Tables 478, 482, in Rusk, 1999, 220). But "horizontal" revenue sharing between local governments is far less prevalent, and multijurisdictional revenue sharing is very rare.

Since the tax on local property is the primary source of municipal government revenues, certain types of development—office buildings, corporate headquarters, up-scale housing—are attractive because they almost always generate more revenue than it costs local government to provide services to them. However, *all* taxpayers in the region pay state and federal taxes toward the state and federal funds that subsidize development in affluent areas, and therefore all municipalities in the region should be permitted to share in the tax returns that accrue.

Revenue Sharing

A successful example of revenue sharing is Twin Cities, Minnesota. The Twin Cities region is one economy. Commercial-industrial developments concentrate in only a few locations, drawing workers and customers from the regional market that extends beyond the city itself. Access to these firms, primarily state and federal highways, is a major determinant of where these developments locate. Cities in the metro area with such access are the ones most likely to attract commercial-industrial development (see www.metrocouncil.org/metroarea/FiscalDisparities/index.htm/2012).

In 1975, the Minnesota legislature began to implement a tax-base sharing plan. State legislation required that all taxing jurisdictions in the Twin Cities metropolitan area (seven counties; 186 cities, villages, and townships; 48 school districts; and about 60 other taxing bodies) contribute 40% of the increase in assessed value of commercial-industrial property into a common pool. The pool is taxed at a common rate, and revenues are redistributed among all local governments on the base of each jurisdiction's population and its tax capacity—the per capita market value of commercial and industrial property—in relation to the tax capacity of the region as a whole. A municipality with below-average tax capacity receives a relatively larger distribution from the regional fund, and a jurisdiction with above-average tax capacity receives less.

By 1998 the annual fiscal disparities pool had reached $410 million, about 30% of the region's total commercial-industrial property tax receipts. Of the region's municipal governments, 137 were recipients, and 49 were contributors. Over the years the contributors have been the Twin Cities' wealthiest suburbs, and the major recipients were Saint Paul, inner-ring suburbs, and the financially stressed outlying towns and villages (see www.metrocouncil.org/metroarea/FiscalDisparities/index.htm/2012).

Tax-base sharing is a much more cost-effective means of reducing tax-base inequity than existing state aid programs. On average, tax-base sharing reduces inequities by a greater amount than current state aid programs with a pool of money that is less than one-third the amount of current aid.

As in the "Twin Cities," the political battles for regional changes such as tax-base sharing need to be fought in state legislatures because state representatives and senators make the rules for local governments' land use (that is, sprawl controls, local zoning powers, and intergovernmental agreements).

More Equitable Education Funding

I will argue now that good models already exist on which to base regional revenue sharing to support urban schools. State education funding and state-distributed federal transportation money are already spread throughout metropolitan areas, and their equalizing possibilities could be greatly expanded. Early 2000s experience in Michigan, Washington, Texas, Illinois, and Vermont demonstrates that state initiatives to reform educational spending can achieve many of the same equities sought by metropolitan tax sharing. Most of the educational financing reforms in these states have shifted school funding from local property taxes to broadly based taxes collected by the state (Yaro, 2000).

Indeed, advice from a regionalist would be that states assume the entire cost of public elementary and secondary education from taxes collected at the state level rather than by locally collected funds. Education expenses represent more than two-thirds of most municipal budgets; shifting education finance to broad-based, state-collected taxes paid into a common pool, for example, could eliminate inequities that arise out of municipal property and other tax-base differences (New York's Third Regional Plan, put forward in 1989 by the states' prestigious Regional Plan Association, advocated just that).

Currently, education in the U.S. is administered by 13,600 school districts (U.S. Department of Education, 2012). If these were consolidated and added to the state-wide education administrative functions that already exist, both financial disparities and racial/economic segregation could be reduced. Moreover, metro-wide districts should be established. Metropolitan districts (such as Albuquerque, described above) are among the least segregated (Orfield, 1996, p. 832; see also Orfield, 2002). Small, all-minority districts like Hartford, Connecticut (19 square miles) and Newark (23 square miles)—if blended into their surrounding counties—could be desegregated and their funding merged into much larger systems.

Regional districts would allow for economies of scale, and would foster the implementation of potentially important equalizing policies like the provision in the federal "No Child Left Behind," which allows children in failing schools to enroll in successful district schools. In current city districts, successful schools to which to transfer are few and far between, and there are few if any seats available.

As I will elaborate in the final chapter of this book, in order to advocate for equalizing educational policies, *central cities and urbanized suburbs need to form political coalitions*. The potential clout of such coalitions resides in the fact that almost two-thirds of metropolitan poverty populations live in these urbanized, at-risk suburbs and central cities.

I believe there is ample evidence for the utility of metropolitan housing and finance reform as strategies to improve urban school systems. Affordable housing to which lower-income urban families could move would alleviate the concentrated poverty that typically overwhelms urban schools. And policies that would spread more equitably the considerable resources of some to the benefit of all municipalities in a region would increase the ability of urban districts to pay for high-quality programs, personnel, and facilities.

But when we think about the financial distress of urban school systems, we generally do not see a direct link between their poverty and the wealth of affluent suburban districts; we generally believe that the money affluent earners make is theirs to keep, does not flow from the labors of the urban working class, and should not necessarily be shared to educate "other people's children." We tend to blame the poverty of poor districts on city or state politicians, district mismanagement or graft, or on teachers, administrators, and the families who live there.

Yet as I have shown, federal economic and tax policies are culpable, and create a link between suburban wealth and urban poverty. Suburban owners and other shareholders of companies operating in cities take home profits and dividends that accrue in part from low wages paid to the workers in those companies. General Electric, for instance, had $15.13 billion in U.S. profits in 2002, a figure that analysis found gave them about $45,000 in profit per worker that year.

Business professionals, executives, and well-paid managers also derive salaries from monies that are available because of company profits. The tenacity with which owners of small businesses fight attempts to raise the minimum wage, and with which executives of large corporations seek sources of cheaper workers across the globe, testify to the link between low wages, higher profits, and therefore better salaries and dividends.

Moreover, as we have seen, wealth produced in both urban and suburban businesses has long depended on infrastructure supported by taxes paid by residents living throughout the metropolitan region. Indeed, urban residents continue to contribute to affluent suburbs through taxes used for further development in outlying municipalities, as well as through tax income lost at all government levels because of corporate write-offs and relocation incentives. We must remember that it is federal tax dollars—paid by city residents as well as others—that have provided the billions funding telecommunications, electronic, aerospace, medical and other research labs, most of which are located in affluent suburban job centers (federal subsidy that developed the computer and internet industries—beginning in suburban Palo Alto—is just one of many examples).

It seems only fair, then, that metropolitan tax-base sharing be more widely instituted. Distributing tax resources equitably throughout a region would return to low-income municipalities a portion of their past and continuing contributions to suburban affluence—and would better finance urban schools and neighborhoods. When we think, therefore, about where to obtain funding for urban school systems, we should remember that wealthy suburbs are, and have been at least in part dependent on profits earned in the cities and on city residents' tax dollars. I would argue, therefore, that parents in poverty urban schools have a right to financial recompense from the coffers of America's Scarsdales, Shaker Heights, and Beverly Hills.

Social Movements and New Policies

The policies I have promoted so far in this book are not likely to be popular with political and economic elites or, indeed, with many in America's middle class. Public policy theorist Theda Skocpol (1991) has argued that broad popular support of a social policy—especially by the middle class—is necessary for its adoption and survival. One of the examples she uses is Social Security, which is beloved by the middle classes, she argues, and therefore secure as national policy.

It may be true that middle-class support is necessary for the passage and survival of a social policy. But it is also the case that most, if not all, legislation that has favored the middle class, the poor, the working class, and minority communities—including Social Security and Medicare—were adopted in large part because of popular protest and public demand—or in response to social crisis and the contention which followed or threatened to follow. In the early years of the 20th century, for example, after massive protest beginning in the 1870s, the 12-hour work day became a federal maximum. Later, in the 1930s, after tumultuous organizing by a plethora of groups, legislation creating long-term mortgage loans for those without sufficient cash to purchase homes, public housing programs, and various worker protections—as well as social security—was passed. (Medicare was included in the 1960s, following concerted political organizing by seniors.)

Only as a result of the assassination of Martin Luther King, Jr., was the nation's first Fair Housing law passed (Massey and Denton, 1993). Billions of dollars were provided to the cities only after a decade of civil rights mass mobilizations and riots in over 100 American cities. The whole host of civil rights legislation—not only the 1964 Civil Rights and 1965 Voting Acts, but the programs of the Great Society and War on Poverty (Model Cities, Elementary and Secondary Education Act, Head Start) and federal aid for community development in the 1970s were only adopted after decades of political struggle by civil rights activists, community residents, and supporters.

Even the more recent passage of Empowerment Zone legislation to assist urban neighborhood economic development was approved in response to the riots following the trial that acquitted the officers who beat African American Rodney King in Los Angeles. The legislation had been proposed in the early 1980s, but only after the riots in Los Angeles was it passed in 1993 (see Davis, 1993; Lemann, 1994).

Thus, public contestation certainly seems necessary if we are going to fulfill the redistributive potential of American democracy and U.S. education. The challenges and possibilities of protest and a new social movement for economic and educational rights, which could enable us to adopt both federal and regional leveling strategies such as those promoted here, are subjects that occupy the entirety of Part IV. First, however, it is prudent to see what we can learn from efforts that have already been made to improve cities and their neighborhoods in metro areas across America.

8

REGIONAL AND LOCAL
CHALLENGES TO INEQUITY

So far I have been describing macro structures (federal and regional policies and regularities of practice) that affect our conduct and daily opportunities. I have argued that the policies I have described act to keep people (in particular, people of color) and neighborhoods poor—and therefore pauperize local schools, as well. I turn now to the locality in which people negotiate these realities. As my view suggests, the local (in cities and urbanized suburbs, for example) is not only a product of neighborhood and urban cultures and municipal regulations and policies, but is also shaped by federal and regional decisions both current and historical (some of which I have discussed at length). Federal policies that sustain urban minority poverty, and metropolitan arrangements that spread resources unequally throughout regions, have circumscribed the life chances of residents in urban neighborhoods today.

A central argument of this book has been that we need to significantly improve economic opportunities and conditions in urban neighborhoods in order to provide infrastructural support that will nurture systemic, long-term school reform. In *Ghetto Schooling* I argued similarly that:

> if we do not resuscitate our cities, we face an impossible situation regarding school reform: Attempting to fix inner city schools without fixing the city in which they are embedded is like trying to clean the air on one side of a screen door.
>
> *(Anyon, 1997, p. 168)*

If we accept the premise that a strong neighborhood is important for school reform to take hold, then we must ask how we can accomplish urban rejuvenation. By what methods can we improve low-income neighborhoods and the lives of residents?

This has been a question many have tried to answer. The present chapter critiques strategies of the main long-term players: Federal efforts since the 1960s, and efforts by philanthropic foundations and Community Development Corporations (CDCs) over the same decades. These efforts have failed to revitalize urban neighborhoods largely because they have tried to change localities and individual residents *without challenging the underlying federal and regional rules of the game.*

In addition to CDCs, grassroots community-based organizations have a long history of attempting to solve the problems faced by residents of urban neighborhoods, and they have not been particularly successful in providing increased economic opportunities there. Some significant recent successes have occurred, however. These successes result mostly from coalitions of political, labor, community, and religious groups that combine—*across the municipalities of a metropolitan area*—to *systematically challenge federal and regional policies and arrangements that build barriers to economic opportunity.*

This chapter describes some of these coalitions, and argues that they offer a working model that school reformers could emulate. Urban and suburban district cooperation, as well as regional and state coalitions, and even federal linkages will be necessary to combat the large-scale, corporate-fed reforms that have brought reductive and restrictive practices to education—especially urban education.

Regional coalitions demonstrate, in the long tradition of political protest in America, that organized public contestation across broad spheres of the population is necessary if we are to build a strong foundation in poor areas—not only to lessen poverty, but to ensure that curricular, pedagogical, and progressive school reform can take hold and have meaningful consequences for student futures.

Federal Programs

Since 1960, hundreds of federal programs—announced with much fanfare and promise—and ostensibly geared to elimination of neighborhood poverty, unemployment, and dilapidated housing, have been implemented to varying degrees in cities. Such programs include (among others) Model Cities, Urban Renewal, Job Training Partnerships, Empowerment Zones, Enterprise Communities, and the recent "mobility programs" such as Hope VI (a HUD program advertised as replacing high-rise public housing with mixed-income communities, which I have already critiqued).

Numerous scholars have argued that these and other federal urban efforts of the last several decades have kept assistance to relatively superficial "quick fixes," and have confined treatments to the area within a neighborhood's boundaries—limiting remedies to what regionalists call *in-place* or *place-based* strategies. As I have described in previous chapters, it is clear that these programs have not been able to stem the growth of poverty or concentrated poverty in cities and urbanized suburbs, as both have increased significantly in the last decade.

I would argue that an important reason the federal urban programs failed is that they left unaltered the basic macroeconomic policies and regional arrangements that define the underlying parameters, or rules, maintaining poverty and inequitable arrangements. This is not to say that there have been no federal programs addressing urban problems that have been worthwhile. Several, if fully implemented, would prove extremely useful: For example, the Community Reinvestment Act of 1977, intended to outlaw redlining by banks and realtors; the Federal Fair Housing Law, passed in 1968 (and its stronger iteration of 1989), which made a wide range of racially discriminatory practices in real estate rental and sales illegal; or the federal Transportation Efficiency Act-21, which reformed the Federal Transit Act of 1998 by (in part) providing options for states to establish regional reverse-commute approaches to public transportation between inner-city workers and suburban jobs, and to give communities input into where these rail lines should be placed.

We saw in earlier chapters that the equity potential of federal transportation and housing anti-discrimination programs has been severely curtailed by non-implementation. And reliable studies document that the Community Reinvestment Act is not being fully implemented either. I mentioned in Chapter One that the disingenuous marketing of banks and other mortgage buyers during the housing bubble was aimed in particular at low-income buyers of color, particularly immigrant non-English speakers. Vast numbers of those mortgages sank underwater and the houses returned to the bank or speculators during the Great Recession.

Good policy is not enough; public pressure must be continually brought to bear to achieve just implementation.

As I have noted throughout, concentrated poverty still marks many city neighborhoods, and now characterizes segregated suburbs as well. As in the poorest neighborhoods during the 1960s (e.g., Harlem, New York; South Central Los Angeles; and Roxbury-North Dorcester, Boston) poverty rates of 50%, and labor force participation rates of *under* 50% characterized these neighborhoods before the Great Recession and after (Wallin, Schill, and Daniels, 2002, pp. 2, 274; Gittell and Gardner, 1997, p. 10; Venkatesh, 2004; Anyon 2011a, 2011b).

During the last four decades, various groups have attempted to fill the void left by inadequate federal programs. Philanthropic foundations, CDCs, and a variety of grassroots, neighborhood-based organizations (NBOs) have been active in low-income neighborhoods over the years. The following sections assess these efforts and highlight not only the pitfalls of local efforts but some of their promising strategies.

Philanthropic Foundations

Over the years, much hope has been placed in foundations to improve city neighborhoods. The nation has more than 56,000 grant-making foundations. Relatively few philanthropic foundations fund urban community development organizations and projects: Ford, Rockefeller, Surdna, North Star, Charles Stewart Mott, William and Flora Hewlett, Hyams, Stern, Hazen, Edna McConnell Clark, Pew Charitable Trusts, Annie E. Casey, John D. and Catherine T. Macarthur, Joyce, and Unitarian Universalist Veatch at Shelter Rock, are the best known.

At their worst, foundations fund discrete, categorically determined projects unconnected to others, for a short amount of time, dropping them to fund the next "flavor of the month." One year, for example, welfare reform is in, and criminal justice is out; domestic AIDS is out, and global AIDS is in.

At their best, foundations fund comprehensive, longer-term programs with a regional focus that have as a goal to foster responsiveness in urban and rural government agencies. To date, there have been only a few exemplars: The five-city Neighborhood Jobs Initiative of the Rockefeller Foundation, the federal-state endowment of California Works for Better Health Initiative, and Annie E. Casey's Jobs Initiative (JI) (Policy Link, 2001) have been more successful than most—although the services provided did not bring most participants out of poverty because employers did not raise wages (Fleischer, 2001).

I agree with the authors of an important book when they argue, "The Revolution will not be Funded" (INCITE!, 2009). Foundations answer to the corporations that give them money; it is extremely unlikely that these corporations would attempt to fund radical change of the progressive kind, whose main goal is to spread wealth around.

Conservative Foundations

The foundations mentioned above are more "liberal," center/left of center, in many of their programs. There are, however, a number of politically conservative foundations: Lynde and Harry Bradley, Smith Richardson, Sarah Scaife, John M. Olin, Earhart, Claude R. Lame, JM, Charles G. Koch and brother David, Carthate, Phillip M. McKenna, and Henry Salvatori. These foundations have had a huge impact on federal macroeconomic policy.

One of the most impressive successes of conservative funding has been shaping federal economic policy of recent decades. When Ronald Reagan assumed the Presidency, conservatives seized the moment. Four private institutions—the National Bureau of Economic Research, Hoover Institution, American Enterprise Institute, and Center for the Study of American Business—led an organized campaign for "trickledown" policies. Using TV sound bites, magazines, radio, and scholarly journals, they argued that large tax cuts would generate revenues by stimulating the national economy.

This supply-side economic theory laid the basis for what became the economic recovery tax act of 1981, legislation that reduced federal income tax rates by 25% over a three-year period. This tax cut, however, produced a loss of $1 trillion to the Treasury Department by 1987, and helped to create unprecedented federal deficits during the 1980s. The federal deficit was itself used politically to justify:

a frontal assault on the revenue base of the modern welfare state by creating a zero-sum legislative environment, pitting individual programs against each other in the fight for revenues while rendering an expansion of federal social policy extremely difficult. This conservative victory set the stage for some of the most aggressively anti-poor legislation in a century, and ushered in a right-wing revolution.

(Covington, 1998, p. 16; see also Klein, 2007)

Conservative funding in politics increased exponentially with the passage of the Citizens United bill, which allowed foundations and other corporations to donate as if they were individuals.

We have more recently seen venture philanthropy in education, as well. Conservative foundations have fueled the school choice movement, and charter schools in particular (Scott, 2009). Also active are conservative groups that—although not philanthropies—utilize corporate monies to fund positions and policies they like. The American Legislative Exchange Council (ALEC) is one of the most notorious. ALEC was co-founded in 1973 by the late Paul Weyrich—who also founded the Heritage Foundation and Moral Majority. ALEC's membership rolls include large corporations and nearly 2,000 state legislators across the country. ALEC's lobbyists create model bills that advance a pro-business, socially conservative agenda. ALEC members take the bills they have crafted and work with individual legislators to get the agenda adopted.

A review of internal ALEC documents shows that this is only one facet of a sophisticated operation for shaping public policy at a state-by-state level. The records offer a glimpse of how special interests effectively turn ALEC's lawmaker members into stealth lobbyists, providing them with talking points, signaling how they should vote and collaborating on bills affecting hundreds of issues like school vouchers and tobacco taxes.

(McIntire, 2012)

ALEC also sends talking points to its lawmakers to use when speaking publicly about issues like President Obama's health care law. In March of 2012, on the day that Supreme Court arguments on the law began, ALEC sent an e-mail to legislators with a bullet-point list of criticisms of it, to be used "in your next radio interview, town hall meeting, op-ed or letter to the editor" (McIntire, 2012).

Groups that fund ALEC include Johnson and Johnson, Wal-Mart, ATandT, and the right-wing activist Koch brothers.

Critics have accused ALEC of buying school boards, and forcing through legislation on privatization, corporate school reform, and union busting (Ravitch—http://dianeravitch.net/; Anderson and Donchik, 2013).

The state of liberal philanthropy in urban neighborhoods in the early 21st century is less secure than that of conservative groups. Liberal/left CDCs and grassroots organizations compete for a very small pot of money to carry out projects that are important for people in the neighborhood. This provides an extremely important service, filling a void left by governments. But funding by philanthropies is not going to save city neighborhoods.

Community Development Corporations (CDCs)

After the elections of Nixon and Reagan, governments largely abandoned inner-city neighborhoods to the care of community and faith-based organizations. The CDCs (some faith-based, some not) have worked hard to provide residents with housing, marketable skills, and jobs. There are approximately 4,000 CDCs nation-wide. About half of those serve urban areas, with the other half split equally between suburban and rural areas. Most CDCs today are small, with 60% of them employing ten or fewer staff members, and they continue to serve a predominantly poor population. Housing is the most common activity, with between 80% and 90% involved in the development or financing of affordable homes. However, commercial real estate development and business enterprises are increasingly common activities of these groups. Many are also involved in education, childcare, and workforce development (job training and placement).

The great majority of CDCs produce housing at a very modest rate, with half of those involved in the activity producing or sponsoring fewer than ten housing units a year. The largest 10% of CDCs produce more than 50 units a year—which is, however, twice the amount produced annually by the small, independent for-profit developers who constitute more than 75% of U.S. homebuilders. The most generous estimates indicate that CDCs produced about 30,000 to 40,000 housing units a year during the 1990s—a far cry from what was needed (Dreier, 1999). As one long-time organizer observed, "in two years, a nonprofit developer might build 200 units of housing, while around him 500 units are lost through abandonment or high rents" i.e., gentrification (ibid.).

In order to obtain grants from foundations and government entities, CDCs—as non-profits—are restricted by IRS 501c(3) regulations from engaging in politically partisan activity. CDCs are increasingly dominated by professionals with a technical orientation, have narrow membership bases, and avoid the social activism which characterized their work in the 1960s and early '70s. Competition between CDCs for funds is intense. Foundations seem to be giving larger amounts of money to fewer organizations, and to those that can demonstrate results. CDCs must often have the data and statistics to prove performance.

One of the best-known CDCs is The Dudley Street Neighborhood Initiative in Boston—brought to fame by Peter Medoff and Holly Sklar in 1994 in their book, *Streets of Hope*. Residents of the Dudley Street neighborhood acquired the abandoned land within their neighborhood (which is less than two miles from downtown Boston). The lots had been abandoned in the 1960s and '70s, and the residents claimed eminent domain. The Dudley Street Neighborhood Initiative has grown into a collaborative effort of over 3,000 resident members, businesses, non-profit and religious institutions concerned with revitalizing the area where 24,000 people live. Yet, it remains one of the poorest neighborhoods in Boston. The per capita income is $12,332, and almost a third of the neighborhood's family incomes are below the federal poverty line (see www.dsni.org/history).

In 1999, David Rusk carried out an analysis of 34 CDCs that were the longest-lasting, largest and considered by two national support organizations at the core of the CDC movement to be exemplary. He found that in every case, the target neighborhoods' poverty levels increased between 1970 and 1990, as they did in the vast majority of low-income urban neighborhoods in the U.S. (see also Jargowsky, 1998). He found as well that the median household incomes in the target areas declined over the years, and fell farther behind regional income levels (Rusk, 1999, p. 49). Neighborhood segregation also increased, and the neighborhoods lost people, as some of those who were financially able have moved out.

The continuing poverty in neighborhoods where CDCs have been active does not deny that the physical attributes of local streets and buildings may be in better condition and more attractive than in the 1960s. It is not to deny that many people's lives have been improved by the services CDCs provide. What the persistent poverty does point to is the power of federal policies and regional arrangements to thwart the potential of CDC programs to raise the economic levels of residents. In the many cases where job training and placement is a CDC priority, persistent neighborhood poverty demonstrates that as long as jobs available to men and women trained by the CDCs pay poverty wages, and as long as public transportation routes bypass outlying job centers or business investment is withheld from urban neighborhoods, residents will remain poor.

The ability of CDCs to eliminate poverty in urban areas is not only delimited by federal and regional systems. Many CDCs have become clients in their city's patronage system of political spoils, and no longer challenge the basic rules of the game as they did in the 1960s and '70s.

Veteran political activist and scholar Peter Dreier argues that CDCs have failed in their larger mission to revitalize urban neighborhoods because they are isolated and unconnected to social movements:

> [T]he vast majority … are not part of a network linking them to wider political constituencies. They are politically isolated in their own communities, unable to work simultaneously on local, state, and federal issues…. They are not, in other words, part of a movement.
>
> *(1999, p. 186)*

Grassroots Organizations

There are over 7 million grassroots organizations that could be instrumental in challenging federal and metro-area rules of the game. Despite the popular perception that poor areas are devoid of agency and organization, poor urban neighborhoods are home to many of these associations. Researchers in one lower income Chicago neighborhood, for example, found over 150 associations. Among the 150 associations were such groups as the Dickens Block Club, Act Now, Amistad Spanish Speaking Youth, and Damen Ave. Revitalization Effort (Kretzmann and McNight, 1997). Urban housing projects are not devoid of citizen associations, either. In Cabrini-Green public housing project in Chicago, for example—which journalists and politicians long described as devoid of community—researchers identified extensive social networks and neighborhood institutions, many organized and run by residents. A selected list of community-based groups includes four religious congregations, a legal services group, youth sports organizations, tutoring and college preparation, pre-school, day care, a newspaper, counseling, and job training (ibid.).

The existence of active resident organizations in poverty neighborhoods belies the stereotype of a passive, unconcerned population. Citizen participation in organizations is present; what is missing, however, is the coordination of these groups across neighborhoods of the city, and the region.

A particularly frustrating result of recent years is that the work of CDCs and community organizers gets washed away by the tsunami of gentrification—as affluent families move to a neighborhood and upscale rents, businesses, parks, and schools follow. And low-income families can no longer afford to live there (see Lipman, 2011; Brenner, Marcuse, and Mayer, 2012).

Models of Local-Regional Collaboration

In many of the largest metro areas, *a new form of grassroots organizing* has begun to make important inroads into equity by joining labor unions, political and religious associations, and community development organizations across neighborhoods, across regions, and sometimes across states. These metro area collaborations have successfully confronted governments, banks, developers, and other corporations in regions where a focus on neighborhood-by-neighborhood organizing did not work. The coalitions develop a wide enough power base, with diverse constituents, to challenge the metropolitan and federal policies that often determine the local problems. These regional associations no longer let governments off the hook, demanding that politicians and bureaucracies at varying levels carry out their responsibilities to residents, as in more affluent municipalities.

Manuel Pastor et al. (2000), a leading figure in the research on metro area equity activity, has studied examples of regional organizing throughout the country.

Here are two exemplars:

> The Gamaliel Foundation ... is a network of 60 affiliates in 21 states. The Partnership for Working Families, a network spanning 18 affiliates in ten states, including LAANE and Working Partnerships [in Los Angeles], has developed a new model for urban growth and social justice that analyzes

regional sources of inequality and utilizes community benefits agreements as an organizing tool. The Transportation Equity Network, originally founded under the aegis of the Center for Community Change, has brought together organizations such as the Bus Riders Union (Los Angeles), the Northwest Interfaith Federation (Northwest Indiana), the Metropolitan Congregations United (Missouri), and West Harlem Environmental Action (New York) [into joint initiatives] (Swanstrom and Barrett, 2007).

The Right to the City Alliance brings together groups around the country, including Strategic Actions for a Just Economy and the Miami Workers Center, who are fighting gentrification by equating their power-building efforts with regional equity goals and a human rights framing. The Pushback Network, with organizations from eight states, including SCOPE in Los Angeles, links and builds capacity of progressive grassroots organizing efforts focused on electoral strategies and state alliance building.

Another exemplar is Jobs with Justice (JWJ). JWJ provides insight into how a regional coalition of community-based groups can challenge federal and metro area policies. JWJ is a campaign for workers' rights and economic justice.

> Jobs with Justice is a national network of local coalitions that bring together labor unions, faith groups, community organizations, and student activists to fight for working people. Our members are in the streets in 46 cities in 24 states across the country.
>
> *(http://www.jwj.org/ accessed January 18, 2013)*

JWJ was founded in Miami in 1987 by several unions that realized that unless they worked together they would be defeated. JWJ was founded during the anger and frustration resulting from President Reagan's firing of the striking air traffic controllers in 1982, and the subsequent efforts by Eastern Airlines to squash the machinists and flight attendants unions (Center for Community Change, 1998).

The Massachusetts JWJ has 70 member organizations, two-thirds of which are unions. The coalition includes Association of Community Organizations for Change Now (ACORN), local tenants organizations, a local Women's Alliance, as well as religious, political, and immigrant groups. In 1998 they began an ultimately successful Right to Organize campaign involving members of the Haitian community, which makes up a large portion of health care employees in the metro area.

The Buffalo, New York, JWJ has been involved in a number of hard-fought efforts to protect workers from layoffs and poor working conditions. When the Service Employees International Union (SEIU) attempted to organize janitors for better wages at the Marine Midland Bank Building in Buffalo, JWJ organized support from a range of organizations. The protests culminated in a series of high profile events, including an announcement by the Buffalo Area Metropolitan

Ministries that it would withdraw its accounts at Marine Midland to support the campaign. The action that finally broke the bank's refusal to raise wages was a prayer vigil and fast the JWJ held on the front steps of a party the bank held for its officers and big clients to celebrate its purchase of rights to the city's hockey arena. The public pressure and embarrassment forced them to give in.

Campaign for a Sustainable Milwaukee and JWJ are two of perhaps 20 such coalitions of local groups joining with others across regions and states. Their organizing strategies flow from the understanding that most local problems have been created by policies and decisions made far from the borders of the neighborhood.

Pastor and his colleagues argue that these regional associations, when aimed at building collective power of residents, could form an important strand in a national social movement for progressive economic and social change: "we have become convinced that the regional equity movement, like the labor and civil rights movements of earlier decades, can offer a language with forward looking and universal appeal" (Pastor, Benner, and Matsuoka 2009, p. 6).

> Such an approach to amassing national power—working one city at a time, one region at a time, one state at a time—seems to parallel the strategy ... taken by the right: work from the local to the state to the national, moving hearts and minds ... in a way that can make a new American politics possible. Thus, regional equity is a tool that is a stepping stone strategy to national transformation.
>
> *(Pastor, Benner, and Matsuoka, 2011, pp. 437–457).*

I agree with the authors, and will argue in Part IV that collaboration across metro areas by labor, educator, housing, and other social justice groups that are connected is an important kind of community organizing, and provides a way to lay the groundwork, "region by region, community by community," for the revitalization of a national progressive movement (ibid.).

However, a caveat is warranted. "The power of an organized and resisting metropolis is important and necessary, but not sufficient to override macroeconomic decisions and policies taken at federal levels – unless joined by other regions around the country" (ibid.).

Resegregation, federal education policies, repressive labor union regulations, the long slide in wage scales, lack of public transit to jobs, and decent jobs themselves are examples of issues that are not only regional but national in scope, and need a national movement to overcome them. *Yet regions can be the building blocks of a larger force for justice.*

In the final chapters, I argue that education groups need to take part in, and model their activity on, these regional organizations—collaborating with unions, CDCs, and other organizing groups on not only local, but regional and national levels.

Regional Campaigns and School Reform

The efforts of regional and state coalitions have not solved the problems of low-income urban residents in Milwaukee, Buffalo, or Massachusetts. Much more certainly needs to be accomplished. The existing coalitions are internally fragile, not connected to one other, and nationally few in number. But they have won wage, transportation, and labor union victories that demand our attention. I believe their method might be usefully employed by those concerned with urban educational reform.

Even though it may not seem to be the case when one is in the classrooms and corridors of a poverty urban school, the fact is that very few fundamental educational problems *originate* in local schools or neighborhoods. As I have argued in Parts II and III, macroeconomic decisions taken at the federal level, arrangements made among metro-area developers and other power brokers, and public policies promulgated by state and city politicians create conditions in urban areas that practically preclude high-quality public schooling. Local remedies therefore rarely suffice—at least not in the long run. Thus, it behooves us to pay attention to the larger collection of forces pressing on urban teachers and students, and to attempt to lift that weight from their shoulders. Building coalitions of groups across neighborhoods of a city, and across inner-city and segregated suburbs, should become a priority. And these campaigns ought to be aimed at unjust regional, state, and federal barriers to effective urban school systems, as well as at school and class size, and pedagogy.

Equity-seeking educational reform groups like the Coalition for Educational Justice in New York; the democratic caucuses of teachers' unions in Chicago, New York, Newark and elsewhere; and the rapidly expanding groups of parents, teachers, and administrators beginning to challenge the massive high-stakes testing juggernaut could join with community-based groups that have recently been active in regional housing, jobs, and other education organizing in cities across the country. The two kinds of campaigns have much in common, and much to learn from each other. Chapters in Part IV describe the surge of education organizing in urban communities, and provide methods for cooperation between these groups and mainstream school reformers.

Neighborhood constituencies are forming in cities across the nation, as educational organizers embolden and conjoin parents and other residents to demand an end to teacher bashing and high-stakes standardized testing, and increases in funding, district accountability, and pre-college opportunities. It remains to connect this educational struggle to other community campaigns for jobs, housing, and public transportation (for example), so that school reform demands will have the power of a social movement behind them. This is the heart of my argument in Part IV.

PART IV

Social Movements, New Public Policy, and Urban Educational Reform

9

HOW DO PEOPLE BECOME INVOLVED IN POLITICAL CONTENTION?

Preceding analyses of federal and metropolitan barriers to the opportunity of urban low-income people of color suggest that, if we are realistic, we will acknowledge the plethora of policy changes that must be accomplished in order to provide meaningful life chances for poor families and neighborhoods. These new opportunities—and their ultimate actualization by residents—will be crucial to the sustainability of urban school reform. Economic access, which improves social standing for parents, students, and communities, will be a prerequisite to full funding and other educational opportunities in urban districts.

But economic justice, this important precursor to systemic urban school reform, will not be achieved without concerted, sustained political struggle. Thus, although activism for economic opportunity is necessary, educational reform must be a target of sustained contention, as well. As civil rights veteran Bob Moses has argued, urban students and communities will have to demand what many people say they do not want—quality education.

How do we carry out the political struggles that are needed? Where can we look for guidance?

My reading of American history, as I have stated throughout, is that social movements are catalysts for the enactment of social justice legislation, progressive court decisions, and other equity policy. In order to think deeply about how we might mobilize a unified force for economic and educational opportunities, I therefore turn to history. We can learn from stories of the past how people developed social movements, and what encouraged actors to get involved. History also reveals relationships between public policy, equity, and contention. In turning to history for assistance, I could have chosen to study the labor movement, women's, or other social struggles. Because of my personal involvement in civil rights, I look there.

Recent historiography of African American protest during *the first half of the 20th century* has led me to two heartening conclusions. First, this early civil rights activity was incredibly important "spade work" that prepared the ground for the mass flowering of protest in the 1950s and '60s. The modern Civil Rights Movement did not spring from untreated soil, as most school books imply. Rather, it grew slowly, developing roots and branches, over the years.

That this long development proved necessary prompts me to view optimistically our own future activity. Since the mid-1980s, a largely unpublicized building of protest for economic rights has taken place in America's cities. This has already prompted new policies—for example, Living Wage laws in 123 cities and counties (with more campaigns in progress). Organizing for educational justice in urban neighborhoods has grown, as well. I will discuss in the next chapter how these campaigns are bearing fruit. These social resistance activities, and the regional organizing I described in Chapter Eight, may also constitute "spade work" for a larger social movement for economic and educational justice—as do the Occupy movement, immigrant youth organizing, and other rebellions simmering just below the surface of media attention.

The second conclusion I reach from a review of American history is that even before a mass civil rights movement prompted far-reaching federal legislation like the 1965 Voting Rights Act, the dialectic between social activism and the promulgation of social justice policy was apparent. This, too, inspires confidence: Early protest for black rights produced new, more equitable policy even in early decades of the 20th century, which led to an increase in activism and, in turn, additional equity policy. There were of course multiple causes of the ascendance of both protest and good policy, but the dialogue between them stands out clearly.

For example, activism by middle-class black women's civic groups and the newly formed NAACP (National Association for the Advancement of Colored People) in the first decades of the 1900s led to the unconstitutionality of the "grandfather clause" as an exemption from literacy tests for voting, and led as well to the end of legal apartheid (legally defined black and white zones of residence) in the Supreme Court decisions *Guinn v. United States* in 1915 and *Buchanan v. Warley* in 1917 (Fairclough, 2001).

Black veterans returning from World War I angrily transgressed the Jim Crow strictures during the 1920s, and in the decade of the 1930s, public protest was continuous, as the Communist Party organized black industrial workers in cities of the South and sharecroppers in the rural counties (Kelley, 1990). After numerous voter registration drives by African American civic leagues and radical youth groups like the Southern Negro Youth Congress (SNYC) in this tumultuous decade, as well as three lawsuits by the NAACP, the Supreme Court declared all-white primaries unconstitutional in 1944 in *Smith v. Allright*. As a result of this decision, southern voter registration drives increased many times over, and by the early 1950s the number of black voters in the South had gone from a few thousand (in 1940) to about a million (Fairclough, 2001). The symbiotic relationship between protest and good policy revealed in this early civil rights history should clarify the efficacy of public contention, and give us hope that our own efforts will yield results.

But how do we get people involved? How did black southerners come to the decision to take part in protest—despite devastating white reprisals? And in our own time, what strategic, conceptual processes prompt people to engage in movement-building? Why did people join the brief but affecting Occupy demonstrations? What brings unauthorized (illegal) immigrant youth into the dangerous fight for legal status and educational opportunity? And what gives teachers, such as those in Garfield High School, in Seattle, the strength to refuse to administer high-stakes testing, knowing the penalties such action could provoke?

To propose ways to think about these questions I turn to social movement theory. The rest of this chapter appropriates developments in the field, and uses examples from civil rights history to illustrate the theoretical constructs I develop.

Theoretical Constructs

Following the tumultuous 1960s, social movement theorists utilized several major concepts to explain how the social movements of that and other decades originate:

1. Changes in the economy or political system provide resources that can be mobilized to develop social movements.
2. Organizations offer insurgents valuable assistance in mobilization of available resources. A large body of evidence finds that organizational strength is correlated with challengers' ability to wrest concessions from governing elites.
3. Framing, a collective process of interpretation, links opportunity and action. Movements frame grievances within collective action frames that lend dignity to claims, connect them with other struggles, and help to produce a collective identity among participants.
4. Repertoires of contention (strikes, marches, sit-ins) are the means by which people engage in contentious collective action. The forms these actions take are a resource that actors can use to press their claims.

This classical approach yielded a research agenda that produced a large body of empirical evidence correlating the factors listed above with increases in activism (see McAdam, 1982; Morris, 1984; Snow, Rochford, Worden, and Benford, 1986; Klandermans, Kriesi, and Tarrow, 1988; Gamson, 1990; Traugott, 1995).

However, classical social movement theory left individual actors out of the equation—and did not ask the question of how individuals actually get drawn into contentious politics. The role of personal agency remained unexplored: What allowed people who have (for years, perhaps their whole lives) been accommodating in their daily lives decide to participate in direct challenges to oppressive conditions?

In addition, classical theory did not assess interactions between the various factors it identified as leading to social movements, and did not identify component mechanisms and processes that might make up each category of explanation. The theory was a rather static, topographical chart of what happened in the various episodes and movements studied.

In 2010 Doug McAdam, Sidney Tarrow, and Charles Tilly published *Dynamics of Contention*, which unpacked the classical concepts of social movement resources and "mobilizing structures." They identified constitutive mechanisms or processes of these and other theoretical constructs, and argued that these interact with one another in any number of ways to produce contentious politics. In this approach the role of human agency is paramount, and explanations focus on the question of what processes involve people in protest.

I have engaged their theory, changed it some, and use the result in combination with several still relevant categories of classical theory to attempt to identify personal and social processes that encourage people to take part in sustained public contention. I have re-cast one other assumption of social movement theory, as well. Most scholarship on political movements partitions social protest into discrete "waves" of contention: Movements emerge, run their course, and abate. Long periods of quiescence or contention contained within the system follow months or years of overtly transgressive protest. This theoretical chunking captures an obvious truth. However, a different, perhaps deeper truth also characterizes movements for social rights in the U.S., and that is their extremely long run. African Americans' political protest against segregation extends over the entire 20th century, and stretches ahead of us now—as do the struggles of Latinos, immigrants, workers, and women. While various time periods witness more legally contained than socially transgressive activity, both kinds are present in most decades.

This continuity of protest over the long haul demonstrates that social movements do not necessarily die. They change and persist. Civil rights struggle, for example, continues—both quietly in courtrooms (regarding affirmative action, a living wage, urban education funding, immigrant and voting rights) and more noisily in transgressive public protest by community groups, parent and education organizers, faith-based organizations, and progressive labor unionists. Movement activities continue in organizing by the multi-regional, multi-state Gamaliel, Justice for Janitors and the Service Employees International Union, and in the flowering of protest and demands by rapidly expanding immigrant groups—among many others.

The following theoretical constructs attempt to capture processes and mechanisms by which people come to such protest and movement building. (Watch the interesting YouTube video produced by an unidentified teacher and students that acts out these theoretical constructs, based on the first edition of *Radical Possibilities*.)

Attribution of Opportunity

The first process I apply from *Dynamics of Contention* has to do with how people interpret changes in the political economy. For such change to encourage social protest, people must view developments as presenting opportunities for waging struggle (McAdam, Tarrow, and Tilly, 2010). The suburbanization of minority poverty, the deterioration of wage and job opportunities, and diminishing rewards for educational attainment—indeed, the ravages wrought by the Great Recession—all need to be seen as openings through which to push for equity. This apprehension of new opportunities sometimes helps people see old arrangements in a new light. Situations that were previously understood as oppressive but immutable can be re-imagined and viewed as useful.

Historical examples of this process include utilization of the 19th (suffrage) Amendment to attempt to register black women in the segregated South in 1920, although it was clear that most whites did not interpret the suffrage amendment to include black women. As I noted in the first section of this chapter, protest in each decade led to new policy and each decision by the Supreme Court and each Presidential Proclamation set people to work to take advantage of the new mandate.

There are less obvious examples of the process of attribution of opportunity, as well. In the 1930s and '40s, blacks were becoming consumers as the cotton economy ailed and more farming families moved to southern and northern cities. Many realized that they had new leverage over businesses where they shopped. "Don't Buy Where You Can't Work" campaigns of the 1930s, sit-ins and boycotts of restaurants and other public facilities by black college students in the 1940s, as well as 1947 Freedom Rides to test interstate bus segregation all took advantage of the economic changes affecting African Americans (for descriptions of these activities see Payne, 1995; Fairclough, 1995; Olson, 2001).

Later, the mass boycotts of white-owned businesses and southern bus companies—whose profits depended on black ridership—were an opportunistic understanding of the companies' dependence on black ridership. Indeed, economic pressure on southern whites—through boycotts or sit-ins, for example—often brought quicker results than dealing with city politicians, or long, drawn out legal challenges (Raines, 1983; Payne, 1995; see also Morris, 1984; Fairclough, 2001).

Occasionally political and economic governing groups are destabilized by world or domestic events. This weakening of the legitimacy of the government can be appropriated for ways they might enhance the possibilities of social protest. Most U.S. labor history exemplifies this: Workers and allies responded to the economic and social crises produced by industrialization in the late 19th and early 20th centuries—and again during the Great Depression—and successfully organized for new laws that benefited labor, urban education, and women's suffrage. We see in the emergence of the Occupy movement in the fall of 2012 the same process of destabilization and crisis leading to radical response, in this case the Great Recession and its rapid erosion of wages, jobs, and educational benefits.

The converse occurs as well: Concerted protest can foster the destabilization of elites and thereby stimulate change: Think of the movement against the Vietnam War and how this broad-based effort destabilized President Lyndon Johnson's administration, the ruling political and economic coalitions, and ended the war.

Indeed, it is sometimes necessary for social activists to create crises in order to force concessions from governing groups. The following description of civil rights demonstrations in Birmingham in 1963 illustrates this case.

The strategy of the civil rights campaign in Birmingham was to paralyze the city through massive direct action. The plan was to bring out enough demonstrators and create mass arrests that would fill the jails. "The mobilization and deployment of thousands of protesters was key; without them social order could be maintained and the movement would fail" (Morris and Staggenborg, 2002). At a crucial stage movement leaders were not able to bring out enough demonstrators to fill the jails and the campaign seemed to be in jeopardy. Strategists mobilized thousands of youth to engage in demonstrations. "The children filled the jails, clogged public spaces, and provoked the use of attack dogs, billy clubs and fire hoses, thereby precipitating the crisis needed to win the struggle" (Snow, Soule, and Kriesi, 2006).

Political pressure caused disorder, destabilized the governing regime, and achieved massive social change in Birmingham.

Appropriation of Existing Organizations, Institutions, and Cultural Forms

Closely related to attribution of opportunity is the process whereby people appropriate existing organizations, institutions, and cultural forms to make them more radical, to change their function, purpose, or manner of operating, so that they are more useful for transgressive politics (McAdam, Tarrow, and Tilly, 2010).

The southern black church during the 1950s and '60s is a salient instance of this process. Until the 1950s, most black church leaders in the South (but not all congregants) saw their churches as preparation for salvation, not as a way to change the present. In the 1950s, urban (and then some rural) congregants and pastors appropriated the church and transformed it into a major tool of the civil rights struggle. The extensive committee structure and community activities of women members were appropriated for civil rights; the format and activities of the Sunday service were altered somewhat to provide the structure and tone of mass political meetings; extensive, widespread church networks among pastors were energized and organized for planning and sharing protest information (see, for example, Morris, 1984).

Cultural forms such as music can be appropriated, as well. In 1946, the African American gospel song, "I'll Overcome Some Day," (the melody of which derives from the older 19th century spiritual, "No More Auction Block for Me") was sung by several hundred black employees of the American Tobacco Co. in Charleston,

South Carolina, when they were striking. One day a woman on the picket line, Lucille Simmons, changed the pronoun "I" to "We," and the singing continued using the plural. When a group of the strikers visited the Highlander Folk School, Pete Seeger heard them sing the song, and taught it to Guy Carawan and Frank Hamilton, who—almost three decades later—introduced it to the founding convention of the Student Non-Violent Coordinating Committee (SNCC) in North Carolina. The song, "We Shall Overcome," became the familiar anthem of the Civil Rights Movement (Candovan and Candovan, 1983; Payne, 1995).

These institutions and cultural forms were already part of the black experience. Only minor, but crucial, alterations in focus, purpose, or mode of functioning needed to be made.

Outsiders and Bicultural Brokers

Exogenous organizations can be appropriated, as well. The U.S. Communist Party was an organization that originated outside the South. When it moved into southern cities and rural areas, it brought resources to black workers and farmers that they did not have: It provided a place and a forum for discussion, and a framework for understanding the roots of poverty and racism and for placing these in larger perspective. It assisted members in challenging the hegemony of white supremacy and black elites, and created an atmosphere in which people could analyze, discuss, and criticize their society. The party offered an assurance of support and protection for transgressive activity; the presence of an organization engendered a sense of power in the local population (Kelley, 1990).

Southern blacks appropriated the U.S. Communist Party and made it into a "race organization." The party was composed mostly of poor blacks, rather than whites from the North. The party and the Congress of Industrial Organizations (CIO) unions they organized became broad-based movements with a strong civil rights agenda, saturated in black local culture, paying little heed to national or international communist party dicta. Most of the members were semi-literate and devoutly religious, and long before congregants in the 1950s were appropriating aspects of the black church to the political struggle, southern Communist Party members were doing so. They developed strategies such as disguising political meetings as church meetings, and keeping minutes by underlining pertinent words or phrases in the Bible. They transformed church songs into labor songs: "Give Me That Old-Time Religion," for example, became "Give Me That Old Communist Spirit" and later was transformed into a song about the Scottsboro Boys.

In the 1930s, black college students in the radical Southern Negro Youth Congress (SNYC) and later in the 1960s Student Non-Violent Coordinating Committee (SNCC) who traveled into the farm country of the South to organize sharecroppers and tenant farmers were "bicultural brokers" who brought perspectives gained from city living and higher education to the support of local people.

Many important and well-known events in later southern civil rights history were brokered by bi-cultural men and women with northern experience—A. Philip Randolph, SNCC convener Ella Baker, Eleanor Holmes Norton, Bob Moses, James Farmer, Andrew Young, and Martin Luther King, Jr. had all lived in the North.

Aldon Morris and Suzanne Staggenborg make a related point when they argue that African American leaders such as Martin Luther King, Jr., who were relatively new to a city could be more effective than local leaders in pulling people together because they were not entrenched in any one faction in the city or area (2002, p. 43).

Creation of Regional Organizations

The role of organizations in social movements has been hotly debated. Frances Fox Piven and Richard Cloward, for example, contend that organizations weaken social movements, because political insurgency tends to be abandoned as groups build hierarchy and procedure, and cooperate with government bureaucracies in attempts to further the interests of their members (1979). Alden Morris, on the other hand, demonstrates that without the strength and reach of the well-organized, hierarchical Southern Christian Leadership Council (SCLC), and its ability to bring local groups together in the South, the Civil Rights Movement might have faltered. Most likely, successful social movements need different kinds of organizations at different times, and even different kinds of organizations contemporaneously. But an umbrella group is crucial. Series of protests do not become a movement without some form of organization to coordinate and create synergy and overall direction (Morris, 1984).

The analysis in Part III of this book demonstrates the importance of regions in the maintenance of inequity in the U.S. The Civil Rights Movement in the 1950s and '60s in the South was prescient in its regionalism. One of the most important features of the Civil Rights Movement in those decades was what Morris calls "movement centers"—civil rights organizations made up of other organizations. These were more than coalitions: They were formally organized but partly autonomous; regional, yet rooted in localities. SCLC, formed in 1957 by groups that had collaborated to guide the Montgomery bus boycott, may be the best example. This regional organization was able to provide strength to local struggles by sending in resources, and acting as a "rudder," as King put it, to the movement. Regional groups connected local problems to state national issues, and were crucial in creating a national movement (see Fairclough, 1995; also see Morris, 1984).

Other regional organizations (Congress of Racial Equality (CORE), SNCC, and the Council of Federated Organizations (COFO), a coalition of all the civil rights groups in Mississippi) were less formally structured than SCLC, but their spread over wide areas gave them a broad reach and allowed them to create a synergy between small groups of civil rights workers.

Leadership Development

The development and role of leadership in social movements is not well theorized (Aminzade, Goldstone, and Perry, 2001; Morris and Staggenborg, 2002). Scholars debate what kind of leadership works best—individual or group, hierarchical or democratic, indigenous or exogenous, or a mix (Marx and Useem, 1971; Ganz, 2000; Morris and Staggenborg, 2002).

But one thing is certain: Civil rights leaders in the 1950s and '60s did not drop from the sky fully formed. They emerged out of participation in the struggle. Martin Luther King, Jr., for example, emerged as a leader during the Montgomery Bus boycott of 1955–56, as the following account makes clear.

E.D. Nixon and fellow civil rights leaders in Montgomery had been examining the backgrounds of people arrested for refusing to give up their seats on city buses for several years, and finally found a perfect candidate in NAACP activist Rosa Parks (Raines, 1983). Until her arrest and the resulting boycott, most black ministers of Montgomery had shied away from public attempts to fight segregation (Olson, 2001). But at Parks' arrest, the riders of Montgomery's buses—mostly women, going to and from their jobs as maids, cooks, beauticians, and cleaning ladies—erupted with fervor, and seemed ready to boycott the buses with leadership from the ministers or without them.

At Dexter Ave. Baptist Church, newly arrived 26-year old Martin Luther King, not yet finished his doctoral dissertation, resisted the attempts of his friend Reverend Ralph Abernathy to get involved. King refused, saying he was not ready to take on a commitment to social protest; he wanted to dedicate himself to developing his preaching and prove himself to his well-educated congregation. But he did agree to open his church to a planning meeting.

When King and Abernathy arrived at the church for the meeting, they were met with hundreds of women (and some men) who were ready to go ahead with a boycott. In the wake of their enthusiasm, Montgomery's black leaders formed a new group to develop the boycott (the Montgomery Improvement Association), and Abernathy was astonished when newcomer King accepted the Presidency.

The boycott lasted over a year, and would ultimately involve the vast majority of Montgomery's 50,000 citizens—not only maids and cooks, but beauticians, janitors, teachers, doctors, and college professors. It was the largest prolonged defiance of racial discrimination in the country's history (Olson, 2001). And it was from his work during those turbulent days that Martin Luther King, Jr., emerged as a leader.

King and other well-known leaders who traveled the country generating support for civil rights were dependent on the organizing work of local leaders, most of whom were neighborhood women. These women were the ones who "establish[ed] the links and connections with grassroots organizations that provided the mass support" for the large protests; they formed "bridges" between regional and local groups (Collier-Thomas and Franklin, 2001, p. 3; see Barnett, 1993; Robnett, 1997).

The participants in most of the mass mobilizations in the South were not well-educated or middle class. Most were working class and poor. As Charles Payne's research demonstrates, they were sharecroppers, day laborers, laundresses, and cooks. They were "yardmen and maids, cab drivers, beauticians, barbers, custodians and field hands" (1995, p. 133). It was these people who made up the mass of the movement, and from whom local leaders emerged.

Over the many decades of civil rights history, participation in Citizenship Schools developed activist leaders. Begun by African American women's groups in the 1920s, utilized by the Communist Party and SNYC in the 1930s and early '40s, then picked up by Septima Clark and Ella Baker in the '50s, Citizenship—or Freedom Schools, as they came to be known—not only taught civics and literacy for voter registration, but discovered and developed local community leadership (Kelley, 1990; Collier-Thomas and Franklin, 2001). Citizenship Schools were highly successful, and were subsequently developed by CORE, NAACP, and SNCC. Almost 900 of the schools operated in the South between 1961 and 1970 and many women (and a few male) leaders emerged from those schools. Teachers frequently became grassroots leaders, and in many cases they replaced local clergy as community leaders; Andrew Young and *Sweet Honey in the Rock* singer Beatrice Reagon got their start in the movement here (Rouse, 2001).

Other leaders emerged from their participation in more confrontational protest: Fannie Lou Hamer, for example, a challenger of Lyndon Johnson and leader of the Mississippi Freedom Democratic Party in 1964, had a sharecropping background, and developed leadership skills through immersion in the struggle to develop an alternative political party to the Democrats in Mississippi.

It is entirely possible that without the movement, many local women would not have had a forum through which to develop as community leaders; and it is probably true that without their leadership, the movement would not have developed the mass base that it had. Many experienced activists argued that "[voter] registration drives were more successful to the degree they could be locally organized and staffed, which [the activists] attributed to the importance of 'intimate knowledge of [the] conditions, psychology and people' involved" (quoted in Payne, 1995, p. 247).

Centrality of Youth

Twentieth-century civil rights protest often involved young people, some in high school and many in college. James Farmer and other CORE activists in the 1940s were graduate students in their twenties, as was Martin Luther King, Jr. in 1954. The 400,000 American blacks who fought in World War I and their black descendants in World War II were most likely in their late teens or early twenties (Vincent, 1972). Most members of SNYC in the 1930s, and SNCC in the '60s were college students. Indeed, throughout the 20th century, sit-ins, boycotts, and "freedom rides" were planned and carried out primarily by students and other youth. High school girls and boys often took part—and sometimes played leadership roles—in civil rights activity in southern cities and farmlands (see, among others, Payne, 1995; Chafe, Gavins, and Korstad, 2001; Olson, 2001).

Writing about Greenwood Mississippi, Bob Moses argued that:

> We can't count on adults. Very few who 'have the time' and are economically independent of the white man are willing to join the struggle, and are not afraid of the tremendous pressure they will face. This leaves the young people to be the organizers, the agents of social and political change.... [I]t is a sign of hope that we have been able to find young people to shoulder the responsibility for carrying out the voting drive. They are the seeds of change.
>
> *(quoted in Payne, 1995, p. 250)*

Student movements in the U.S., France, Italy, Mexico, and Spain in the 1960s—and in Tiananmen Square, China, in 1989—attest to the leadership of youth in the struggle for social justice. Indeed, it is doubtful that social movements would develop at all without central participation of the young. As I will discuss in detail in Chapter Ten, the crucial role played by youth is one of the reasons that concerned U.S. educators should be at the center of efforts to build a social movement.

Community Organizing

Although the fact is not often acknowledged, one of the most important strategies of civil rights work throughout the 20th century was community organizing (see Payne, 1995, for full development of this theme). Working in neighborhoods, using local networks and contacts to urge residents to participate in resistance activities, was central to civil rights protest both North and South. Barely more than a teenager in 1916, Septima Clark taught and organized rural families on St. John's Island in North Carolina; Ella Baker mentored a Socialist group in 1920s Harlem; Socialist A. Philip Randolph and other union organizers went door-to-door for the Pullman Porters in 1920s Chicago; the Communist Party organized men, women, and families in communities North and South; SNYC college students registered sharecroppers to vote in the 1930s and organized southern farm workers; and Robert Moses and other young SNCC workers lived and worked in rural communities in the 1960s. All of these activities were part of the tradition of community organizing.

Experienced community organizers describe the strategies they used to "open up a town" to voting drives. One registration worker:

> frequently found that the real leaders were not the people in places of position. An elderly woman of no title and with no organizational support

might be highly influential simply because she was noted as a kind of personal problem-solver. Sometimes, such a person, because of her effective-
ness in small matters and the trust consequently built, could be a key figure
in efforts to persuade people to register to vote in a difficult area.

(quoted in Payne, 1995, pp. 248–249)

Another community organizer said he would go for the persons who were
economically independent of whites and their reprisal:

the undertaker, the grocers, the preachers. Then he would go to the school
principal.... Having made contact with these, he would assume that he had
discovered the ... community leaders.... He would regard the deacons of
the churches ... as very important to anything he undertook.

(Payne, 1995, p. 249)

In other cases, neutralizing black middle-class leaders was an important first
task:

I would do this to neutralize them. They do not usually oppose having the
job done–they want it done, but they don't want to be embarrassed if some-
one else does it and they are left out. After seeing [the middle-class leaders]
I would find people prepared to work hard for recognition. Then I'd try to
wed the two together and monitor the group.

(Payne, 1995, p. 250)

Community organizing, not often thought of as a civil rights tactic, was in fact
an important strategy throughout.

Social Construction of New Identities Through Participation in Transgressive Politics

Re-imagining economic change, institutions, and cultural forms as potentially
oppositional does not by itself bring social change. And developing "critical consciousness" in people through information, readings, and discussion does not by
itself induce them to participate in transgressive politics—although it provides a
crucial base of understanding. To activate people to create or join a social movement, it is important to actually involve them in protest activity of some kind
(McAdam, Tarrow, and Tilly, 2010; see also Payne, 1995; Meyer, 2002, among
others).

To make this point, the authors of *Dynamics of Contention* argue that people
do not "become political" and then take part in contention; rather, participation in contention creates new, politicized identities: "*[I]dentities modify in the
course of social interaction*" (McAdam, Tarrow, and Tilly, 2010, p. 126). In other

words, shifts in political identity do not so much *motivate* contentious political action as develop as a logical *consequence* of it. One develops a political identity and commitment—a change in consciousness—from talking, walking, marching, singing, attempting to vote, "sitting in," or otherwise demonstrating with others.

Not only do personal identities change as people become involved in protest, but gradually new categories of social actors can emerge: Participation by individuals over time in concerted struggle creates new political categories and groups. The rebellions that created the French Revolution also created the "sans-coulottes," (who refused to wear the pants of elites as a protest) and ultimately produced the "French citizen" as a class of political actors. Indeed, McAdam, Tarrow, and Tilly (2010) argue that "contentious politics always involves the social construction of 'politically relevant categories' such as (for example) feminists, civil rights activists, or 'suffragettes'" (p. 58).

As southern sharecroppers began to register to vote, and continued in this politically contentious activity, a new collective identity was constructed by them individually and as a group: They came to see themselves, and they became—individually and as a "class"—a new category: Black citizens who were entitled to representation, entitled to their "rights."

Such "signifying work" was evident at the close of the successful Montgomery bus boycott in 1956. As Martin Luther King, Jr., noted, the courageous, organized, successful actions of the participants in the boycott "had rendered the conventional identities—members of this or that congregation [or] 'our Negroes', for example—inadequate descriptors" of the celebrants (McAdam, Tarrow, and Tilly, 2010, p. 319). After the boycott, King described the "new Negro": "[W]e walk in a new way. We hold our heads in a new way" (p. 319). The boycott not only changed the laws in Montgomery, but helped to create, and became an expression of, "a new collective identity among Southern blacks generally"—a result of mass participation in the 381-day boycott (p. 320).

Creation of Innovative Action Repertoires

As people participate in contention, they develop new strategies of action out of everyday activities, routines, and cultural forms. During the French Revolution, for example, barricades—that were originally erected to protect neighborhoods from thieves—were turned into protection from authorities trying to quell the neighborhood rebellions (ibid., p. 41). Sit-down strikes from the labor movement in the 1930s became sit-ins at lunch counters and other public facilities throughout the South in the next decades.

Other creative uses of everyday activity as strategies of rebellion used over the centuries have included effigies, boycotts, and nonimportation; petitioning, attacks on a wrongdoer's house, assaults on a miller's grain store, collective use of public space; occupation of buildings, songs, industrial sabotage, legal action, violent encounters, organized public demonstrations, rent strikes, refusal to pay taxes, inter-state bus rides, and "die-ins" (by gay activists). Clothing has been used as a form of protest—the sans-coulottes of the French Revolution, and women's "bloomers," for example.

Strategic repertoires are often created "on the spot," in the heat of action. They include slogans and symbols that resonate with the protesters' demands, and have powerful connotations. For example, the call for "black power" was coined in 1966 during a march to protest the killing of NAACP activist James Meredith in Mississippi. One of the SNCC marchers, Willie Ricks, shouted "power for black people." Shortened to "Black Power," it was picked up and chanted by other marchers, and ultimately made famous by Stokely Carmichael and the Black Panthers (The Staff of Black Star Publishing, 1970).

We see that as political identities emerge from participation in protest, repertoires of action and altered cultural forms develop concurrently, as people take part in contentious politics.

Appropriation of Threat

The infamous Bull Connor—who began his crusade against integration and civil rights activists as Birmingham City Commissioner in the late 1930s—was but one of tens of thousands of southern officials who for many decades attempted to intimidate blacks and ward off protest with violence (Fairclough, 2001). Television transmission of this violence in the 1960s helped to delegitimate such tactics in the mind of the nation. Civil rights demonstrators learned how to make use of the violence by kneeling in a prayerful position in the face of it—not only as a means of protecting themselves, but as a way of highlighting a peaceful posture and the unfairness of the officials' behavior. Protestors were appropriating Connor's violence for their own ends.

Non-violent civil disobedience was a strategy long used by black activists. As Adam Fairclough reminds us, "the practice of staging nonviolent protests in the hope that the oppressor would react violently [and thus discredit himself] was fundamental to the Ghandian concept of *satyagraha*, or civil disobedience" (2001, p. 277). Martin Luther King, Jr., described this concept and his and the SCLC's use of it in his Letter from Birmingham City Jail: "Nonviolent direct action seeks to create … a crisis and establish such creative tension that a community that has constantly refused to negotiate is forced to confront the issue" (276). When the SCLC launched demonstrations in Bull Connor's Birmingham in 1963, they were using this tactic, and appropriating official violence. To do this, they needed to attempt to appropriate the media. Andrew Young explained, "We wanted the world to know what was going on in the South. We had to craft a concise and dramatic message that could be explained in just sixty seconds. That was our media strategy" (278). Blatant provocation of violence by the protestors would have destroyed the sympathy of television viewers.

Members of SNCC in 1964 appropriated the social status of affluent white college students from the North in order to obtain federal protection for civil rights workers. SNCC invited 1,000 students from elite colleges to Mississippi to participate in extremely dangerous rural voter registration drives during the summer of 1964 (see McAdam, 1988; Payne, 1995; Carson, 2001; Fairclough, 2001). The federal government had not fulfilled the promise of the 1957 Civil Rights Bill to protect civil rights workers, and the murder and beatings of black civil rights participants continued.

As SNCC executive staff meeting minutes reveal, members knew that the death of a white college student would attract national attention. One staff member argued, "We must bring the reality of our situation to the nation. Bring our blood to the White House door" (Fairclough, 2001, p. 285). The disappearance and ultimate death of three civil rights workers—two of whom were white northerners—created a national uproar, and forced the FBI into supporting protestors in the South.

Appropriation of Social Networks

Doug McAdam analyzed the applications of the northern college students who applied to be part of Freedom Summer. He found that of the 1,000 applicants accepted into the program, those who came South to participate had:

> much stronger links to the Summer Project than did the no-shows. They were more likely to be members of civil rights (or allied) groups, have friends involved in the movement, and have more extensive histories of civil rights activity prior to the summer ... in fact nothing distinguish[ed] the two groups more clearly than this contrast [in 'social proximity' to the project].
>
> *(McAdam, 1988, p. 65; see also McAdam, Tarrow,*
> *and Tilly, 2010, p. 132)*

McAdams' analysis suggests that belonging to a social group or network increases a person's chances of participation in contentious politics; and in this phenomenon we also find important evidence that initial participation makes *further* participation more likely.

In the South, leaders of civil rights groups used local networks to publicize and implement transgressive activity. They found that the best way to spread the word about upcoming demonstrations was to request that ministers announce it at Sunday morning services. During bus boycotts in Baton Rouge in 1953, and later in Montgomery, dense networks of residents provided carpooling for people to get to work (Morris, 1984). Later, networks of black college students in campus NAACP chapters were behind the rapid spread of sit-ins to cities throughout the South in 1960 and '61.

Cross-class and Cross-generation Alliances

Although it is the case that, generally speaking, social groupings make their own movements—workers, the labor movement; middle-class white women, the feminist movement; gays and lesbians, their own—sympathizers from other groups are often involved, as well. Civil rights struggles throughout the 20th century have involved the participation, to varying degrees, of whites and blacks from all social classes. Consider the African American and Caucasian professionals in the 1900s NAACP and black women's civic organizations; the middle-class pioneers such as A. Philip Randolph in the 1920s and '30s; middle-class black college students of the 1930s and '40s, and black and white college students of the '60s; consider white elites who "defected" to enter the struggle full time (Allard Lowenstein, Anne Braden, and Bob Zellner, for example).

Civil rights history was also blessed by a number of family activist traditions. Long-time activist Ella Baker was inspired by her mother's involvement in the black Baptist women's missionary movement of the early 1900s; 1960s radical Angela Davis learned social justice from her mother, a 1930s SNYC member and teacher who was close to the Communist Party. Malcolm X's father was an admirer of Separatist Marcus Garvey in the 1920s; Martin Luther King, Jr., Septima Clark, and many others had parents who were social activists (Kelley, 1990, pp. 203, 234; Collier-Thomas and Franklin, 2001, p. 44; also Olson, 2001).

Charles Payne notes that many of the core activists in Mississippi came from families with traditions of overt defiance or activism: James Meredith, Medgar Evers, Fannie Lou Hamer, and Robert Moses (1995, pp. 233–234). Discussing the movement in Greenwood in the 1960s, Payne remarks,

> The people who formed much of the core of the movement ... frequently came from families with similar traditions of social involvement or defiance, subtle or overt. These were the people who joined earliest and often the people who worked hardest. In [some] cases defiance takes the form of explicit political involvement pre-dating [the arrival of civil rights workers]. In other cases, it takes the form of self-conscious attempts to shape the way in which children thought about race and in ways that go beyond the familiar custom of telling children that they were just as good as whites.... The common thread is a refusal to see oneself as merely acted upon, as merely victim.
>
> *(ibid.)*

There are certainly many activist families whose history we do not yet know. But these examples suggest that a good deal of political learning and development takes place outside of educational institutions, and is an important source of movement building.

Communities have memories, as well, and these can be an important source of support for movement building. In the 1960s, young Stokely Carmichael and a handful of other SNCC organizers moved into the black belt Lowndes County where in the 1930s the Communist Party had worked. To Carmichael's surprise, poor farmers of all ages, especially older ones, came to the first meetings "enthusiastic and fully armed" (Kelley, 1990, pp. 229–230). Some of the residents had been participants in battles in Lowndes County 30 years before, when the Communist Party had organized there. Charles Smith, one of the 1960s black leaders in Lowndes County, was a former Communist Party member active in 1935, and had been a labor organizer on the docks in Mobile. He turned his home into SNCC's living and working quarters and offered sustenance and leadership. As Robin Kelley notes, "The radical thirties were part of the collective memory of the [Lowndes] County's families" and facilitated the protests of the 1960s (ibid.).

Social Contradiction as an Impetus for Radical Action

The ghetto explosions in American cities of the late 1960s were in part a result of dashed expectations of the millions of southern blacks who had fled Jim Crow hoping to find freedom and jobs in the North and were dearly disappointed by what they encountered. This profound disappointment is an example of the power of social contradictions to stimulate revolt. Other contradictions have also stimulated activism.

Rising education levels have often been associated with rebellion against social strictures—as, for example, when the pre-professional training that became widely available to women in college courses in the 1960s bumped up against corporate hiring procedures and "glass ceilings" that well-educated women experienced upon their arrival in business and professional life. This contradiction between preparation in the face of discrimination and a lack of opportunity motivated many to join the modern women's movement. The influx of black southern college students in the 1930s and '40s, also emboldened by new knowledge, were motivated to participate more fully in civic and economic protest.

The labor movement, too, has been informed by contradictions: The contrast, for example, between the ideology and practice of democracy in the civil sphere versus the loss of personal rights in the workplace. This has long been a source of frustration, and has certainly motivated workers over the years to take part in labor union organizing.

War, as well, often points up contradictions in American society and stimulates rebellion. In 1919, Du Bois explained the consequences of fighting for the freedom of others when one's own was not assured. He argued that this experience in World War I would change forever the consciousness of the black soldiers: They would "never be the same again....You need not ask them to go back to what they were before. They cannot, for they are not the same men anymore" (in Bates, 2001, p. 28).

The contradiction between U.S. rhetoric of freedom and the reality of brutal oppression of black citizens in the South haunted U.S. foreign policy during the Cold War that dominated foreign relations by 1947. Federal officials were caught in the contradiction of criticizing the Soviet Union for oppression that was becoming more and more evident at home. This contrast certainly contributed to the relatively strong support of civil rights Presidents Truman and Eisenhower (Dudziak, 2000, p. 11).

A contradiction that fueled the Occupy movement was that many college graduates had borrowed huge sums of money to obtain a degree because of its promise of a good job, only to find, with the Great Recession, few such jobs available.

National Consensus and Certification of the Legitimacy of Goals

As news of the mass mobilizations grew in the 1950s and '60s, and especially as television stations broadcast pictures of whites beating and hosing black protesters, a national consensus formed that the goals and values of the protesters were legitimate. The overwhelming size of the 1963 March on Washington for Jobs and Freedom—250,000 strong and the largest demonstration in the nation's history—lent moral backing to the Civil Rights Movement and forced the active support of President Kennedy and other federal officials for Congressional civil rights legislation—namely the Civil Rights Act of 1964, Voting Rights Act of 1965, and, later, the 1968 Fair Housing Act (Williams, 2003).

Federal government certification of the legitimacy of the civil rights crusade had developed slowly—beginning with Franklin Delano Roosevelt's edict #8802 in 1941. The *Brown* decision's rejection of the "separate but equal" doctrine in 1954 put the U.S. government on the side of public integration, and legitimated the intense political struggle for equal educational and other public rights that followed.

An important federal acknowledgement of the movement itself came in the form of the 1957 Civil Rights Act, which made interfering with a person's right to vote illegal. This act empowered the Justice Department to investigate the harassment and murder of activists (although it was tragically slow to do so) (Fairclough, 2001).

Without national consensus and without certification by a federal authority—and the protection this would provide—white southern violence and the states' rights which allowed it would probably have escalated to the point where blacks would have found it difficult if not impossible to maintain the struggle. National consensus and certification by authorities are important if movements are to reach their national potential (McAdam, Tarrow, and Tilly, 2010).

Final Thoughts

Three notes should be appended to this discussion of theoretical constructs.

1. Anger is mobilizing; but shame, despair, and resignation are not. As social movement scholar Sydney Tarrow explains,

Some emotions like love, loyalty, reverence, are clearly more mobilizing than others, such as despair, resignation, and shame. Some, like anger, are 'vitalizing,' and are more likely to be present in triggering acts of resistance, whereas others, like resignation or depression, are 'devitalizing,' and are more likely to be present during phases of demobilization (1998, p. 111; see also Gamson, 1992; Melucci, 1999).

2. Distant goals are not always enough to involve people in protesting oppression. Sometimes, people only reach the point of being "street-marching mad" when something they count on is threatened or is going to be taken away. For instance, during the winter of 1962, in reprisal for local black protest, authorities in the Mississippi Delta engineered an end to government surplus food. Robert Moses reports that this government food had been the only thing between the sharecroppers and starvation; the families had little to lose, and they fought back. And "[s]uddenly, Greenwood had a mass movement" (Moses and Cobb, 2002, p. 63).

3. Finally, as activist-scholars Frances Fox Piven and Richard Cloward have argued, in order to get involved in transgressive politics, people must hold at least some hope of being successful (1979).

Social movement theory and the history of political movements—in this case civil rights—provide a rich tapestry of possibility. Images of suffering, rebellion, and victory grace the walls of the American past. If we are willing, we can appropriate this brocade, and design the future with it.

Knowledge of history and theory, in other words, should give us hope; and could provide confidence that with appropriate effort, we can lift economic and educational burdens that oppress the U.S. poor.

But, you may respond, we live in a conservative time, with government suspicion of protest heightened, motivated by terrorism and war; the current landscape is not hospitable. History reminds us, however, that rarely does the status quo invite rebellion. It takes the active appropriation of whatever conditions exist to begin transforming the present. The next chapter argues that the present is, in fact, rife with radical possibilities.

10

BUILDING A SOCIAL MOVEMENT

I have described numerous federal and other public policies that maintain poverty and segregation, and thereby severely delimit educational opportunity in urban school systems. This suggests that solutions to the problems of city schools should not be limited to reforms addressing class size, standardized testing, and small schools. Indeed, we need solutions to the problems of urban education that are considerably more comprehensive—that provide strong supports for schools, communities, and their reform. We need policies that deal with the complex causes of the poverty of the schools in which teachers and students, neighborhoods, and families are caught. Joblessness, low wages, and concentrated segregation of poor families of color all create formidable barriers to urban educational equity and success.

How are we going to obtain policies that will help us to remove macroeconomic and regional barriers to systemic school change? We need to double or triple the minimum wage (and let the economists squirm); create decently paying jobs in cities, and transportation to where most jobs are located; tax great personal and corporate wealth to pay for this public investment; and share proceeds among rich and poor municipalities in U.S. metro areas. Most of these programs would threaten America's corporate elites and the politicians dependent on their largesse, and may indeed appear impractical to sympathetic readers.

Critical social scholars on the Left usually end their books with a list of policy recommendations, but rarely risk putting forth strategies for the policies' realization. Authors may feel there is too much risk involved in charting a path that may appear incendiary to elites, or impractical.

I am taking this risk. I have been arguing that to obtain policies that could set the stage for economic and educational justice, we need to apply the pressure that a social movement can provide; this and the final chapter make explicit suggestions for implementing that goal.

Consider that before the Civil Rights Movement, many southern whites said that sharecroppers and tenant farmers did not *want* to vote—they were "apathetic"; or they were "content"; and some black farmers told Robert Moses and other civil rights workers that they had not wanted to get involved in "dat mess" (Moses and Cobb, 2002, p. 17). Yet sharecroppers and tenant farmers were central to the mass movement that emerged in the 1950s.

Interestingly, the decade of the 1950s was not a radical time. McCarthyism and the prosecution of former radicals certainly must have given would-be activists pause. Yet a mass movement did develop in that decade, and in a little over ten years wiped away the most egregious racist policies and practices. It is true that the Civil Rights Movement did not eliminate all barriers to voting (think of Florida, in the 2000 Presidential election and the 2013 judicial damage to the Voting Rights Act); and it failed to remove basic determinants of racial injustice such as lack of jobs, poverty wages, segregated housing, and underperforming city schools. But the primary goal of the Civil Rights Movement was voting and citizenship rights, and in that it was, in the main, successful. The movement ultimately changed federal and state laws, American mores of acceptability, many institutional practices, and U.S. culture. *To argue that the Civil Rights Movement failed, is to trivialize the mass oppression that went before.*

It is our turn now, and perhaps we can move the task forward with the millions of African Americans, Latinos, and immigrants who continue to suffer from economic and educational injustice. We could increase the radical outcome of this moment in history by working to create a social movement that would force the issue on education, jobs, and housing. Building a social movement is of course a monumental task, but I would argue it is no greater a task than that faced by our compatriots in 1950.

Indeed, the beginning years of the 21st century are—at least in regard to civil rights and education—not unlike the 1950s, with both times being ostensibly conservative while at the same time having potentially revolutionary legal structures at the ready. By 1954 and the *Brown* decision that separate public facilities are unconstitutional, over 30 years of effort had resulted in significant Supreme Court and Presidential policy providing legal ground for black citizenship—and an impetus for further activism.

Similarly, the year 2000 brought with it 25 years of legal battles at the state level to remove urban educational inequities. Over 70% of these court cases have been successful and many new state mandates have been written by the courts; more than a few await full funding. In regard to jobs and housing there are multiple anti-discrimination laws on the books (most resulting from the Civil Rights Movement) which have not been fully enforced, but the very existence of which could provide important leverage for new demands.

The emergence and rapid uptake of the message of the Occupy movement in the fall of 2012—"We are the 99 percent"—also suggests that beneath the surface of a population stunned by the Great Recession and its consequences—in a politically conservative time—there is deep dissent and the possibility of open revolt against the 1%. It remains, of course, to organize that revolt, and link it to the concerns of poor communities and the African American, Latino, and immigrant populations.

Other similarities between the 1950s and now include the fact that in 1950 there was a stable urban black working class at the same time that a much larger group of black farming families had been made economically redundant by the industrialization of agriculture, demise of labor-intensive cotton farming, and the absence of protective federal or state policy. These millions of displaced workers—and their urban working-class peers—formed an important constituency of the mass insurgency. Today we are in an analogous period of the black political economy: A small group of blacks are in middle-class positions—one result of the civil rights struggle, resulting progressive policy, and of course hard work—while the vast majority have again been economically disenfranchised, this time by policies that regulate the terms of an information economy and remove opportunity from urban communities. These millions, too, could provide a mass base for a new social movement.

It may seem that the despair and sense of futility alleged to characterize America's current urban poor are similar to the fatalism that was said to keep rural blacks from mass rebellion in the segregated South. Even if this is the case, it is also true that fatalism provides but a fragile dam against the onslaught of a mass social movement. We can, like organizers of earlier decades, mobilize the underlying rage, and channel the energy that is released.

Indeed, there are already a number of existing smaller social movements in urban areas and metro regions—constituted primarily by the people of color who live there. There is more activism in 21st-century urban neighborhoods than at any time since the Black Panthers and Young Lords of the 1960s. This chapter will describe four current but not well-known movements, and will then suggest, using lessons from a theorized history, what we could do to build a unified and strengthened movement for economic and educational justice. The final chapter puts urban educators at the center of this effort.

Already Existing Social Movements

We do not have to build a social movement for economic and educational rights from scratch. Four separate but interrelated movements have been growing rapidly since the early 1990s. They include—in addition to the regional movements Manual Pastor has described—renewed community organizing for economic justice in cities and metro areas across the country, an increasingly sophisticated movement of education and parent organizers in urban neighborhoods and across large cities, an active group of progressive labor unions whose members are immigrant and other minority workers, and an emerging movement of organized inner-city youth—which includes increasing numbers of young undocumented immigrants. The Occupy movement of 2012 might have been included here, but its distance from poor and minority neighborhoods, and its lack of focus, may have already limited its life span—although as I have noted, Occupiers effectively raised the consciousness of Americans to economic inequality and the greed of corporate executives such as bankers, hedge fund operators, and other financial investors.

Community Organizing

A good number of the 7.5 million grassroots groups in this country advocate for progressive causes; and most of the 3,000 Community Development Corporations are politically liberal as well. (I wouldn't count the conservative Tea Party as a "grassroots group," since it is so well funded by the Koch brothers.)

Many grassroots groups and CDCs organize residents in their neighborhoods. But the community organizing movement has been led by two large, well-established progressive groups—the Association of Community Organizations for Reform Now (ACORN) and the Industrial Areas Foundation (IAF). Both are regional, multi-state organizations.

Until 2010, ACORN was the nation's largest organization of low- and moderate-income families, with about 150,000 member families organized into 750 neighborhood chapters in 60 cities across the country (www.acorn.org). ACORN organized low- and moderate-income communities for over 30 years around such issues as affordable housing, public safety, predatory lending, living wage, community reinvestment, and most recently, education.

They were skilled at public demonstrations that call out parents and community residents in high-profile, media-covered events. *The New York Times* gave extensive coverage to ACORN's successful effort to organize Brooklyn, New York, parents to vote against privatization of a local school by Edison, Inc. ACORN and the parents then began pressuring the Board of Education to provide increased resources to the school. ACORN then launched ambitious political campaigns aimed at state legislatures, including a press for $10 million from the state of Illinois to increase parent engagement in Chicago school reform.

From 1999, ACORN engaged in a major effort to protect urban neighborhoods from predatory lending by companies such as Wells Fargo. Predatory loans are made in concentrated volume in poor and minority neighborhoods where better loans are not readily available. The loss of equity and foreclosure when the loans cannot be repaid at the high interest can devastate already fragile communities. ACORN campaigned to stop these abuses by promoting state legislation and federal regulation, putting pressure on particular offenders, and education and outreach in communities.

They played a leading role in passing city and state legislation to restrict this practice, winning reforms from federal regulators, and waging an ongoing fight to block a bill in Congress aimed at pre-empting state and local protections. ACORN organized thousands of victims of predatory loans to tell their stories and to get involved in efforts to keep others from encountering the same problems. These ACORN members protested at lending company offices and the homes of CEOs, rallied outside legislative sessions, and testified in city, state, and federal hearings. At the same time, neighborhood actions prevented foreclosures and forced lenders to repair the worst loans, empowering ACORN members to keep pushing for bigger victories.

Another community organizing group with a strong national presence is the Industrial Areas Foundation (IAF). Founded in 1940, the IAF is the nation's largest and longest-standing network of local faith and community-based organizations (Cortes, 2011, 2007; Anyon, 2011a). The IAF is an organization of organizations, primarily of churches in low- and moderate-income neighborhoods in the Southwest, Chicago area, and in the Northeast (Boston, New York, Philadelphia, and Paterson, New Jersey). IAF employs about 150 full-time professional organizers. There are about 60 IAF locals in 20 states and the District of Columbia. These groups are made up of nearly 3,000 congregations and associations and tens of thousands of ministers, pastors, some rabbis, women religious leaders, and state and metropolitan lay and civic leaders. Between 3 and 4 million Americans are members.

The IAF is descended from the organization of the same name started by Saul Alinsky in 1940 in Chicago. The IAF does not organize around issues until it has organized a neighborhood. They begin by meeting with leaders and members of churches and associations that reflect the racial and religious diversity of a community. They are financially independent, in that local leaders and institutions must commit their own dues money of $250,000 for organizing projects before they may pursue foundation money. The IAF trains neighborhood residents and leaders from local congregations in ten-day institutes that develop residents' skills of organizing, writing petitions, negotiating with city hall, and public speaking. The "iron rule" of the IAF is "Don't do for others what they can do for themselves" (Gecan, 2002, p. 10; see also Shirley, 1997, 2002; Warren, 2001).

Member congregations of the IAF are organized in a federated regional and state structure that gives them power on a larger level without abandoning the priorities and ultimate authority of local organizations. State IAF networks cannot dictate to local affiliates. State policy is developed by leaders from the local organizations as they meet to build relationships, or social capital, bridging across localities and local racial groupings. With its federated structure, the IAF overcomes the limitations of local organizing, and yet does not become a national or regional organization that has no real ties to its local constituents.

The IAF used this strategy with success in Texas in its school reform efforts—the Alliance Schools program. By 1999, the program covered over 100 schools, and had pressured the state legislature to substantially increase the funding, resources, and technical expertise of each school. There has been improvement in test scores. However, the main success of the Alliance initiative is the development of a culture of engagement, protest, and organization among the parents and communities in which the schools are located. IAF affiliates in Albuquerque, Tucson, Phoenix, and Omaha, in addition to the rest of the Southwest, have joined the IAF in these efforts. In Brooklyn and Bronx, New York City, IAF founded three public high schools; in the 1990s, two were among the highest performing schools in the city (Gecan, 2004).

Education Organizing

The second already existing movement is community organizing specifically for school reform, or education organizing—which describes the actions of parents and other community residents to change neighborhood schools through an intentional building of power (Oakes, Rogers, and Lipton, 2006; Rogers and Orr, 2010). Larger groups doing education organizing are part of the IAF/ACORN universe described above, but many additional groups are involved as well.

Education organizing aims to create social capital in communities, and to encourage parents and other residents to utilize their collective strength to force system change. Education organizing attempts to build leadership in parents by providing skill training, mentoring, and opportunity for public actions (Coalition for Educational Justice, 2011). Parents conduct community and school surveys, speak at rallies, mobilize other parents and community residents, and plan and enact campaigns aimed at school and district personnel and practices.

Because education organizing gives parents a base of power outside of school—typically in alliance with other community groups—parents are not dependent on school personnel for approval or legitimacy (Fruchter and Hyde-Keller, 2011). When successful, parent organizing in poor communities yields the clout that parents create among themselves in affluent suburbs—where, with their social and cultural capital, and economic and political influence, they closely monitor the actions of district educators and politicians (Reneé and Mcalister, 2011).

Several studies of parent organizing groups in low-income neighborhoods around the country document their rapid increase in number and influence (Gold, Simon, and Brown, 2002; Mediratta, Fruchter, and Lewis, 2002; Su, 2009; Coalition for Educational Justice, 2011).

Eighty percent of 66 parent organizing groups studied by the Collaborative Communications Group are working not only in local neighborhoods, but in regional or state coalitions formed to improve district or state education policy. One such group is Mississippi-based Southern Echo, which has grassroots community organizations in Tennessee, Arkansas, Louisiana, South Carolina, Kentucky, Florida, North Carolina, and West Virginia (Warren and Mapp, 2011).

Southern Echo is an exemplar in several ways: It is regional, multi-generational, and led by—and connected to—former civil rights and labor union activists. The group describes itself as a "leadership development, education and training organization working to develop new, grassroots leadership in African American communities in Mississippi and the surrounding region" (Warren and Mapp, 2011, p. 27; see also http://southernecho.org/s/?page_id=5). Until 1992, their work focused on jobs, affordable housing, and rebuilding community organizations. When they shifted their attention to education in the early 1990s, they began to organize around minority rights in education.

Southern Echo worked to create a force that could put pressure on state education officials. They provided training and technical assistance to help community groups carry out local campaigns, created residential training schools that lasted two days or more; published training manuals; and delivered hundreds of workshops in communities. One result of the work of Southern Echo and an affiliate, Mississippi Education Working Group (MEWG), is that on October 23, 2002, the Mississippi State Board of Education agreed to fully comply with federal requirements for providing services to special education students—for the first time in 35 years. Echo leaders report that this was "the first time the community came together to force legislators, the state board of education, superintendents, special education administrators and curriculum coordinators to sit down together" (Warren and Mapp, 2011, p. 33).

A particularly impressive education organizing group in the North is the Logan Square Neighborhood Association (LSNA) in Chicago—founded in the 1960s to work with the variety of problems local residents faced in their community. In 1988, when the Chicago School Reform Act created local schools councils, LSNA began to assist parents and community members in working to improve their schools (Mediratta, Fruchter, and Lewis, 2002). Among the accomplishments of the LSNA and parents are: Construction of seven new school buildings, evening community learning centers in six schools, mortgage lender programs to offer incentives for educators to buy housing in the area, parent training as reading tutors and cultural mentors of classroom teachers, the establishment of bilingual lending libraries for parents, a new bilingual teacher-training program for neighborhood parents interested in becoming teachers, and collaboration with Chicago State University to offer courses at the neighborhood school at no cost to participants. Mediratta, Fruchter, and Lewis report that the extensive parent engagement and LSNA's other initiatives:

> have contributed to achievement gains at its member schools. In its six core schools, the percent of students reading at or above the national average in 1990 ranged from 10.9 percent to 22.5 percent. By 2000, the percent of students reading at or above national average ranged from 25.4 to 35.9 percent.
>
> *(2002, p. 28)*

The final example of education organizing comes from South Bronx, New York. This group, Community Collaborative for District 9 (CC9), is an important instance of coalition building—between parents, community-based organizations, the teachers union, and a university partner (Mediratta, Fruchter, and Lewis, 2002; Fabricant, 2010). Organizational members include ACORN (which has been organizing parents in Districts 7, 9, and 12 for over a decade); the New York City American Federation of Teachers (AFT); Citizens Advice Bureau (a local Congressional Budget Office (CBO) providing educational services to residents for 30 years); Highbridge Community Life Center (a CBO providing job training and educational services since 1979); Mid-Bronx Senior Citizens Council (one of the largest CBOs in the South Bronx); parents from New Settlement Apartments; Northwest Bronx Community and Clergy Coalition (which unites ten neighborhood housing reform groups); and New York University Institute for Education and Social Policy (which conducts research and evaluation and provides other technical assistance to CBOs and education organizing groups).

The CC9 coalition researched educational best practice to determine what reform they were going to pursue. They decided that stabilizing the teaching force was critical, and that increased staff development and lead teachers at every grade level in the schools would give teachers skills to be more successful with their students and thus encourage them to remain in district classrooms. The coalition then organized residents, petitioned, demonstrated, and engaged in other direct action campaigns to obtain New York City Department of Education funding to pay for the reforms. At every step, neighborhood parents were in the forefront. In April, 2004, New York City provided $1.6 million for lead teachers and staff development throughout the ten-school district.

The CC9 campaign was based on attempts to improve education by organizing in one district in the South Bronx. Several years after its conclusion, the organizers were faced with the following district-wide facts, as they took stock of almost a decade of mayor-led school reform in New York City:

- Only 23% of New York City high school graduates are prepared for college and the world of work.
- Less than half of all New York City students can read and write at state standard, and only a third of black and Latino students can, compared to nearly two-thirds of white students.
- In many schools in East Brooklyn, Harlem, and the South Bronx, less than a quarter of students are reading, writing, and doing math at state standards.
- Only 45% of New York City high school students graduate in four years with a Regents diploma, which will soon be the only diploma available.
- Just 36% of Latino students and 37% of black students graduate in four years with a Regents diploma, and just 28% of young black males do.
- National tests show only modest progress in New York City since 2003, and no closing of the achievement gap.

(www.nyccej.org/facts, 2011)

These statistics demonstrated to organizers that their efforts should be directed at the entire New York City district, not just the South Bronx. A city-wide group, Coalition for Educational Justice (CEJ), formed, with the following constituent groups:

Highbridge Community Life Center. This group has been providing a wide range of educational and social services since 1979, including job training programs and entitlement assistance to families living in the Highbridge neighborhood of the Bronx.

Make the Road New York. A major force for social change in New York City, this group has more than 9,000 members who lead the organization in Brooklyn, Queens, and Staten Island. Make the Road New York offers a variety of services and strategies for neighborhood improvement, including organizing for civil rights and economic justice, legal services, educational programs, and youth development.

New Settlement Apartments. Founded by South Bronx parents in 1997, the New Settlement Parent Action Committee (PAC) organizes for educational justice and safety with dignity in the lowest performing school districts in New York City. PAC develops local and district-wide campaigns, builds the leadership and skills of South Bronx parents, and offers monthly "Know Your Rights" workshops that benefit the entire community. PAC is a program of New Settlement Apartments which owns and operates nearly 1,000 units of housing and provides educational and community service programs to thousands of children, youths, and adults.

New York Civic Participation Project. This is a collaboration of labor unions and community groups organizing union members in the neighborhoods where they live. The member organizations—SEIU Local 32BJ, AFSCME DC-37, HERE Local 100, the National Employment Law Project, and Make the Road by Walking—represent hundreds of thousands of workers and decades of success fighting for immigrant and worker rights in New York.

New York Communities for Change. This organization is a community-based membership group committed to organizing in New York City's lowest-income neighborhoods. Their goal is to empower communities to impact the political and economic policies that directly affect them. They want to build organizations that have the strength to create positive change through leadership development, direct action, negotiation, legislation, and voter participation.

United Federation of Teachers Brooklyn Parent Outreach Committee. This committee of the New York City teachers' union works to strengthen home-school collaborations and increase parent involvement and responsibility.

The Community Involvement Program of the Annenberg Institute for School Reform. The Annenberg Institute has supported community organizing for school reform in New York since 1995. It provides a wide range of strategic support to the collaboratives, including data analysis, research, and training.

One of the strengths of CEJ is its parent leadership. Another is its collaboration with unions that organize in communities, not just workplaces. As of early 2013, CEJ had won the following for New York City students:

Academic Intervention Services: After city test scores plummeted, a CEJ-led campaign resulted in a Department of Education initiative of $10 million to provide additional tutoring to struggling students at 532 schools across the city.

Middle Grades: CEJ's efforts led to the establishment of a Middle School Success fund of almost $30 million to support comprehensive reform in low performing middle grade schools.

Science Labs: The Brooklyn Education Collaborative won $444 million from the Department of Education to build science labs in every middle and high school.

Teacher Quality: The Community Collaborative to Improve District 9 Schools created the Lead Teacher Program, which puts master teachers in schools to support the development of other teachers. The program has expanded to include more than 100 schools city-wide

A current focus of CEJ is on alternatives to school closures (New York City Coalition for Educational Justice, 2010). A goal of this group should include, it seems to me, expanding their work to affiliation with groups organizing for jobs and housing (for example).

Progressive Labor Unions

The progressive wing of the labor movement is the third of the already existing social movements I describe here.

Although many unions have traditionally maintained an exclusionary stance toward minority workers, it is also true that others have worked strenuously for social justice. In the past, these "social justice unions" were instrumental in the passage of major civil rights legislation, the abolition of child labor, the establishment of the 40-hour work week and the eight-hour day, the minimum wage, Social Security, occupational safety and health standards, higher wages for industrial and other organized workers, and protection from business abuses that are allowed by federal law.

Currently, unions with large numbers of minority workers, generally the more progressive unions, have been collaborating with community organizations in large urban centers and metro regions, and have experienced a good deal of success.

Justice for Janitors, which I have already described, is a national organization that has become in many cities "a civil rights movement—and a cultural crusade" (Kelley, 2002, p. 52). Over the last two decades, the Justice for Janitors campaign of the Service Employees International Union (SEIU) has become a symbol of social movement unionism and immigrant rights activism. SEIU is the fastest growing union in the country.

As historian Robin Kelley remarks,

> Justice for Janitors succeeded precisely because it was able to establish links to community leaders, to forge an alliance with black and Latino organizations, churches, and progressive activists from all over the city. They built a powerful mass movement that went beyond the downtown luxury office buildings and the [local union] headquarters into the streets and boardrooms.
>
> *(p. 53)*

Other progressive unions include the Hotel Employees and Restaurant Employees (HERE), American Federation of State, County, and Municipal Employees (AFSCME), and the Chicago Teachers Union (CTU).

In late August 2012, teachers around the country, weary of high-stakes testing they deemed of little value, and angry at frequent attacks on their abilities, were heartened by a mass strike of Chicago teachers. The strike was successful in garnering massive support not only of Chicago teachers, but of the public, as well. The group that leads the union, CORE, or Caucus of Rank and File Educators, considers the union a social justice organization that must involve itself in neighborhood concerns beyond education. CORE had been organizing in neighborhoods for issues that affect the entire working class, not just teachers. And they argued that the real problem motivating the strike was not just teachers' issues, "but the city's priorities of tax cuts for business, instead of money for education" (Hagopian, 2012, p. 5). Many have attributed the CTU's success and city-wide support to this uptake of issues of interest to poor communities, and their previous organizing within such communities (ibid.).

Democratic or progressive caucuses in other teacher unions are also leaning toward "social justice unionism," and issues that affect the entire working class:

- New York: Movement of Rank and File Educators (MORE): http://more-caucusnyc.org
- Massachusetts: Educators for a Democratic Union (EDU): www.educators-forademocraticunion.com
- Seattle: Social Equality Educators (SEE): www.socialequalityeducators.org
- Newark: New Caucus: www.newarkeducationworkerscaucus.com
- Progressive Educators for Action (PEAC): www.progressiveeducators.org/PEAC/Main.html

It remains to be seen if the widely heralded strike of the CTU will spark militant union tactics nationwide.

Youth Organizing

Contradicting popular stereotypes of inner-city youth as dangerous and uninterested in education is the fourth of the existing movements. Increasing numbers of African American, Latino, Asian, and unauthorized immigrant teenagers in cities across the country have been organizing for the right to courses that prepare them for college, for better educational funding, and for a resolution of other social justice issues like an end to police violence and mass incarceration of their peers. In the 1990s there was a surge in youth organizing—with a reported 500 well-established groups around the country by 2002 (Wimsatt, 2002, pp. 3–4).

Kavitha Mediratta and colleagues (2008) noted in a national study of education organizing that "youth are a growing presence in community organizing for school reform, and youth-led organizations are winning changes that lead to an improved learning environment and more equitable policies and practices in schools and districts around the nation." Mediratta, Cohen, and Shah (2007) found that in addition to creating policy and school changes, the process of youth organizing resulted in empowered, educated, and engaged students.

Below is a sampling of youth organizations working for educational equity and justice.

Baltimore Algebra Project (Baltimore, MD)

www.baltimorealgebraproject.org
Begun by civil rights activist Robert Moses, the Baltimore Algebra Project is now a youth-run non-profit organization that tackles math illiteracy and seeks to empower youth within the Baltimore school system. The project employs youth, both high school and college students, as classroom instructors, teacher assistants, tutors, and organizers. It has been involved in three campaigns: advocating a national Student Bill of Rights, fighting the school-to-prison pipeline, and quality food justice.

Boston-area Youth Organizing Project (BYOP) (Boston, MA)

www.byop.org
BYOP organizes high school students across the Boston metropolitan areas. With chapters in some 22 high schools from suburbs to inner city, BYOP has worked to improve student–teacher relations and clean up school facilities, as well as lobbied in the community to reopen recreational facilities and extend the hours of public transportation passes. BYOP is sponsored by City Mission Society and is partnered with Greater Boston Interfaith Organization.

Californians for Justice Education Fund

www.caljustice.org
Californians for Justice (CFJ) is a statewide grassroots organization that works for racial justice and brings together youths and adults pushed to the margins of the political process. Its campaigns have included "Improving School Health and Conditions," Dismantling the "Prison Track," and "Equalizing Funding and Resources," among others. The current campaign, "Campaign for Quality Education," includes a "Tax the 1%, Education for the 99%" petition. CFJ engages youth through student-led high school teams, summer leadership academies, student "know your rights" trainings, and skill building in media and policy work.

Inner City Struggle (East Los Angeles, CA)

www.innercitystruggle.org

Inner City Struggle (ICS) is a youth-driven organization fighting for educational equity and justice in East Los Angeles. ICS has a database of over 20,000 youth, parent, and community members who have signed up in support of ICS campaigns, ranging from increasing the number of counselors in the areas four high schools and pressing officials to honor their commitment to making the area's "A–G" curriculum the standard to winning state funds to reduce class sizes and educating voters about its "Education Not Incarceration" vision.

Padres & Jóvenes Unidos (Denver, CO)

www.padresunidos.org

With roots in the struggle for educational justice, Padres Unidos has evolved into a multi-issue organization led by people of color who work for educational excellence, racial justice for youth, immigrant rights and quality health care for all. Jóvenes Unidos, the youth initiative of Padres Unidos, emerged as young people became active in reforming their schools, ending the school-to-jail track and organizing for immigrant student rights. Both Padres and Jóvenes Unidos build power to challenge the root cause of discrimination, racism, and inequity by exposing the economic, social, and institutional basis for injustice as well as developing effective strategies to realize meaningful change.

Seattle Young People's Project (SYPP) (Seattle, WA)

www.sypp.org

SYPP encourages and supports youth-led projects for social change. Its youth members, all under 19, vote on proposed projects that other young people introduce. Once a project passes a vote of SYPP's membership, it becomes an officially sponsored "initiative." Since 1992, young people at SYPP have arranged speaking engagements; held teen forums; met with teachers, administrators and politicians; posted flyers; held phone banks; coordinated conferences; led rallies; organized press conferences; and published newspapers and "zines."

Sistas and Brothas United (Bronx, NY)

www.sistasandbrothasunited.org

Sistas and Brothas United (SBU) was founded in 1998 as the youth organizing arm of the Northwest Bronx Community & Clergy Coalition (NWBCCC). Neighborhood youth saw the need for young people to take ownership of their schools and communities to change the social-economic gap that exists between low-income black and brown communities and wealthier white communities.

Focusing on educational justice as their bread and butter issue, SBU leaders began organizing their local community schools, building a solid base of students who fought for student safety, equitable resource allocation, and for a college prep curriculum for all students. Over a decade later, SBU leaders continue to fight for a quality education for all students Bronx-wide, city-wide, and nationwide.

Students Against Testing

www.nomoretests.com
Students Against Testing is a nationwide network of young people who resist high stakes standardized testing and support real-life learning. The website spells out the group's ten reasons for opposing standardized testing and details action students and others can take. The site also offers downloadable fact sheets and flyers, order forms for free bumper stickers, and an extensive set of links to pertinent research, articles, resources, and organizations.

- The four social movements described each have somewhat different foci, although their goals are closely related. There is some overlap in personnel, and occasional collaboration. But the four movements are largely separate, and have relatively few members overall. Yet most are organizing in communities and connected across regional metro areas.
- Given that these movements are not yet national, we need to think about how we could get more people and groups involved. Given that the movements are not conjoined, we need to think about how to unify them into one large force.

Lessons from History and Theory

To consider these strategic problems of movement building, I apply lessons extracted in the theoretical exposition of the last chapter. Initial theorizing yielded a set of categories—Attribution of Opportunity, Appropriation of Existing Organizations, Institutions, and Cultural Forms, etc.—and these constructs should prove useful for thinking about the present. Following this application, the last and final chapter of the book will place concerned educators in the center of attempts to build a movement for social justice.

Attribution of Opportunity

We can view current confluences as presenting multiple opportunities for radical political intervention, even when it may not seem that they do.

The new geography of minority poverty—covering central city and segregated suburbs—is one development that can be utilized strategically. This demographic offers possibilities for cross-place collaboration that potentially involves almost two-thirds of the poor people in large U.S. metropolitan areas. As I have noted, there are already a number of organizing efforts that are regional in scope but very few that take an explicit city-suburban focus. One that does is the *Gamaliel Foundation*—a multiracial, city-suburban church-based alliance centered in Chicago—described in Chapter Eight.

Urban-suburban coalitions of distressed, segregated school districts could force the issue of equitable funding in metro areas and the many states that have had legal challenges to the constitutionality of existing school finance. Comprehensive state education reforms already on the books (e.g., Kentucky and New Jersey) or in process (e.g., New York and California) demand, for their ultimate success, that urban communities and supporters organize around them and get people "in the streets" to demand passage and full implementation. Lawyers can win legal mandates, but only demonstrations and public outcry can obtain full implementation.

The New Jersey funding equity court case, *Abbott v. Burke*, for instance, which mandates extensive state investments to compensate for economic disadvantage, has not been fully implemented by the State Legislature in over 25 years of continual litigation on the part of lawyers for the states' urban school districts. There has been no organized constituency of urban residents to press for full enforcement of the law. In 1991, by contrast, well-organized and highly vocal middle-class and affluent taxpayers massed at the state capital in demonstrations against a proposed tax hike to pay for the court mandate. The governor responded by repealing the tax increase (Anyon, 1997).

An economic development that has potentially powerful consequences for progressive organizing is the collapse of the traditional well-paying working-class job. As chapters in this book document, an increasing percentage of jobs available to low-income workers pay poverty or poverty-zone wages. This development provides a rationale for organizing for better economic policies, as well as for low-income student access to college preparation courses and funds to complete college. The collapse of working-class job opportunities could also provide a basis for organizing for meaningful, non-racist programs of vocational education for the non-college bound student. As I have noted, figures demonstrate that most jobs in the U.S. do not require college, but rather on-the-job training. Public schools could become a meaningful part of the preparation for these positions if they offered programs combining academic study with realistic vocational training and job placement—combined, crucially, with union support for minority workers and better starting salaries. All these could be strategic organizing goals among low-income students and families.

And for some working- and middle-class college graduates, a central motivating force for joining the Occupy movement was the collapse of job and pay opportunities for those who had borrowed large sums of money to complete college.

There are technological developments that could also be appropriated in urban communities. In late 2002 and early 2003, the internet-based group, Moveon.org, successfully utilized the internet to organize demonstrations in cities across the country against the invasion of Iraq. During the 500,000-strong demonstration against the Republican National Convention in New York City in early September 2004, activist groups coordinated over 150 protests using cell phones and text messaging. As other authors have pointed out, internet access, email, and cell phones have enhanced movement building by increasing the networking and communication capabilities of movement-building groups (see Castells, 1996, 2000; Melucci, 1999; McAdam, Tarrow, and Tilly, 2001; Rheingold, 2002). The World-Wide Web and cell phones are increasingly utilized by urban residents, especially youths, and could be widely appropriated to political ends.

Appropriation of Existing Organizations, Institutions, and Cultural Forms

As the next chapter illustrates in detail, public educational institutions in the U.S. can be sites of appropriation as movement-building spaces. Education in the U.S. has always had a contradictory nature. On the one hand, schools have been primary agents of social control and the reproduction of class, gender, and racial advantages and disadvantages. However, education also has had—and continues to have—potentially liberatory, egalitarian, and transformative functions as well. This contradictory nature of schooling holds out promise that concerned educators can make central contributions to the transformation of society through their work in schools. Many authors have developed extremely important ideas about ways in which teachers can utilize critical pedagogy and create democratically run schools (Darder, Baltodano and Torres, 2008; Apple, Au, and Ganden, 2009, among many others). I will add to this rich tradition in Chapter Eleven with activities educators can use to engage students in public contestation and political campaigns, thereby increasing the appropriation of classrooms and schools as movement-building spaces.

Outsiders and Cultural Brokers

Residents of urban neighborhoods—low-income youth and beleaguered poverty-wage workers—should not be expected to organize a movement alone. Bicultural, bi-class brokers, such as progressive teachers, social workers, and other minority and white professionals concerned with social justice, need to take advantage of their own relatively privileged status to provide spaces and opportunities for low-income urban residents to air grievances, discuss and strategize, and—most important—engage in contentious politics.

Groups can also act as brokers. Groups already active in existing movements can build bridges by brokering relationships, coalitions, and convenings that could get people talking about uniting for social justice. Called intermediaries, such brokers as Local Initiatives Support Corporation in the community development field, Center for Third World Organizing in the community-organizing field, and

Southern Echo in education, could perhaps play these roles. Well-regarded unions like SEIU and HERE, or groups with a national base like IAF and ACORN could act as intermediaries to call people to conference to discuss a united movement for economic and educational opportunity.

Creation of Regional Organizations

As the Civil Rights Movement confirmed, groups that work on a regional level are more likely to make inroads on injustice than groups that work only in their neighborhood.

And larger umbrella groups (like the Southern Christian Leadership Conference) that can pull people and organizations together over large geographical regions can reach national audiences. Without an umbrella group, there can be a cacophony of messages and dissipation of effort.

Intermediaries and their representatives could form an umbrella group to assist smaller movements to coalesce and reach scale. An umbrella group should have its own funding. It might obtain money from progressive unions, church groups, or established civil rights organizations.

Leadership Development

As I argued earlier, leaders emerge from the struggle itself. Those who work with adults and youths need not only involve them in contentious politics, but should set up situations where leadership can emerge, be nurtured, and developed. Nascent leaders can be identified in neighborhood and church-based organizations and after-school groups. As in the Civil Rights Movement, if we involve current youths in political struggle, and if we support them in opportunities to lead, they will develop leadership abilities, skills, and experience. These acquisitions constitute social capital in the best sense of the word: Skills and knowledge that will assist people in making changes to society from which they will truly profit.

Centrality of Youth

Urban youth have a powerful critique of education and white society. Hip Hop lyrics express their complaint: The group Dead Prez states that minority youth are urged to stay in school and get a job, but are not told that "the job gonna exploit you every time." Hip Hop icon Tupac Shakur wrote that whites would "*rather see us locked in chains*" than in school or decent jobs.

Most Hip Hop lyrics are replete with violent epithets, and words and phrases—like nigger and bitch—that many adults find offensive. But until its commodification and spread to white suburban teenagers in the late 1990s, when it lost much of its political edge, this language—that is, Hip Hop discourse—was a form of overt rebellion and transgression against mainstream white and black middle-class

America. It expressed the anger, angst, and frustration of many young people of color (Dimitriadis 2001; Kitwana 2002, among others). Hip Hop, as Todd Boyd remarks, "is a testament to overcoming the obstacles that American life often imposes on its Black and Latino subjects, and in this, it is a model of what 'we shall overcome' means in the modern world" (2002, p. 152).

The rebellion in early Hip Hop also gave the lie to any stereotype of universal fatalism among young people in cities. The lyrics revealed instead a broad-based rebellion that is now finding its political voice in the emerging youth movement.

The youth organizations described previously are examples of how some in the "hip hop generation" have appropriated this cultural stance, and the music, to work for social change. Nascent political attitudes embodied in this cultural form are crucial tools for any social movement that could be developed in the forseeable future. To build a movement, adults both inside and outside of schools need to assist youths in turning this rebellion into informed, organized resistance.

Social Construction of New Identities Through Participation in Transgressive Politics

Let me reiterate this important point from Chapter Nine: As people march, sit-in, prepare petitions and speeches, meet with politicians and school boards, and otherwise engage in contentious politics, they typically develop identities as activists and, ultimately, if a movement develops, identities as part of that movement. As I have argued, we do not typically get people involved in activism or social movements through exposure to critical pedagogy, social justice curricula, or books like this one, although these are crucial to providing information and analysis. Rather, as labor movements, peace movements, and civil rights activists will tell you, people are radicalized by actually *participating* in contentious politics.

Robert Moses describes how involvement in civil rights work changed him:

> I was a 26-year old teacher at … an elite private school in the Bronx…. It was the sit-in movement that led me to Mississippi for the first time in 1960. And that trip changed my life. I returned to the state a year later and over the next four years was transformed as I took part in the voter registration movement there.
>
> *(Moses and Cobb, 2002, p. 4)*

The power of participation to encourage activism implies that an initial component of building a social movement is to personally involve students, other youth, and adults in public protest and other strategic activities with which they can advocate for better opportunities.

The final chapter works at length with this understanding. It provides a variety of ways in which participation in social movement organizing can teach urban youth not only that they can improve their communities, but that they are persons of worth, quality, and intelligence. Through political participation, youths become enmeshed in constructive social networks, develop positive personal identities, and improve their communities.

Creation of Innovative Action Repertoires

The repertoire of activities expressed in social movements develops over time, with each generation utilizing strategies of those who went before them and creating new ones out of their own experiences.

As the previous chapter demonstrates, community organizing was an important strategy in the repertoires of civil rights activists throughout the 20th century. The four movements already existing today also utilize community organizing as a central method of building power. Without a constituency, based in actual neighborhoods, towns, and cities, there is no movement. And without organizing, there is no constituency.

Even though the message of the Occupy movement regarding the massive wealth and power of the 1% spread quickly across the globe, even though masses of people across the U.S. demonstrated against invading Iraq organized throughout the country in early 2003, and many activists fought the "Battle of Seattle" in 2000, these campaigns were not part of sustained community movements with organized constituencies. And they will not be, unless time and effort are spent to build bases in towns and cities around the country. Community organizing is a strategy that must remain central to any attempt to build a national social movement.

Other strategies that might be useful in urban education struggles today include sit-down strikes of families and children in school buildings until demands for funding are met; "sick out" strikes, where students and families boycott schools until the threat of government withdrawal of funds because of absenteeism leads officials to meet demands; and picketing school, district, and political leaders at their homes. Or, students and community members could chain themselves to the metal fences surrounding urban schools. Hunger strikes may be necessary. The refusal of the teachers in Seattle's Garfield High School in 2013 to administer high-stakes tests is an important tactic.

We could emulate the Freedom Rides of the Civil Rights Movement and of the minority unions in 2003—when a coalition of black and immigrant workers hired buses to drive from California to Washington, D.C. They stopped in cities along the way to bring attention to the problems workers face. They achieved much media attention and could have affected pending legislation affecting immigrant workers.

We could appropriate this strategy, filling yellow school buses with students and families and driving through the city stopping at schools and neighborhoods that need urgent attention. We could organize street corner discussions and rallies at each stop, highlighting what needs to be done.

In the theoretical discussion of Chapter Nine I noted that civil rights history demonstrates that economic pressure has typically been a potent strategy in struggles against more powerful groups. Urban education is big business. Expenditures in each city for school district payrolls, testing, purchases, facilities and maintenance, technology, and other goods and services are paid by taxpayers and keep hundreds of thousands of people employed nationwide—and keep many business owners solvent. Perhaps there is a way to learn from the Civil Rights Movement about the power of the economic boycott. Perhaps new strategies will emerge that threaten recipients of district monies with loss of income, and taxpayers with wasted resources, unless community demands are met. Useful, additional actions will arise during contestation, and urban youth will no doubt be instrumental in creating starkly expressive strategies.

Appropriation of Threat

Most urban youth do not engage in violence; and most violent acts that are carried out by blacks and Latinos involve other residents of low-income communities. But the "thug" stereotype follows urban males throughout the media, and many whites fear them. We could appropriate this stereotype, and whites' perceptions of dangerous minority males. Political organizing in the youth movement demonstrates that urban teenagers can move from anger, despair, and street life to well-informed resistance and organized political campaigns for equity. We would be remiss if we did not point out to whites the diminution of the threat of violence by these youths that such politicization embodies.

Appropriation of Social Networks

This theoretical construct asks us to consider the power that would be generated if even half of the 7.5 million grassroots organizations and the several thousand Community Development Corporations (CDCs) were aligned together, acting toward the same goal. Linked by a common agenda, these groups would constitute a vast national network. Such a network would be a significant strand of a social movement.

There are other networks that could constitute other strands: The Leadership Conference on Civil Rights (LCCR), a venerable organization of 180 civil rights groups, represents the older generation of activists. Members have vast accumulated experience. They have produced a *Handbook for Activists* and a *Grassroots Tool Kit*, and maintain active student chapters on college campuses. The Leadership Conference has authored two prospective legislative bills that could lay the foundation of a platform for educational and economic justice (see www.civilrights.org).

As we know, the African American church has long provided networks supporting social justice mobilizing. Some argue, however, that the church may not be able to play a similar role today. Sociologist Omar McRoberts (2003) studied a low-income section of Boston, and found that in contrast to the past, African Americans in the congregations of churches in that area do not typically live in the neighborhoods where they worship; they merely rent the buildings for services. Therefore, they are not as available or concerned about "social uplift" in the neighborhood where the church is located. McRoberts argues that black churches therefore are not likely to take part in sustained political struggle to improve the inner city.

But as Andrew Billingsley (2002) demonstrates in *Mighty Like a River: The Black Church and Social Reform*, there also exist well over a thousand mostly large, well-established African American churches in U.S. cities, and a majority of them are deeply involved in community outreach. Billingsley argues that among black churches, "community outreach activities are much more common than is generally believed, especially in urban areas.... [A] majority of contemporary black churches have not abandoned community issues since the civil rights era" (2002, p. 89).

Indeed, some of the most productive CDCs and community-based organizations today are part of, or offshoots of, religious organizations. And faith-based organizing (e.g., in the IAF, PICO, GAMALIEL, and other faith-based networks) is an important part of movement building today.

I noted when discussing social networks in the last chapter that the Civil Rights Movement was blessed with many family activist traditions. However, indications are that there is little agreement between elders and the young in African American communities today. There is often distance, suspicion, and even hostility that builds up around social goals and means. As in the 1960s, when white activists expressed contempt for people over 30 years old, today African American youths are often estranged from their civil rights forebears.

But it is crucial for movement building today that we overcome the boundaries of age, because men and women who fought the battles of the civil rights, labor, and community development movements in the 1950s and '60s have much to teach those who would be political today. And the organizations these elders built over the years could provide a national network of "safe houses" and operational nodes in a national movement.

Social Contradictions as an Impetus for Radical Action

The penultimate theoretical construct is the role of contradictions in stimulating political contention. Social justice teachers know that political and economic contradictions can be a fecund source of anger and ideas for discussion, political education, and consciousness raising. They can also catalyze action among the people affected.

As I have pointed out, for example, African Americans and Latinos are obtaining more education than ever before, but their situation in the economy has deteriorated. This highlights the new truth that an historic faith in education as the path to middle-class status is no longer assured. This is anger-producing, and therefore may be catalyzing—if we utilize it as such.

Another contradiction of urban schooling that could be mobilizing is that even though society urges minority youth to "stay in school," perseverance (unless one has the funds to complete college) is likely to get a high school graduate very little. Many students are aware that without available jobs and decent pay, lacking a college degree, and in the face of employer discrimination, the promises of education are severely compromised.

These and other contradictions plaguing folks day after day, if used strategically, can become mobilizing points for youths and their families. I will demonstrate in the final chapter numerous ways educators can assist youths and their families to move from knowledge of the social traps they experience to concrete political contention to change the situation.

Legitimation

For ultimate success, the goals of a social movement should appear legitimate to a broad swath of the public. There may not be wide acceptance of the idea of, say, a wealth tax on the super rich. However, if people were made aware of how much wealth a very few have, how much tax they paid in the past, and how much money equitable taxing might produce, a consensus for a wealth-tax might develop.

But I do believe that there is a consensus among Americans that urban students deserve quality education. Moreover, the repeal of welfare and the "discovery" by policy makers that the jobs former recipients can obtain do not provide funds sufficient to support a family has created the basis for another emerging consensus—that full-time work should bring a person at least a living wage.

For maximum power, the various movements today—and the many grassroots and social justice groups that constitute them—need to unite, and acknowledge that the problems they tackle can be best resolved if they are tackled as intimately interrelated issues. For as I have been at pains to point out, the obstacles that urban residents face are complex and interrelated. The problems of urban education, jobs, poverty, housing segregation, police brutality, and incarceration are tangled together in the fabric of everyday living in poor neighborhoods. These issues form a formidable knot of many tightly wound strands. Only when the knot itself is undone will the threads come free.

11

PUTTING EDUCATORS AT THE CENTER OF A SOCIAL MOVEMENT FOR ECONOMIC AND EDUCATIONAL JUSTICE

If I were writing for an audience of labor union organizers, immigrant parents, social workers, or civil rights lawyers, I would describe how they—in the work they do every day—could be crucial to building a social movement for economic equity and justice. But I write primarily for educators, and so this chapter is written for that audience. The unfair political economy remains the main target, yet each of us can contribute to its reshaping by efforts where we live and work. Educators who are concerned about the mounting corporate pressures shaping the educational enterprise in this country are central to social movement building, as is education itself.

A most important characteristic of urban education is its theoretical "location." Urban schools are at the center of the maelstrom of constant crises which beset low-income neighborhoods. Education is an institution whose basic problems are caused by, and whose basic problems reveal, the other crises in cities: Poverty, joblessness and low-wages, lack of health care, housing and transportation, and racial and class segregation. Therefore, a focus on urban education can expose the combined effects of these public policies, and highlight not only poor schools, but the entire nexus of constraints on urban families. And educational institutions, not only reflecting but contributing to an unequal political economy, are targets of mobilization as well. Organizing centered on severing the links between education and neoliberal goals would challenge federal and regional political economic policies and practices as one part of an overall plan to improve local educational opportunity.

The reasons to organize in the economic arena have become more urgent as the Great Recession lingers, and reasons to organize in education have multiplied as private decision making and profit taking drives the enterprise. We have seen, since the publication of the first edition of this book in 2005, the explosion of neoliberal, corporate-sponsored educational reforms like high-stakes testing as a means of accountability, privatization apparent in reforms like the spread of charter schools, attacks on teacher unions, and school closings that provide a premise for profit-making ventures by hedge funds and other high-flying investors (Lipman, 2011; Ravitch, 2013, among others).

An additional reason education is a good place to organize is that, even though education is not guaranteed by the U.S. Constitution, it is often construed as a civil right, and can be located ideologically in the long and powerful tradition of civil rights struggle (Moses and Cobb, 2002; see also www.civilrights.org). This legitimacy may lend movement building by educators an acceptance that could affect public attitudes toward new policies regarding the need for jobs, decent wages, and affordable housing.

Further, many people involved in the movements described in the last chapters live in low-income urban areas and have children in under-funded and under-achieving city schools. Like other adults, they are often willing to bear substantial hardship without fighting back; but as parent-organizing in cities across America reveals, these parents will "go to the mat for their kids" (Leigh Dingerson, Center for Community Change, personal communication). This willingness to fight for the rights of their children means that putting education at the forefront may be a good mobilizing tool with which to attract parents' involvement in other issues as well.

Indeed, educators are in an excellent position to build a constituency for economic and educational change in urban communities. Teachers and principals have continual access to parents and urban youth. If they are respectful, caring, hard-working educators, trusted by students and parents, they have a unique opportunity to engage residents and youth in political conversations and activity in the community.

A final reason to connect movement building in education to political-economic justice issues is that there is a rich tradition of liberal/Left advocacy to build on. I, like many others, entered teaching "to change the world." There are teachers in every city today who teach a critical, thought-provoking curriculum, and who utilize the classroom to discuss issues their students face. Hundreds of scholarly books and articles have been written offering insight and inspiration to teachers who concern themselves with social justice. In addition, there exist widely read progressive publications like *Rethinking Schools*; proactive organizations like National Coalition of Educational Activists and Educators for Social Responsibility; professional conferences that enrich critical teaching; and democratic, progressive caucuses in teacher unions in large cities throughout the country. There is possibility here, and great promise in the work of these educators. We can take this work further in our appropriation of the institution for radical purposes.

Thus, I believe that those of us in education who have social justice as a goal can play a crucial role in movement building for both educational and economic rights of the poor. We can do this in our daily lives, as we "cast down our buckets" where we are. We can commit to the radical possibilities in our everyday work in schools, despite the onslaught of institutional mandates. To assist in this effort, the present chapter supplements the existing critical pedagogical literature with strategies used by community and education organizers.

Throughout, I want to remember that to turn anger and despair into a commitment to struggle for justice, we cannot stay in the classroom; we must engage our students in actual political contestation. In the fall of 2012, when Occupy Wall Street was in its prime, several of my doctoral students who were teachers took their high school classes to evening demonstrations sponsored by Occupy and attended, in New York City, by tens of thousands of people. The students were excited and uplifted by the crowds and the fervor of the chanting and singing. I was there too, and as I looked in the faces of these young people, I saw the possibility that they—through such activity, and with the help of their teachers— might begin to see themselves as political actors for radical justice.

Student Self-esteem and Politicization

As noted earlier, studies indicate that fear, despair, and negative valuations of the self can be immobilizing, and may keep social actors who have cause to get involved in political contention from participating. Feelings of efficacy, righteous anger, and strength, on the other hand, are more likely to lead a person to activism. A first step in movement building in urban schools, then, is to help students appreciate their own value, intelligence, and potential as political actors.

African American and Latino scholars write tellingly about the fears harbored by many students of color that they fit the stereotypes white society has of them— that they are incapable of high academic achievement, not interested in education, and to blame for their lack of advancement (e.g., Boykin and Noguera 2011; Steele, 2011).

An important mechanism is that this "stereotype threat" can prevent students' full engagement in academic work, as they fear failure and fulfillment of the stereotype. This is tragic in and of itself. But I want to point out that blaming oneself, rather than locating causes of failure in the wider structure of opportunities, has another consequence: It can also mitigate against a perceived need to change the system.

Theresa Perry argues that in order to undermine the ideology and practice of victim blaming, educators need to create a *counter-narrative* to the story of failure and low intelligence of students of color. She notes that we could learn from successful all-black schools in the antebellum South, where teachers emphasized the relation between education and freedom: "Freedom for literacy, and literacy for freedom" (2003, p. 92). Perry exhorts teachers to counter the damaging dominant social narrative by building an intentional classroom community spirit of education for "racial uplift, citizenship and leadership" (ibid., p. 93). In order to demonstrate to students that they are capable and worthy, "teachers must explicitly articulate, regularly ritualize, and pass on in formal public events the belief in minority students as scholars of high achievement and as of social value" (ibid., pp. 99, 100). A supportive and trusting environment provides "identity security" to students, who are then emotionally more ready to challenge the stereotypical myths (also Steele, 2011).

As Paolo Freire taught us (1992), and Lisa Delpit reminds us (2006), we must also teach working-class and minority students the culture and knowledge held by powerful whites and the middle and upper classes, so the students may problematize their own positions and work against aspects of the system that oppress or subordinate them. Poor and non-white students need to understand the codes of dominant cultural capital and be able to parse them. Early research of my own suggested that affluent white students are taught a much more analytical approach to society and its processes than students in other social classes (Anyon, 1980, 1981).

A healthy education of this sort would urge minority students toward a stance of *entitlement* regarding the responsibility of governments to provide equal opportunities; and this would encourage them to hold the system accountable. Thus, a politically energizing education for African Americans must explicitly recognize and acknowledge with students that they and their families are *not* yet free—and that social change is necessary. This is one reason a history of both oppression and resistance is so important. Students who are knowledgeable about dominant forms of power and how this power affects them can better move from self-blame to informed efforts at change of the system. Teachers and administrators who would assist students in this development could begin by working with the community of which the students are a vital part.

Working with the Community

Teachers, administrators, and other professionals in urban public schools are not usually from the neighborhood. Their social class and often their race differentiate them from students, families, and other residents. In this sense, most of those who work to appropriate the educational institution for social justice are outsiders and bicultural brokers. They can contribute important resources and knowledge to that which students and families already possess. In education organizing across urban America, educators are increasingly playing a brokering, bridge-building role, as they join with parents and communities to combat policies that oppress.

When educators work with community residents as equals and as change agents to develop community power, movement building is taking place; and as research I reported in the previous chapter confirms, schools typically improve and student achievement increases. Research suggests that there are several reasons for this raised student achievement, including community pressure for more resources and district accountability, increased parental engagement, and improved staff development and pedagogy (Gold, Simon, and Brown, 2002; Rogers and Orr, 2010).

I would like to highlight two other—related—causes of the increased achievement. First, education organizing has been shown to lower the rate at which students move from one school to another (mobility), sometimes by as much as 50%. Studies show that in schools where educators work closely with the community as partners in change, parents and students often report that they do not want to leave the school because of their involvement in and satisfaction with the activities (Whalen 2002; Hohn, 2003).

Another reason for increased achievement in schools where parents and educators work together as change agents may be an increase in trust and respect between the parties. Tony Bryk and Barbara Schneider (2002) demonstrated convincingly that trusting relationships in daily interactions in low-income urban schools are correlated with raised achievement over time.

Community organizers regularly utilize several strategies that teachers and administrators might incorporate to work for change and build personal relationships and mutual trust. Teachers can involve parents and other residents in one-on-one conversations designed to identify their concerns, can hold meetings in parents' homes where groups of residents address these concerns, and can engage parents, other community members, and educators in "neighborhood walks"—during which participants tour the area around the school and reach a common understanding and vision of what changes are needed.

School principals who work with the Industrial Areas Foundation often say that "an angry parent is an opportunity"—an opening to organize the community for increased accountability "of officials and politicians (IAF Principal Claudia Santamaria, Cambridge, MA Conference, 2/04)" (Ayers et al., 2008). If a parent is angry about something, other parents may be as well, and the opportunity presents itself to get them together and organize to change what causes the anger. Community anger is also most likely connected not just to education, but to lack of job opportunities, low wages, etc., and provides a way to connect the issues with parents.

Some education organizers also work with parent groups and teachers to monitor district and state programs and policies by carrying out research that identifies discrepancies between stated goals of district, city, or state policies and programs, and the actual experience of students and teachers; stated goals of officials in other areas of the city's administration—such as job development, housing, or health care—can be related to outcomes as well. These can also be useful as the basis for calling officials to account.

Acquiring Community Organizing Skills

The foregoing strategies provide an introduction to working with parents and communities as partners for change. This section provides advice on how to organize parents in extended issue campaigns.

In 2012, the Center for Education Organizing at Annenberg Institute prepared a pamphlet entitled, "Getting Started in Education Organizing." Other guides have been developed as well. Chicago-based Cross City Campaign for Urban School Reform (Cahill, 1999) and the Institute for Education and Social Policy in New York (Zimmer and Mediratta, 2004) prepared advice based on many years of organizing experience that is useful for educators interested in carrying out issue campaigns with community members. The advice I offer in this chapter adheres to some of their guidelines. But crucially, I differ from them somewhat in my insistence on connecting education issues to other social justice issues such as decent jobs and housing, health care, and transportation.

Zimmer and Mediratta (2004) offer the following advice to educators interested in organizing for school reform:

1. Choose issues from the bottom up. Issues to pursue should come from parents, students, and other residents. Knock on doors in two-people teams (for example, one parent and one teacher or principal) to identify issues important to the community; and recruit people for home meetings to discuss the issues they feel are important and what to do about them. Visit area congregations to discuss local problems, and develop relationships with members and clergy. Systematic personal contact, and the building of personal relationships are key to successful engagement of residents.

2. Begin to build a community constituency for long-range reform through immediate, specific, and winnable issues. Frame broad demands like "better schools" more specifically to attract particular constituencies: Bilingual programs for Latino parents; after-school job training and placement for parents and high school students. Building a base among parents and community members will provide a force and legitimacy to the demands you will make. Because you also want to develop working relationships with other educators, it may be best to start with a neighborhood issue like jobs and housing rather than one that directly targets problems in the school.

3. Locate key school and district personnel who can assist you in gathering data to document the problems you want to address. Work with local community-based organizations to see what system information they already have. Collaborate with them, if possible.

4. Develop a program of needed changes and present this to authorities. Plan demonstrations and other activities that attempt to obtain concessions, promises, and behavioral responses from those in power in the district and city.

5. Develop a plan for what to do when people in power ignore you, refer you to others, delay you, try to pacify and placate you, or try to divide and conquer your group. Officials may try to discredit you or pursue action against you. Or they may attempt to buy off your leaders, or propose a substitute that does not meet your needs. Some of the strategies you could consider when

this happens may be cooperative, like setting up meetings; but some may be confrontational—like pickets, demonstrations, political theatre, press conferences, etc.

6. Keep the pressure on administrators and officials by demonstrations and actions of various sorts. A "presence in the streets" is necessary to hold their attention and get results.

I want to emphasize again that whenever possible, link educational issues to community ones regarding jobs, housing, transportation, and investment (for example). Not only—as I have been insisting—is education reform without economic reform insufficient to sustain better schools in a neighborhood, but successful education organizing in a neighborhood without other reforms can improve schools in low-income areas to the point that housing values rise, businesses increasingly invest in the neighborhood, and low-income residents are pushed out by higher rents. This occurred on two blocks in Chicago's Logan Square area, in part because of the success of education organizing by LSNA (Halsband, 2003; Hohn, 2003).

Gentrification resulting from education organizing and improved local schools is a reminder that without other public policy changes (in this case housing policies to maintain low-income housing or policies providing better-paying jobs), successful school reform in low-income urban neighborhoods can have unfortunate, unintended consequences.

Collaboration between Mainstream School Reform, Community Groups, and Education Organizers

One way to link school reform to community groups is for education organizers to collaborate with those working to provide resident services and neighborhood development. The following project description is an example of how vital the synergy could be if curricular and pedagogical reforms were coupled with financial and social support of students outside of school.

In Washington, D.C., Othello Poulard and the Center for Community Change created such a system. With foundation funding, they provided extensive supports for 8th through 12th graders living in five local housing projects. Poulard and the Public Housing Graduates Demonstration program (PHG) built a system of daily after-school tutoring in each project building. They hired skilled, long-term tutors. Poullard provided emotional support and guidance with trained neighborhood residents serving as "Mighty Moms" or "Mighty Pops," hired as long-term mentors. They kept an eye on the students and helped them with personal problems. "Big Brothers" and "Big Sisters" were provided and offered emotional and academic support. PHG exposed the students to colleges as well as middle-class culture, and trained them to use computers; the program provided computers for the students' homes. PHG offered athletics, and taught the youth how to avoid pregnancy and deal with violence. They provided health care, and financial support. As in middle-class and affluent families, youths were paid an allowance. They received $100 a month in 10th and 11th grade, and $200 a month in 12th grade. To qualify for the allowance they had to participate in almost daily after-school activities, along with weekend college readiness sessions and field trips. They also had to produce journals and detailed time sheets. They lost money every time they did not fulfill requirements (Center for Community Change, 2001, pp. 1–4).

The results of this extensive support system were extremely encouraging. Whereas before the program only 40% of the public housing students who entered the 8th grade ever graduated from high school, 89.6% of PHG's students graduated by the end of a three-year evaluation, as compared to 63% of students who attended the same schools but were not in the program. PHG participants had a significantly higher grade point average and higher test scores than a control group; 70% of PHG students applied to college or trade school; all were accepted and every one who applied for financial aid received it. Over three years, only one 12th grader failed to graduate because of pregnancy or incarceration (ibid., p. 5; for other examples, see Reneé, 2011).

We know all too well that over the last few decades traditional school reform in U.S. cities has shown considerably less success than its proponents hoped for. One important reason for disappointing results is that most mainstream urban school reforms have no public constituency—the reforms are not successful in part because the community is not behind them, and often actively mistrusts them. Community organizing can create the political will to create and implement meaningful reforms. Indeed, success would most likely be assured if politicians and education reform groups were to work with community members to come to a consensus as to what changes are needed.

One way to reach this consensus is for school reformers to create proposals for change on the basis of recommendations made by community research. Such research typically documents inequities in a powerful, personal manner, and highlights inadequate provision for low-income students and schools.

In March 2013, admissions figures for the elite Stuyvesant Public High School in New York City revealed that out of 963 students accepted, just nine were black and 24 Hispanic. The previous year, the school accepted 51 black and Hispanic students. In the mid-1990s, ACORN carried out and published three studies demonstrating that the vast majority of students in New York City's three elite competitive high schools came from three white, middle-class districts, and that almost no low-income districts sent students to the special schools (Association of Community Organizations Now, 1996, 1997). These powerful reports could have been the basis for meaningful, community-backed school reform if taken up by mainstream educational organizing groups.

It is also the case that education organizers have much to learn from educators. As political activists, education organizers typically are not trained in education, and need to know more about curriculum and pedagogical best practice, and how public schools work internally, in order to know what classroom reforms to advocate for, and how to work with administrators once they get their attention. Community pressure is not always enough (Mediratta and Fruchter, 2003). Moreover, in order to work with school boards, mayors, and state legislatures, community organizers must be knowledgeable about educational research, practice, and jargon.

Any effort to create a social movement with potential to affect current policy and practice regarding urban schools and economic access must get concerned actors from different spheres together, working in concert. Equity-seeking school reform networks, progressive caucuses in teacher unions, community activists advocating for school and neighborhood improvement, and regional social justice organizations described earlier are on the same side; they should acknowledge their commonalities and collaborate in the interest of increased opportunity and change (Weiner, 2012).

I have already mentioned the powerful video about parents and community groups working together. For solid advice about working such a campaign, see the film's Viewer's Guide (2011, Parent Power: Education Organizing in NYC, 1995–2010—Screening Toolkit; available for download at http://annenberginstitute.org/publication/parent-power-education-organizing-nyc-1995-2010-%E2%80%93-screening-toolkit).

Importantly, politically progressive classroom teachers are central here. They are in a position to work with both kinds of groups as they mentor youth activism for educational and economic justice.

Classrooms as Movement-building Spaces

Secondary school teachers, in particular, can make a powerful contribution to movement building by engaging students in civic activism. Both the insurgent immigrant youth movement, the Civil Rights Movement, and successful youth efforts to reduce the voting age from 21 to 18 (legalized in 1971) demonstrate that activism by young people can make a huge impact on American society. The activities in this section provide teachers with teaching strategies to assisting urban teenagers move from self-blame or angry rebellion to well-informed political engagement.

But, you might respond, urban students are not interested in political activity. To that I reply that behavioral resistance to extant, typical methods of teaching does not necessarily transfer to alternative, more appealing methods. Indeed, I believe it is the case that most urban teens *want* an education—a high-*quality* education. College readiness is the top priority of urban youth who are involved in organizing. A comprehensive assessment of 49 youth groups in 18 states found that the issues youths most frequently address have to do with education. Most (61%) want college preparation from their high school; the next issue is criminal and juvenile justice (49%), and then economic justice (18%) and immigrant rights (14%). Moreover, programs already run by organizations in urban communities to encourage teenage activism typically attract youths who are alienated from school. Teachers, then, may not find it difficult to interest students in political projects; and they may find that those considering dropping out can be brought back in (Weiss, 2003; see also Wheeler, 2003; www.theinnovationcenter.org).

Numerous benefits accrue to youths who work for increased opportunities in their communities. Studies have documented that civic activism by low-income students of color typically fosters teenagers' positive personal development, and improves their academic engagement and, therefore, achievement (see, for example, Roth, Brooks-Gunn, and Murray, 1998; Ginwright and James, 2002;Forum for Youth Investment, 2004; Hilley, 2004).

There are several other benefits, as well. Organizing urban youth to work with others to improve their schools and neighborhoods gives teenagers *connections*, embedding them in constructive community networks. This connectedness is a worthy alternative to that offered by most street gangs.

In addition, by organizing others to work responsibly for social change, minority youth counter the view that they constitute a social "problem." Teens also are encouraged to understand how the poverty of their families and their peers arises from systemic rather than personal failings. And it provides them with the concrete lesson that they can bring about changes in society, giving them a foundation for pursuing this kind of activity as adults.

A final benefit to working with students on political projects that aim to achieve youth and family rights puts educators and students on the same "team," and increases trust between them which, as we have seen, has been found to increase academic achievement (Bryk and Schneider, 2002).

An example of teachers organizing students demonstrates several of these positive outcomes. In 1995, youth at Gratz High School in Philadelphia started the first chapter of what became a city-wide Student Union (PSU). The original impetus for organizing was students' complaints about inadequate textbooks and dirty bathrooms. When the students asked administrators why there were no new textbooks, they were told it was their fault because "students tear them up." When students complained about the bathrooms, they were told "students mess them up." Students' first reaction was to agree with school administrators that they were themselves to blame. However, with their advisor's help they learned to take partial responsibility for disrespecting school property, and were also encouraged to ask themselves the following questions: "Why didn't they consider it their school and their property? Why did they deface their school as if they didn't respect it or own it? Why didn't they feel comfortable at school?" After years and years in a failing system, the students were frustrated and self-blaming. Their advisor assisted them as they got to work to advocate for changes in the school.

Since 1995, many changes have resulted from PSU's activism in Philadelphia high schools, including new student governments, creation of school ombudsmen to stop the harassment and abuse by school security officers, a district level student platform on planned school reforms, a rally of 2,450 students at City Hall which helped to defeat (at least temporarily) planned privatization of Philadelphia high schools, new networks of organized students in other city schools, and a statewide campaign to increase school funding to the level of nearby affluent suburbs (American Youth Policy Forum 2002, p. 103).

As in research studying the benefits of youth organizing in Los Angeles, many of the Philadelphia students who became involved as activists and leaders had been on the verge of dropping out, but remained in school when it became clear that they had a voice. A number of teachers reported that these new youth leaders became academic "stars." Teachers and administrators reported respect for students who organize (Hayasaki, 2003).

The following classroom activities can develop in students many of the skills utilized by community organizers in their movement-building work. The activities begin with research in the neighborhood, and lead to the development of issue campaigns to bring about new policy.

Map Community Assets

Finding and documenting community resources that could be useful for making the neighborhood a better place to live and work is an important first step. The classic source for asset mapping is Kretzmann and McNight (1997). These activist-scholars point out that a thorough map of community begins with an inventory of the "gifts, skills and capacities of the community's residents ... few of which are being mobilized for community-building purposes" (ibid., p. 5).

In addition to identifying the gifts and skills of individuals, households, and families, student researchers will compile an inventory of formal and informal institutions. These include churches, ethnic and religious associations, tenants groups, political organizations, and advocacy and activist groups, among others. Politicians and political parties should be included, as should local branches of corporations, Chambers of Commerce, and other interest groups. Mapping should also include businesses such as banks and restaurants, and public institutions such as libraries, parks, community colleges, and other types of schools; and non-profit institutions such as hospitals and social service agencies. Physical characteristics, as well, are part of a community's assets—vacant and occupied land and buildings and other infrastructure such as streets and transportation systems.

Students travel in pairs or small groups to catalogue these assets. Then, the class as a whole raises important questions: How might the assets held by individuals, associations, institutions, and the physical environment be connected to each other? How might the community begin to imagine and institute new uses for these strengths? Mapping the environment means looking carefully at the political and cultural resources that can be mobilized to solve the particular problems faced by the community.

Teachers could focus the mapping on locating "opportunity structures" within the neighborhoods. These comprise an interrelated and interdependent web of systems (such as education and health care), markets (such as employment), and structures (such as transportation)" (Powell, 2000). Maps can be made of the locations of jobs and day care providers, the availability of transportation, and access to a variety of social services. Maps can reveal key demographic information such as poverty rates, race/ethnicity, age, language, employment status and rates, the cost of land development, who develops it, levels of criminal activity, school achievement levels, the price of housing, and the location of any job training services. The spatial depiction of these systems provides a useful tool for students and teachers who want to identify impediments and assets related to solving problems that people in the community face (www1.umn.edu/irp/programs/oppmapping. html, 1–3; see also www.communityyouthmapping.org).

Power Analysis

Asset mapping is not an end in itself. It should be the basis for a "power analysis." Such an inquiry assesses the causes and solutions of current problems—whether they extend from the neighborhood and city to the metropolitan or federal levels.

A power analysis identifies a problem faced by students or other community residents and asks the following kinds of questions: Who is impacted by the problem? Who makes the decisions that affect the immediate situation? Who makes decisions that determine what those individuals or groups do and say? What kinds of informal influence or formal power do they have? What kinds of informal influence or formal power do community residents have over the situation? Whose interests are affected by decisions that have been made? Who are potential allies in an attempt to solve the problem? (See William Domhoff's website for many tips on how to study local and larger power networks: www2.ucsc.edu/whorulesamerica/power/wealth.html.)

To the asset map a group has made will be added specific individuals and organizations that could work together to solve the problem. As the map shows categories of assets who are actual people with names, work, interests, and relationships to others, it becomes a *power* map (Bass and Boyte, 1995, p. 6). As described below, the power map becomes a basis for political campaigns to improve the community.

After teachers and students map and analyze community issues and resources, they share their analysis with other community residents, to begin to build a base of support. They could share it with school and government officials, as well, in initial attempts to obtain improvements.

In general, students' research can be disseminated in any number of ways. For example, in Oakland, California, a group of teachers, students, parents, and community members prepared a report together which compared state spending on education (proposed cuts) and prisons (proposed increases). After confronting officials with their data, they put their report on the World Wide Web (www.may8.org; see also Bloom, Chajet et al., 2003; www.whatkidscando.org/studentresearch).

Upon completion and sharing of research reports, students and teachers should not end their involvement in the issue. Indeed, they are just beginning. Movement building requires an on-going relationship with the community. Students should continue their engagement with community issues by using their research to assist in developing issue campaigns with residents.

Developing an Issue Campaign

As I will point out in more detail later, activities teachers utilize to develop skills of political analysis and activism in high school students typically involve well-regarded pedagogical strategies. The process involves techniques of *problem-solving* (analysis, or involving students in thinking about a situation to determine issues, problems, and sources of problems and where the power that determines the existing situation comes from); *collecting data and analyzing it*; and *taking reflective action* (taking some action to learn about and communicate findings through writing, graphing, etc., and reflection on what has been accomplished in order to continue).

A key in developing an issue campaign with students is to break the overall task—say, a campaign for immigrant students' rights—into manageable pieces, and to obtain a student to take responsibility for each piece. It is also a good idea to set up structures like committees with student leaders, to facilitate many youths having chances to develop skills. Have older teens teach younger ones. In some cases, college students help high school students plan issue campaigns.

In all organizing work with teenagers, make use of their own cultural modes. For example, my niece, who was a youth organizer in Oakland, California, took a group of her students to a concert by the Hip Hop group Dead Prez, a politically progressive group that does not utilize sexual imagery or descriptions of violence. She reported that attending the concert was an "incredible political education" for the students because they related so well to the medium in which the political message was delivered (Yolanda Anyon, personal communication, February 25, 2004).

The following description of how to develop an issue campaign with students is taken from an interview with experienced youth organizer Kim McGillicuddy, one of 13 founding members of Youth Force in the Bronx. McGillicuddy now works with Youth Justice Coalition to Free LA. This group was formed to deal with what they call "California's undeclared war on youth." The group is led by youths aged 8–24 who have been arrested, detained, incarcerated, or put on probation or parole.

McGillicuddy advises that a successful campaign with young people has a number of steps: It starts with identifying the students' constituency. Who do they feel they represent—immigrant students? Families? All community residents? Youths then conduct a strengths and needs assessment, identifying and mapping constituents' needs, skills, resources, and vision for change. Youths can develop, conduct, transcribe, and assess surveys, interviews, and personal stories. Next, youths scan existing research in relation to concerns or issues identified in their community research. They obtain demographic data, Geographic Information Systems (GIS) data, and evaluate research done by others. Often research requires investigating primary sources, something few schools teach or expect from urban students.

With the teacher's help, the class analyzes the data that surfaced from research activities—looking at everything they have found. They use their asset and power maps. Through discussion, they decide whether they want to act on the concerns. If so, they begin to identify the specific issues the class will take on, and determine short- and long-term organizing goals. The goals may be worded as a youth platform or campaign demands.

Base-building is the next step. Youths determine what sort of organizational structure will best serve that goal. Base-building also means creating and implementing recruitment and communications strategies in the neighborhood, creating informational curriculum, debating whether decisions will be made by majority rule or consensus, facilitating meetings, and recording and communicating decisions.

After researching the problems, identifying the issues, sketching out demands, and beginning to educate the larger community, youths now further develop the campaign's power analysis, including researching targets of the campaign. They ask: Who is the person or group that has the power to give us what we want? What do they believe? How have they voted in the past? From where do they gain their strength—financial resources, advice, support? Where are they vulnerable? Who are their allies, and yours—and who can we move? The answers to these questions, combined with the other analyses already done, should produce a short-term strategy, a long-term vision, and a final list of demands—all of which should be used to measure the group's success.

Teacher and students then develop their campaign action plan—including selecting tactics that will most effectively impact targets. Full debate is necessary to choose tactics, and the pros and cons of everything from taking one's demands to the target with an appointment if possible, to civil disobedience if necessary. Invite community-based organizations to become involved. If, as is likely, the issue has to do with education, invite both education organizers and school reform groups to join in.

Students may want to support their platform, or those of others with which they agree, by demonstrating publicly. They should be encouraged to use electronic means such as cell phone texting and social media such as Facebook to build support for their platform.

During demonstrations and other activities that develop a political campaign, youths build strong communications and media skills. The details, responsibilities, and opportunities are enormous—organizing community forums and school assemblies; educating residents door-to-door; writing one's own stories or creating one's own media such as newsletters, CDs, and videos; educating and cooperating with journalists; organizing meetings with city officials; testifying at public hearings; and integrating cultural expression into outreach (through open microphones, spoken word, slap tags, etc.)—all these develop their communication skills.

Even the rallies and marches that the class may undertake involve lots of duties: Deciding when, where, and why to rally; getting speakers and helping them to develop effective messages; setting up a sound system; getting permits from police, sanitation, and the parks department; handling security and negotiating with police; training people as marshals, coordinating legal support if there's a chance of arrests; and coming up with chants and posters.

The group is writing constantly: Producing research reports, newsletters, websites, curricula, petitions, education guides, scripts for popular education skits, grant proposals, speeches, dialogue for videos. And because the youth are writing for a public audience, they are more concerned about getting it right; they are learning about the power of words well expressed. They learn math: They produce budgets, order supplies, fill vouchers, make requisitions, create estimates, enter data, crunch numbers, and prepare for reviews of their figures. And they practice critical thinking—learning to ask hard questions, make connections, and gather evidence. They learn tolerance for others while discovering and coming to appreciate their own identity and agency.

McGillicuddy notes that many urban youth "struggle with the oppression that they have suffered as well as the hurt that they have caused others, and gain the understanding that their own liberation is dependent on the liberation of other people." She reports that:

> many of the youth who become involved in organizing are not just leaders, but local heroes. Few other 'youth development' activities offer young people the chance, for example, to help rid their community of a toxic waste site or a corrupt police chief. What better way for youth to overcome the isolation and anger they feel in communities where too many people clutch their bags and cross the street to avoid [them]!
> *(Interview of Kim McGillicuddy by What Kids Can Do staff, May 2003 (www.whatkidscando.org/feataurestories/YOinterview.html); for other resources see Funders' Collaborative on Youth Organizing: www.fcyo.org)*

Most teacher-led activities will take place at the local level, in schools and communities. As I have suggested for the Civil Rights Movement, without local organizing there would not have been a mass movement—and so today. However, it is also true that without connection to city-wide, regional, state, and national momentum and groups, many of the "wins" resulting from neighborhood organizing can be easily overruled by officials.

The next section asks education organizers to take the lead in pulling together not only progressive teachers and youth, but all others engaged in struggles for economic and educational opportunities in U.S. cities.

Regional and National Convenings

The education-organizing field is an increasing presence in U.S. cities. A sizeable number of groups are active, and many are part of regional and national networks like IAF, and PICO. Yet the effect is not national. We need to find a way to use these networks to challenge policies and practices at the metropolitan and federal levels—since these are where underlying determinants of urban poverty and poor schools originate.

Thus, because of the intricate connections between urban education and these deep structural issues, moving to scale in educational organizing and reform will require collaboration with the already existing political movements for economic rights—jobs and housing, transportation, and progressive unions, fair taxation, and immigrant concerns.

Moreover, it is also the case that collaboration with educational campaigns would strengthen these other movements. The Immigrant Freedom Ride in 2003, for example, was an exciting collaboration of progressive labor unions and other immigrant groups; and the tour across the country, making the case to audiences along the way, captured media attention and may have an impact on federal legislation regarding immigrants' wages and civil rights. But the campaign could have been considerably stronger if children of immigrants and their exclusion from an education that allows them access to jobs with decent wages had been linked.

How do various campaigns obtain unity of purpose and coordination of activity—these important prerequisites to a large-scale movement? One lesson of the Civil Rights Movement is that "umbrella groups" are essential to coordinating those involved in local activism, and in bringing the struggle to regional and national scales. Currently, there are groups in each of the existing movements that function like proto-umbrella groups. These entities, commonly called intermediaries, offer a wide range of supports to local organizations. They assist with research, policy and organizational development, training, legal assistance, alliance-building, and fundraising.

Among the intermediaries in the education organizing field that I believe have the capacity to join together to call others to the table are the democratic caucuses of teacher unions in Chicago, New York City, Newark, and other cities; and Southern Echo.

Numerous education blogs attempt to connect progressive, equity-minded educators. Many of these are national in scope and readership, and could be utilized in attempts to convene broad coalitions and convenings:

- ows-public-education-committee@googlegroups.com
- nyceducationnews-SUBSCRIBE@yahoogroups.com
- nyceducationnews@yahoogroups.com
- EducatorsforSocialJustice@yahoogroups.com
- Grassroots-Education@googlegroups.com

- ice-mail@yahoogroups.com
- march-4-education-ny@googlegroups.com
- pubedco@googlegroups.com
- ufterstostopthewar@googlegroups.com
- saveourschoolsmarch@gmail.com
- network-edliberation.org
- realworldeducators@yahoo.com
- Rethinking Schools rs@criticalteach.org
- nnat@yahoogroups.com
- NYCoREUpdates@yahoogroups.com

As a new organization representing the youth and education movements, an umbrella group could reach out to unions, living wage proponents, housing, and other community organizations, and begin a process of conversing that could lead to national conferences—the goal of which would be to discuss a national movement that would unify the various campaigns under one banner with a common agenda.

Long ago, community-organizing icon Saul Alinsky pioneered the use of conventions to establish unified agendas and strategies among groups, and such an approach seems crucial to the creation of synergy and impact today.

Conclusion

When I was a child, I listened to my parents' stories of organizing in factories, and of being harassed by the police. One time, a sympathetic television newscaster agreed to announce, falsely, that my father had been killed, to waylay police efforts to find him. Growing up in the household of former 1930s radicals, I got my politics with mother's milk. Over the years it seemed natural to get involved in social movements to right the wrongs I saw around me.

But most Americans do not have family lessons in organizing and political transgression. The majority of people who have come to politically Left beliefs have had to acquire them on their own, many though exposure to movements already in progress, some through radical professors in college or teachers in high school. Moreover, the ideological battering most people receive as school children, the mangled news they imbibe from newspapers and television, and racial and class distortions pouring from the media make the chances of developing a faith in transgressive equity politics difficult.

We can change those odds. My argumentation has aimed at a more radical consciousness in readers, particularly regarding poverty and urban education. I tried to develop an analysis that would explain how macroeconomic and regional policies and practices create conditions in urban areas that cannot be overcome by school reform alone. Several chapters delineated how public policies regarding jobs, wages, taxes, public transportation, housing, and investment prevent even equity-seeking educational policies from having a sustained positive effect and consequence. I argued, as a result, that public policies regarding economic equity ought to be among the strategies we propose in our attempts to increase urban school quality.

Following this explication of the power of macroeconomic policies and regional arrangements to trump urban school reform and conventional educational prescriptions, I presented an array of theoretically and historically derived processes whose enactment could involve increasing numbers of Americans in movement building.

Finally, I offered suggestions specifically for urban educators, whose position in city schools yields strategic theoretical and practical advantages in organizing youth and communities. I took the liberty of suggesting that education organizers should instigate national unity by calling the various other (regional) social movements together.

There remains a final point. Whether one is born to radicalism, or acquires it along the way, the premises on which it rests affirm the deeply rooted causes of, and connections between, social problems. A radical frame provides the understanding that, for example, economic exclusion and educational underachievement flow fundamentally from systemic causes, even in the face of what appears to be individual failure. And a radical analysis points toward concrete, long-lasting solutions.

In 1967, at the height of the Vietnam War, Martin Luther King, Jr. argued that civil rights, poverty, and war are all part of the same problem. He preached that Americans need to fight these as part of the same struggle. But, he said, in order to do that we must "recapture the revolutionary spirit" of freedom and equality which defines true democracy (King, 1999).

If those of us who are angry about injustice can recapture the revolutionary spirit of which King spoke, and if we can act on it together, then we may be able to create a force powerful enough to produce economic justice and the basis for real, long-term school reform in America's cities.

BIBLIOGRAPHY

Ackerman, Bruce and Alstott, Ann. (2011, September 7). Commentary: class warfare? Yale Law School Review.

Addy, Sophia and Wight, Vanessa. (2012, February). Basic facts about low-income children, 2010: children under age 18. National center for children in poverty. Mailman school of public health. Columbia University. Available at www.nccp.org/publications/pub_1049.html.

Albright, Len, Derickson, Elizabeth S., and Massey, Douglas S. (2011, June 15). Do affordable housing projects harm suburban communities? Crime, property values, and property taxes in Mt. Laurel, New Jersey. Available at http://ssrn.com/abstract=1865231.

Allard, Scott W. (2001, September). *Place, race and work: The dynamics of welfare reform in metropolitan Detroit*. Brookings Center on Urban and Metropolitan Policy. Washington, D.C.: Brookings Institute.

Allegretto, Sylvia. (2011, March 23). The state of working America's wealth, 2011. Economic Policy Institute Briefing Paper #292.

Alloway, Kristen and Gebeloff, Robert. (2002, February 17). Jersey's rising property tax dilemma. *The Star-Ledger*.

Amato, Michael, Moore, Colleen F., and Magzamen, Sheryl. (2012, October). Lead exposure and educational proficiency: Moderate lead exposure and educational proficiency on end-of-grade examinations. *Annals of Epidemiology, 22(10)*, 738–743.

American Youth Policy Forum. (1997). *Some things do make a difference for youth: A compendium of evaluations of youth programs and practices*. Washington, D.C.

American Youth Policy Forum. (2002, May 17). *Youth action for educational change: A forum brief*. Washington, D.C.

Aminzade, Ron, Goldstone, Jack, and Perry, Elizabeth. (2001). Leadership dynamics and the dynamics of contention. In Ron Aminzade (Ed.), *Silence and voice in contentious politics* (pp. 126–154). Cambridge, MA: Cambridge University Press.

Anders, Gideon. (2002, June). *False hope: A critical assessment of HOPE VI public housing redevelopment program*. Oakland, CA: National Housing Law Project with the Poverty & Race Research Action Council in Washington, D.C.

Anderson, Gary and Montoro Donchik, L. (2013). Privatizing schooling and policy-making: The American Legislative Exchange Council (ALEC) and new political and discursive strategies of education governance. Paper presented at the Annual Meeting of the American Educational Research Association, San Francisco, April 29, 2013.

Anderson, Sara and Cavanaugh, John. (2011, November 22). America is not broke. Washington, D.C.: Institute for Policy Studies.

Anyon, Jean. (1980). Social class and the hidden curriculum of work. *Journal of Education, 162(1)*, 7–92.

Anyon, Jean. (1981). Social class and school knowledge. *Curriculum Inquiry, 11(1)*, 3–42.

Anyon, Jean. (1994a). Teacher development and reform in an inner city school. *Teachers College Record, 96(1)*, 14–31.

Anyon, Jean. (1994b). The retreat of Marxism and socialist feminism: Postmodern and post-structural theories in education. *Curriculum Inquiry, 24(2)*, 115–134.

Anyon, Jean. (1995a). Race, social class, and educational reform in an inner city school. *Teachers College Record, 97(1)*, 69–94.

Anyon, Jean. (1995b). Inner city school reform: Toward useful theory. *Urban Education, 30(1)*, 56–70.

Anyon, Jean. (1995c). Educational reform, theoretical categories, and the urban context. *Access: Critical perspectives on culture and policy studies in education* (New Zealand), *14(1)*, 1–11.

Anyon, Jean. (1997). *Ghetto schooling: A political economy of urban educational reform.* New York: Teachers College Press.

Anyon, Jean. (2005a, March). What counts as educational policy? Notes toward a new paradigm. *Harvard Educational Review*, 65–88.

Anyon, Jean. (2005b). *Radical possibilities.* New York: Routledge.

Anyon, Jean, with Dumas, Michael, Linville, Darla, Nolan, Kathleen, Perez, Madeline, Tuck, Eve, and Weiss, Jen. (2009). *Theory and educational research: Toward critical social explanation.* New York: Routledge.

Anyon, Jean. (2011a). *Marx and education.* New York: Routledge.

Anyon, Jean. (2011b). Arguing for theory. In Richard Elmore (Ed.), *I used to think … and now I think … : Twenty leading educators reflect on the work of school reform* (pp. 5–10). Cambridge, MA: Harvard Education Press.

Apple, Michael. (2001). *Educating the 'right' way: Markets, standards, God, and inequality.* New York: RoutledgeFalmer.

Apple, Michael, Au, Wayne, and Gandon, Louis (Eds). (2009). *The Routledge international handbook of critical education* (Routledge International Handbook Series). New York: Routledge.

Applebaum, Eileen. (2000). *What explains employment developments in the U.S.?* Economic Policy Institute Briefing Paper. Washington, D.C.: Economic Policy Institute.

Araiza, Olivia E. (2002). *Bridging research and education organizing: Can we strengthen our combined power?* San Francisco, CA: Justice Matters Institute.

Archer, Jeff. (2002, January 9). Group cites needy but high-performing schools. *Education Week.*

Association of Community Organizations Now (1996). *Secret apartheid: A report on racial discrimination against back and Latino parents and children in the New York City public schools.* New York.

Association of Community Organizations Now (1997). *Secret apartheid II: Race, regents, and resources.* New York.

Association of Community Organizations Now (1998). *Secret apartheid III: Follow up to failure*. New York.

Autor, David. (2010). The polarization of job opportunities in the U.S. labor market: Implications for employment and earnings. Center for American Progress and The Hamilton Project. Available at http://econ-www.mit.edu/files/5554.

Ayers, William, Hunt, Jean Ann, and Quinn, Theresa (Eds). (1998). *Teaching for social justice: A democracy and education reader*. New York: The New Press.

Ayers, William, Ladson-Billings, Gloria, Michie, Gregory, and Noguera, Pedro A. (Eds). (2008). *City schools, city kids: More reports from the front row*. New York: The New School.

Bailey, Martha J. and Dynarski, Susan M. (2011, December). Gains and gaps: Changing inequality in U.S. college entry and completion. Working Paper 17633. The National Bureau of Economic Research. Available at www.nber.org/papers/w17633.

Baker, Bruce and Welner, Kevin. (2010). Premature celebrations: The persistence of inter-district funding disparities. Educational Policy Analysis Archives, *18(9)*. Available at http://epaa.asu.edu/ojs/article/view/718.

Baker, Bruce, Sciarra, David, and Farrie, Danielle. (2010, September). Is school funding fair? A national report card. Education Law Center, Newark, New Jersey. Available at www.schoolfundingfairness.org.

Baker, Dean. (2008). The housing bubble and the financial crisis. Real-world Economics Review, 46. Center for Economic and Policy Research, USA. Available at http://paecon.net/PAEReview/issue46/Baker46.pdf.

Baker, Dean. (2010). *False profits: Recovering from the bubble economy*. San Francisco, CA: Berrett-Koehler Publishers. Kindle Edition,

Baker, Dean. (2012, June 13). Fed survey shows middle class took a big hit. Center for Economic and Policy Research. Available at www.cepr.net/index.php/op-eds-&-columns/op-eds-&-columns/fed-survey-shows-middle-class-took-a-big-hit.

Baker, Dean, Pollin, Robert, McArther, Travis, and Sherman, Matt. (2009, December). The potential revenue from financial transactions taxes. Center for Economic and Policy Research, University of Massachusetts, Amherst.

Banchero, Stephanie and Olszewski, Lori. (2000, August 28). 19,000 kids seek new schools. *The Chicago Tribune*.

Bankston, Carl and Caldas, Stephen. (1996). Majority African American schools and social injustice: The influence of *de facto* segregation on academic achievement. *Social Forces*, 75, 535–552.

Barnes, William and Ledebur, Larry. (1998). *The new regional economies: The U.S. common market and the global economy*. London: Sage.

Barnett, Bernice McNair. (1993, June). Invisible southern black women leaders in the civil rights movement: The triple constraints of gender, race, and class. *Gender and Society*, 7, 162–182.

Baron, Harold. (1982). The demand for black labor: Historical notes on the political economy of racism. *Radical America, 5(2)*, 1–46. Cited in McAdam, 1982 (p. 88).

Bartik, Timothy J. (2001). *Jobs for the poor: Can labor demand policies help?* New York, NY: Russell Sage Foundation; Kalamazoo, MI: W.E. Upjohn Institute for Employment Research.

Bartlett, Bruce. (2012, June 12). The fiscal legacy of George W. Bush. *The New York Times*.

Bass, Melissa and Boyte, Harry. (1995). *Making the rules: A public achievement guidebook for young people who intend to make a difference*. Waltham, MA: The Center for Democracy and Citizenship.

Bates, Beth. (2001). *Pullman porters and the rise of protest politics in black America, 1925–1945.* Chapel Hill, NC: University of North Carolina Press.

Belzer, Dena and Srivastava, Sujata. (2011, May). Transit-oriented development and employment. Center for Transit-oriented Development. Available at http://ctod.org/.

Bennett, Larry and Reed Jr., Adolph. (2000). The complexities of a public housing community. In Stephen Steinberg (Ed.), *Race and ethnicity in the United States: Issues and debates* (pp. 127–134). Malden, MA: Blackwell Publications.

Benson, Peter and Leffert, Nancy. (1998). Beyond the 'village' rhetoric: Creating healthy communities for children and adolescents. *Journal of Applied Developmental Sciences, 2,* 138–159.

Berkshire, Jennifer. (2003, February 20). What happens to charities when foundations support trendy issues – and abandon yesterday's hot topics? *The Chronicle of Philanthropy.* Available at http://philanthropy.com/article/What-Happens-to-Charities-W/52532/.

Berlin, Gordon. (2007, May 22). Remarks at National Summit on America's Children. Available at www.mdrc.org/publications/456/presentation.html; quoted in Jimmy Charite, Dutta-Gupta, Indivar, and Marr, Chuck. Studies show earned income tax credit encourages work and success in school and reduces poverty center on budget and policy priorities. June 26, 2012.

Berlin, Ira. (2003). *Generations of captivity: a history of African-American slaves.* Cambridge, MA: Belknap Press of Harvard University Press.

Bernadett, Proctor and Dalaker, Joseph. (2002). *Poverty in the United States: 2001.* Current Population Reports, P60-219. U.S. Census Bureau. Washington, D.C.: U.S. Government Printing Office.

Bernstein, Jared. (2003). *The living wage movement: Pointing the way toward the high road.* Washington, D.C.: Economic Policy Institute.

Bernstein, Jared. (2011, June 29). Getting to a trillion. Available at http://jaredbernsteinblog.com/.

Bernstein, Jared and Baker, Dean. (2002, January 2). Full employment: Don't give it up without a fight. Economic Policy Institute. Available at www.epi.org/publication/workingpapers_full-employment/.

Bernstein, Jared, Brockt, Chauna, and Apade-Aguilar, Mattie. (2000). *How much is enough? Basic family budget for working families.* Washington, D.C.: Economic Policy Institute.

Bernstein, Jared, Hartmann, Heidi, and Schmitt, John. (1999, September 16). *The minimum wage increase: A working woman's issue.* Issue Brief #133. Washington, D.C.: Economic Policy Institute and the Institute for Women's Policy Research.

Berube, Alan. (2003, January). *Rewarding work through the tax code: The power and potential of the Earned Income Tax Credit.* Center on Urban and Metropolitan Policy. Washington, D.C.: Brookings Institute.

Berube, Alan and Frey, William. (2002, August). *A decade of mixed blessings: Urban and suburban poverty in Census 2000.* Washington, D.C.: Brookings Institute.

Billingsley, Andrew. (2002). *Mighty like a river: The black church and social reform.* New York: Oxford University Press.

Blank, Martin, Mellaville, Atella, and Shah, Bela. (2003). *Making the difference: Research and practice in community schools.* Washington, D.C.: Coalition for Community Schools.

Blank, Martin, Brand, Betsy, Deich, Sharon, Kazis, Richard, Politz, Bonnie, and Trippe, Steve. (2003). *Local intermediary organizations: Connecting the dots for children, youth, and families.* Washington, D.C.: Institute for Educational Leadership.

Blinder, Alan. (2009, January 24). Six errors on the path to the financial crisis. *The New York Times.*

Bloom, Janice. (2004). (Mis)reading social class in the journey towards college: Youth Development in Urban America. (Unpublished paper.)

Bloom, Janice, Chajet, Lori, et al. (2003, Fall). Urban students tackle research on inequality: What you thought we didn't know. *Rethinking Schools, 18(1)*, 31–32.

Bobo, Kim, Kendall, Jackie, and Max, Steve. (2001). *Organizing for social change: Midwest Academy manual for activists*. Santa Ana, CA: Seven Locks Press.

Bolger, Kerry and Patterson, Charlotte. (1995). Psychosocial adjustment among children experiencing persistent and intermittent family economic hardship. *Child Development, 66*, 1107–1129.

Boo, Katherine. (2003, August 18). The marriage cure: Promoting wedlock in the projects. *The New Yorker*.

Bos, Johannes, Huston, Aletha, Duncan, Greg, Brock, Tom, and McLoyd, Vonnie. (1996). *New hope for people with low incomes: Two-year results of a program to reduce poverty and reform welfare*. New York: Manpower Development Research Corporation.

Bound, John and Dresser, Laura. (1999). The erosion of the relative earnings of young African American women during the 1980s. In Irene Browne (Ed.), *Latinas and African American women at work*. New York: Russell Sage. Cited in Moss and Tilly, 2001 (p. 6).

Bound, John and Freeman, Richard. (1992). What went wrong? The erosion of relative earnings and employment for blacks. *Quarterly Journal of Economics, 107(1)* 201–232.

Boushey, Heather, Brocht, Chauna, Gunderson, Betheny, and Bernstein, Jared. (2001). *Hardships in America: The real story of working families*. Washington, D.C.: Economic Policy Institute.

Bowles, Jonathan. (2003, April 15). *Think tank: NYC's six closest suburbs gained 39,000 jobs over the past year while the city lost 58,000 jobs*. New York: Center for an Urban Future.

Boyd, Todd. (2002). *The new H.N.I.C.: The death of civil rights and the reign of hip hop*. New York: New York University Press.

Boykin, Wadw and Noguera, Pedro. (2011). Creating the opportunity to learn: Moving from research to practice to close the achievement gap. Alexandria, VA: Association for Supervision & Curriculum Development.

Bracey, Gerald. (1997). *The truth about America's schools: The Bracey reports, 1991–97*. Bloommington, IN: Phi Delta Kappa Educational Foundation.

Bradford, Calvin and Associates, Inc. (2002, May). *Risk or race? Racial disparities and the subprime refinance market*. Washington, D.C.: The Center for Community Change.

Bradley, Robert. (1984). One hundred seventy-four children: A study of the relation between the home environment and early cognitive development in the first 5 years. In Allen Gottfried (Ed.), *The home environment and early cognitive development* (pp. 5–56). Orlando, FL: Academic Press.

Brave, Elina. (2012). Out of reach: America's forgotton housing crisis. National Low Income Housing Coalition. Washington, D.C. Available at http://nlihc.org.

Brenner, Neil, Marcuse, Peter, and Mayer, Margit (Eds). (2012). *Cities for people, not for profit: Critical urban theory and the right to the city*. New York: Routledge.

Briggs, Xavier de Souza, Ferryman, Kadija S., Popkin, Susan J., and Rendon, Young. (2008). Why did the moving to opportunity experiment not get young people into better schools? *Housing Policy Debate, 19(1)*, 53–91.

Bronfenbrenner, Kate and Warren, Dorian. (2011). The empirical case for streamlining the NLRB certification process: The role of date of unfair labor practice occurence. ISERP Working Paper Series 2011.01. Institute for Social and Economic Research and Policy. Columbia University. Available at http://iserp.columbia.edu/content/empirical-case-streamlining-nlrb-certification-process-role-date-unfair-labor-practice-occur.

Brookings Institute. (2008). Tax facts. Washington, D.C.: Urban-Brookings Tax Policy Center.

Brooks-Gunn, Jeanne, Duncan, Greg, Leventhal, Tama, and Aber, Lawrence. (1997). Lessons learned and future directions for research on the neighborhoods in which children live. In Jeanne Brooks-Gunn, Greg Duncan, and Lawrence Aber (Eds). *Neighborhood poverty, Volume 1: Contexts and consequences for children* (pp. 279–298). New York: Russell Sage.

Browning, Edward. (1995, March 24). Bond investors gamble on Russian stocks. *Wall Street Journal*.

Bryk, Anthony S. and Schneider, Barbara. (2002). *Trust in schools: A core resource for improvement*. New York: Russell Sage.

Buchheit, P. (2012, August 27). Add it up: Taxes avoided by the rich could pay off the deficit. Nation of change/Op-Ed. Available at www.nationofchange.org/add-it-taxes-avoided-rich-could-pay-deficit-1346074084.

Bureau of Labor Statistics. (2012a, January 27). Union members summary. Available at www.bls.gov/news.release/union2.nr0.htm.

Bureau of Labor Statistics. (2012b, February 1)2012b. Occupations with the largest job growth. Available at www.bls.gov/emp/ep_table_104.htm.

Bureau of Labor Statistics. (2013, May 22). Employment projections. Available at www.bls.gov/emp/ep_chart_001.htm.

Burtless, Gary. (1995). Employment prospects of welfare recipients. In Demetra Smith Nightingale and Robert Havemann (Eds), *The work alternative: Welfare reform and the realities of the job market*. Washington, D.C.: Urban Institute. Cited in Lafer, 2002 (p. 5).

Byron, Joan, Exeter, Hillary, and Mediratta, Kavitha. (2001, July/August). School facilities provide an entry point for community organizers. *Sheltorforce Online*. Available at www.nhi.org/online issues/118ByronExterMediratta.html.

Cahill, Michelle. (1999). *Community organizing for school reformers: Train the trainers manual*. Chicago, IL: Cross City Campaign for Urban School Reform.

Candovan, Candy and Candovan, Guy. (1983). We shall overcome: An American freedom song. *Talkin' Union*.

Capelli, Peter. (1995). Is the 'skills gap' really about attitudes? *California Management Review, 37(4)*, 18–24.

Cappelli, Peter. (1996). Technology and skill requirements: Implications for establishment of wage structures. In Philip Moss and Chris Tilly (Eds), Earnings inequality: Special Issue of the *New England Economic Review* (May/June). Cited in Moss and Tilly, 2001 (p. 47).

Card, David and Krueger, Alan. (1997). *Myth and measurement: The new economics of the minimum wage*. Princeton, NJ: Princeton University Press.

Carnevale, Anthony, Rose, Stephen, and Cheah, Ban. (2011). The college payoff: Education, occupations, life-time earnings. The Georgetown University Center on Education and the Workforce. Available at http://cew.georgetown.edu/collegepayoff.

Carnevale, Anthony, Strohl, Jeff, and Smith, Nicole. (2009). Help wanted: Projections of jobs and education requirements through 2018. In R.M. Romano and H. Casper (Eds), *Occupational outlook for community college students. New directions for community colleges, number 146* (pp. 21–32). San Fransisco, CA: Jossey Bass.

Carson, Clayborn. (2001). *In struggle: SNCC and the black awakening of the 1960s*. Fourth Printing. Cambridge, MA: Harvard University Press.

Casciano, Rebecca and Massey, Douglas S. (2012a). School context and educational outcomes: Results from a quasi-experimental study. *Urban Affairs Review 48*, 180–204.

Casciano, Rebecca and Massey, Douglas S. (2012b). Neighborhood disorder and individual economic self-sufficiency: New evidence from a quasi-experimental study. Social Science Research. Available at www.sciencedirect.com/science/article/pii/S0049089X1200035X.

Case, Anne, Lubotsky, Darren, and Paxson, Christina. (2002). Economic status and health in childhood: The origins of the gradient. *American Economic Review, 92(5)*, 1308–1334.

Caspi, Avshalom, Wright, Bradley, Moffit, Entner, and Silva, Terrie. (1998). Early failure in the labor market: Childhood and adolescent predictors of unemployment in the transition to adulthood. *American Sociological Review, 63(3)*, 424–451.

Castells, Manuel. (1996). *The rise of the network society*. Cambridge, MA: Wiley-Blackwell.

Castells, Manuel. (2000). *End of millennium: The information age: Economy, society and culture*. Vol. III. Oxford, UK: Blackwell Publishers.

Cauthen, Nancy and Lu, Hsien-Hen. (2001, August). *Living on the edge: Employment alone is not enough for America's low-income children and families*. Research Brief No. 1, Mailman School of Public Health, National Center for Children in Poverty. New York: Columbia University.

Center for Community Change. (1998, June/July). *Organizing, 10* (p. 1).

Center for Community Change (2001, May). *Saved by an education: A successful model for dramatically increasing high school graduation rates in low income neighborhoods*. Washington, D.C.

Center for Responsive Politics. (2011). Most members of Congress enjoy robust financial status, despite nation's sluggish economic recovery. Available at www.opensecrets.org/news/2011/11/congress-enjoys-robust-financial-status.html.

Chafe, William, Gavins, Raymond, and Korstad, Robert. (2001). *Remembering Jim Crow: African Americans tell about life in the segregated South*. New York: The New Press.

Champernowne, David and Cowell, Frank. (1999). *Economic inequality and income distribution*. Cambridge, UK: Cambridge University Press.

Chapman, Jeff. (2003, June 11). *States move on minimum wage: Federal inaction forces states to raise wage floor*. Washington, D.C.: Economic Policy Institute.

Chen, Don and Jakowitsch, Nancy. (2000). *Transportation reform and smart growth: A nation at the tipping point*. Miami, FL: Surface Transportation Policy Project in Collaboration with the Funders' Network for Smart Growth and Livable Communities.

Cherry, Robert and Rodgers, William. (2000). *Prosperity for all? The economic boom and African Americans*. New York: Russell Sage.

Chetty, Raj, Friedman, John N., and Rockoff, Jonah. (2011, November). New evidence on the long-term impacts of tax credits, Statistics of Income Paper Series. Available at www.irs.gov/pub/irs-soi/11rpchettyfriedmanrockoff.pdf.

Chicago Institute on Urban Poverty. (1997). *Does privatization pay?* Chicago.

Christman, Anastasia and Christine, Riordan. (2011, October). Filling the good jobs deficit: An economic recovery agenda for our states and cities. National Employment Law Project. Available at http://www.nelp.org/page/Job_Creation/Filling_Good_Jobs_Deficit_Recovery_Agenda.pdf?nocdn=1.

CIA Factbook, (2012, September 22). Available at https://www.cia.gov/library/publications/the-world-factbook/fields/2172.html.

Citizens for Tax Justice. (2002a, March 15). *Corporate tax payments near record low this year*. Washington, D.C.

Citizens for Tax Justice. (2002b, April 17). *Surge in corporate tax welfare drives corporate tax payments down to near record low*. Washington D.C.

Citizens for Tax Justice. (2011a, June 1). Analysis: 12 corporations pay effective tax rate of negative 1.4% on $175 billion in profits; reap $63.7 billion in tax subsidies—Exxon Mobil, Boeing, Verizon, others illustrate why revenue-raising reform is needed. Available at www.ctj.org/pdf/12corps060111.pdf.

Citizens for Tax Justice. (2011b, September 11). Warren Buffett's effective tax rate is typical of taxpayers with $10 million or more of investment income. Available at www.ctj.org/pdf/buffettrulereport.pdf.

Citizens for Tax Justice. (2011c, November 3) Corporate tax payers and corporate tax dodgers 2008–2010. Available at http://ctj.org/ctjreports/2011/11/corporate_taxpayers_corporate_tax_dodgers_2008-2010.php#.Ub9tDtj45yU.

Citizens for Tax Justice. (2012, April 4). Who pays taxes in America? Washington, D.C.

Citro, Constance and Michael, Robert (Eds). (1995). *Measuring poverty: A new approach.* Washington, D.C.: National Academy Press.

Clemetson, Lynette. (2003, September 2). Census shows ranks of poor rose in 2002 by 1.3 million. *The New York Times.*

Coalition for Educational Justice. (2011). Profiles in school transformation. Annenberg Institute for School Reform at Brown University.

Coleman, James. (1993). *Equality and achievement in education.* Boulder, CO: Westview Press.

Collaborative Communications Group. (2003). *New relationships with schools: Organizations that build community by connecting with schools.* Washington, D.C.

Collier-Thomas, Bettye and Franklin, V.P. (2001). *Sisters in the struggle: African American women in the civil rights-black power movement.* New York: New York University Press.

Community Affairs Department, Federal Reserve Bank of Kansas City. (2002, Summer). CDCs at the crossroads? *Community Affairs, 10* (p. 1).

Congressional Budget Office. (2010, July). Individual income tax returns 2008. Available at www.cbo.gov/sites/default/.../cbofiles/.../43373-AverageTaxRates_screen.

Congressional Budget Office. (2013, February 2). Student loan programs – base line 2013. Available at www.cbo.gov/publication/43913.

Connor, Kevin. (2010, May 11). Big bank takeover: How too-big-to-fail's army of lobbyists has captured Washington. Institute for America's Future, ourfinancialsecurity.org/FinancialReformNews?. Available at www.ourfuture.org/files/documents/big-bank-takeover-final.pdf.

Conon, David. (1995). *Black Moses: The story of Marcus Garvey and the universal negro improvement association.* Madison, WI: University of Wisconsin Press.

Consortium on Chicago School Research. (1996). *Charting reform in Chicago: The students speak.* Chicago, IL.

Cooley, Thomas and Kim Schoenholtz. (2012, April 16). How shape-shifting banks foil Dodd-Frank Act. *Bloomberg Businessweek.*

Cooper, David. (2012, April 13). A rising tide for increasing minimum wage. Economic Policy Institute.

Corbin, Gene. (2003). *Overcoming obstacles to school reform: A report on the 2002 Organizing for Educational Excellence Institute.* Philadelphia, PA: Temple University Center for Public Policy and the Eastern Pennsylvania Organizing Project Research for Democracy.

Corcoran, Mary, Heflin, Colleen, and Reyes, Belinda. (1999). The economic progress of Mexican and Puerto Rican women. In Irene Browne (Ed.), *Latinas and African American women at work* (pp. 105–138). New York: Russell Sage.

Cortes, Ernesto. (2007, April 22). American prospect, 2007 faith, charity, and justice. Available at http://prospect.org/article/faith-charity-and-justice.

Cortes, Ernesto. (2011). Metis and the metrics of success. In Richard Elmore (Ed.), *I used to think … and now I think … : Twenty leading educators reflect on the work of school reform* (pp. 11–18). Cambridge, CA: Harvard Education Press.

Costello, Jane, Compton, Scott, Keeler, Gordon, and Angold, Adrian. (2003, October 15). Relationships between poverty and psychopathology: A natural experiment. *Journal of the American Medical Association, 290(15),* 2023–2029.

Cottrell, Megan. (2012, October 31). The link between lead poisoning and underperforming students. *Chicago Reader*. Available at www.chicagoreader.com/chicago/high-lead-toxicity-in-chicago-public-schools/Content?oid=7819530.

Council of the Great City Schools. (2003). *Beating the odds III*. Washington, D.C.

Cover, Ben, Jones, John I., and Watson, Audrey. (2011, May). Science, technology, engineering, and mathematics (STEM) occupations: a visual essay. *Monthly Labor Review*, pp. 1–15.

Covington, Sally. (1998, Winter). How conservative philanthropies and think tanks transform U.S. policy. *Covert Action Quarterly*, *1*, 12–25.

Crotty, James. (2005). The neoliberal paradox. In Gerald Epstein (Ed.), *Financialization and the world economy* (pp. 77–110). Northampton, MA: Edward Elgar.

Dahl, Gordin and Lochner, Lance. (2008). The impact of family income on child achievement: Evidence from the earned income tax credit. NBER Working Paper No. 14599. Washington, D.C.: National Bureau of Economic Research, Inc.

Danziger, Sheldon and Gottschalk, Peter. (1995). *America unequal*. Cambridge, MA: Harvard University Press.

Darder, Antonia, Baltodana, Marta, and Torres, Rodolpho. (2008). *The critical pedagogy reader*. Second edition. New York: Routledge.

Darder, Antonia, Torres, Rodolpho, and Baltodano, Marta. (2002). *The critical pedagogy reader*. New York: RoutledgeFalmer.

Darling-Hammond, Linda. (2001). *The right to learn: A blueprint for creating schools that work*. San Francisco, CA: Jossey Bass.

Davis, Mike. (1993). Who killed L.A.? The war against the cities. *Crossroads*, *32*, 2–19.

Dawkins, Casey. (2004). Recent evidence on the continuing causes of black-white residential segregation. *Journal of Urban Affairs*, *26(3)*, 379–400.

Delpit, Lisa. (2006). *Other people's children: Cultural conflict in the classroom*. New York: The New Press.

DeLuca, Stefanie, Duncan, Greg, Keels, Micere, and Mendenhall, Ruby. (2010). Gautreaux mothers and their children: an update. *Housing Policy Debate*, *20(1)*, 7–25.

DeParle, Jason, Gebeloff, Robert, and Tavernise, Sabrina. (2011, November 18). Older, suburban and struggling, 'near poor' startle the census. *The New York Times*. Available at www.nytimes.com/2011/11/19/us/census-measures-those-not-quite-in-poverty-but-struggling.html?pagewanted=all&_r=0&gwh=235E4FFCBB28352B04A092C62A19E04C.

Department of Labor (2002). *Occupation projections to 2010*. Washington, D.C.

Diebolt, Claude. (2002). Toward a new social structure of accumulation. *Historical Social Research*, *27*, 85–99.

Dillon, Sam. (2003, April 30). Report finds number of black children in deep poverty rising. *The New York Times*.

Dimitriadis, Greg. (2001). *Performing identity/performing culture: Hip hop as text, pedagogy, and lived practice*. New York: Peter Lang.

Downs, Anthony. (1994). *New visions for metropolitan America*. Washington, D.C.: Brookings Institute.

Downs, Anthony. (1999). Comment on Kenneth T. Rosen and Ted Dienstfrey: The economics of housing services in low-income neighborhoods. In Ronald Ferguson and William Dickens (Eds), *Urban problems and community development* (pp. 463–469). Washington, D.C.: Brookings Institute.

Dreier, Peter. (1999). Comment. In Ronald Ferguson and William Dickens (Eds), *Urban problems and community development* (pp. 178–187). Washington, D.C.: Brookings Institute.

Dreier, Peter. (2000, Summer). Why America's workers can't pay the rent. *Dissent*, 38–44.

Dreier, Peter. (2010, October). Does public housing have a future? *Shelterforce: The journal of affordable housing and community building*. National Housing Institute, pp. 1–3. Available at www.shelterforce.org/article/2023/does_public_housing_have_a_future/.

Dreier, Peter, Swanstrom, Todd, and Mollenkopf, John. (2001). *Place matters: Metropolitics for the 21st century*. Lawrence, KS: University Press of Kansas.

Dudziak, Mary L. (2000). *Cold war civil rights: Race and the image of American Democracy*. Princeton, NJ: Princeton University Press.

Dumas, Michael. (2007). Sitting next to white children: School desegregation in the black educational imagination. Ph.D. unpublished dissertation.

Dumas, Michael and Anyon, Jean. (in press). Toward a critical approach to educational policy implementation: Implications for the (battle)field. In Meredith Honig (Ed.), *Defining the field of policy implementation*. Albany, NY: SUNY Press.

Duncan, Greg and Brooks-Gunn, Jeanne (Eds). (1997). *Consequences of growing up poor*. New York: Russell Sage.

Duncan, Greg and Magnuson, Katherine. (2011, Winter). The long reach of early childhood poverty, *Pathways*, 24–28.

Duncan, Greg and Murnane, Richard (Eds). (2011). *Wither opportunity: Rising inequality, schools, and children's life chances*. New York: Russell Sage.

Duncan, Greg and Zuberi, Anita. (2006, Summer). Mobility lessons from Gautreaux and moving to opportunity, *Northwestern Journal of Law & Social Policy, 1(1)*, Article 5.

Duncan, Greg, Brooks-Gunn, Jeanne, and Klebanov, Pamela. (1994). Economic deprivation and early childhood development. *Child Development, 65*, 296–318.

Duncan, Greg, Huston, Aletha, and Weisner, Thomas. (2007). *Higher ground: New hope for the working poor and their children*. New York: Russell Sage.

Duncan, Greg, Ludwig, Jens, and Magnuson, Katherine. (2010). Child development. In Phillip Levine and David Zimmerman (Eds), *Targeting investments in children: Fighting poverty when resources are limited* (pp. 27–58). Chicago: University of Chicago Press.

Duncan, Greg, Morris, Pamela, and Rodrigues, Chris. (2010, June). Does money really matter? Estimating impacts of family income on young children's achievement with data from random-assignment experiments, *Developmental Psychology*, 1263–1279.

Eavis, Peter. (2013, July 18). Big banks flooded in profits. *The New York Times*.

Economic Policy Institute. (1999, September 30). *Income picture*. Washington, D.C.

Economic Policy Institute. (2000, February 17). *Entry level workers face lower wages*. Washington, D.C.

Economic Policy Institute. (2002a). *Minimum wage issue guide*. Washington, D.C.

Economic Policy Institute. (2002b, July 24). *Economic snapshots*. Washington, D.C.

Economic Policy Institute. (2002c, August 7). *Decline in job openings fuels unemployment*. Washington, D.C.

Economic Policy Institute. (2004a, July). *EPI issue guide: Minimum wage*. Washington, D.C.

Economic Policy Institute. (2004b, July 19). *Higher minimum wage most helps low-earning households*. Washington, D.C.

Economic Policy Institute. (2004c, July 21). *Jobs in the future: No boom in the need for college graduates*. Washington, D.C.

Economic Policy Institute. (2012). Top 1 percent's share of income starting to rise. Center on Budget and Policy Priorities. Washington, D.C. Available at http://stateofworkingamerica.org/subjects/overview/?reader.

Economic Policy Institute. (2013). African Americans. Washington, D.C. Available at http://stateofworkingamerica.org/fact-sheets/african-americans.

Edelman, Marion Wright. (2002, July). *Child watch: The shame of child poverty in the richest land on earth*. Washington, D.C.: The Children's Defense Fund.

Edwards, Ditra and Carlson, Neil. (2003, September 4). Rekindling the movement: 40 years after the dream. *TomPain – Common Sense: A Public Interest Journal*.

Ehrenreich, Barbara. (2001). *Nickel and dimed: On (not) getting by in America*. New York: Henry Holt, Owl Books.

Eisenhower Foundation. (1998). *Background report*. Washington, D.C.

Emery, Kathy. (2002). The Business Roundtable and systemic reform. Unpublished dissertation, University of California Davis.

Entwistle, Doris. (1985). The role of schools in sustaining early childhood program benefits. *Future of Children, 5(3)*, 133–144.

Entwistle, Doris and Alexander, Karl. (1997). *Children, schools, and inequality*. Boulder, CO: Westview Press.

Ettlinger, Michael. (2006). Securing the wage floor: Indexing would maintain the minimum wage's value and provide predictability to employers. Economic Policy Institute Briefing paper. Washington, D.C.: Economic Policy Institute.

EWallstreeter. (2012, December 27). Apple chief's pay package drops 99 percent from 2011. *Wall Street Journal*. EWallstreeter. Available at http://ewallstreeter.com/apple-chief-s-pay-package-drops-percent-from-4792/.

Fabricant, Michael. (2010). *Organizing for educational justice: The campaign for public school reform in the South Bronx*. Minneapolis: University of Minnesota Press.

Fairclough, Adam. (1995). *Race and democracy: The civil rights struggle in Louisiana, 1915–1972*. Athens: University of Georgia.

Fairclough, Adam. (2001). *Better day coming: Blacks and equality, 1890–2000*. New York: Penguin.

Faux, Jeff. (2012, May 23). Who will save the middle class? *The American Prospect*.

Ferguson, Charles H. (2012a). *Predator nation: Corporate criminals, political corruption, and the hijacking of America*. New York: Random House/Crown Business.

Ferguson, Charles H. (2012b, May 23). How financial criminalization crashed the economy, and the culprits got off scot-free. *Huffington Post*. Available at www.huffingtonpost.com/charles-ferguson/how-wall-street-became-a-_b_1536475.html.

Ferguson, Ronald and Dickens, William. (1999). *Urban problems and community development*. Washington, D.C.: Brookings Institute.

Fieldhouse, Andrew. (2011, August 10). Highest-income households can afford to pay more in taxes. Economic Policy Institute. Available at www.epi.org/publication/highest-income_households_can_afford_to_pay_more_in_taxes/.

Fieldhouse, Andrew. (2012, July 20). It's official: Cutting top tax rates doesn't grow the economy, it only grows income inequality. Citizens for Tax Justice. Available at www.ctj.org/taxjusticedigest/archive/2012/09/its_official_cutting_top_tax_r.php#.UccRU9j46z4.

Fieldhouse, Andrew and Pollack, Ethan. (2011, June 1). Tenth anniversary of the Bush-era tax cuts. A decade later, the Bush tax cuts remain expensive, ineffective, and unfair. Economic Policy Institute. Available at www.epi.org/press/news_from_epi_the_bush_tax_cuts_ten_years_later_still_expensive_and_ineffec/.

Fieldhouse, Andrew and Shapiro, Isaac. (2011, May 8). The facts support raising revenues from the highest-income households. Issue brief #310. Washington, D.C.: The Century Foundation and Economic Policy Institute.

FINE Forum e-Newsletter. (2001, Summer/Fall, Updated 2003). *Featured program: Field-based program.* El Paso: University of Texas, *Issue 2* (pp. 4–6).

FINE Forum e-Newsletter. (2003a). *Featured program: Field-based program.* El Paso: University of Texas (pp. 3–5).

FINE Forum e-Newsletter. (2003b, Fall). *Program spotlight: Preparing teachers for urban schools.* El Paso: University of Texas, *Issue 7* (pp. 1–3).

Fine, Michelle. (1991). *Framing dropouts: Notes on the politics of an urban public high school.* Buffalo, New York: SUNY Press.

Fine, Michelle (Ed.). (1994). *Chartering urban school reform: Reflections on public high schools in the midst of change.* New York: Teachers College Press.

Fisher, Peter. (2002). Tax incentives and the disappearing state corporate income tax. *Tax Analysts Reference.* Available at www.tax.org/bestofstate.

Fisher, Robert. (1997). *Let the people decide: Neighborhood organizing in America.* Updated Edition. Farmington Hills, MI: Twayne Publishers.

Fitz-Gerald, Keith. (2011, October 12). Derivatives: The $600 trillion time bomb that's set to explode. *Money Morning.* Available at http://moneymorning.com/.../derivatives-the-600-trillion-time-bomb-thats-set-to-explode.

Fleetwood, Chad and Shelley, Kristina. (2000, Fall). The outlook for college graduates, 1998–2008: A balancing act. *Occupational Outlook Quarterly, (44)3.* Quoted in Lafer, 2002 (p. 61).

Fleischer, Wendy (2001). *Extending ladders: Findings from the Annie E. Casey Foundation's jobs initiative.* Baltimore, MD: Annie E. Casey Foundation.

Folbre, Nancy. (2011, September 5). Public job creation. *The New York Times.*

Forman, Murray. (2002). *The 'hood comes first: Race, space, and place in rap and hip-hop.* Middletown, CN: Wesleyan University Press.

Forum for Youth Investment. (2004, May). *From youth activities to youth action. 2(2).*

Fossey, Richard and Bateman, Mark. (1998). *Condemning students to debt: College loans and public policy.* New York: Teachers College Press.

Foster, John. (2007). The financialization of capitalism. *Monthly Review, 58,* 1–20.

Foster, John. (2008). The financialization of capitalism and the crisis. *Monthly Review, 59,* 1–18.

Fottrell, Quenten. (2012, August 25). Graduates are overqualified, underemployed. *Wall Street Journal.*

Fox, M.A., Connolly, B.A., and Snyder, T.D., (2005). *Youth indicators 2005: Trends in the well-being of American youth.* Washington, D.C.: U.S. Department of Education, National Center for Education Statistics.

Fox, William and Luna, LeAnn. (2010, November). Combined reporting with the corporate income tax: Issues for state legislatures. Center for Business and Economic Research University of Tennessee, Knoxville.

Frankenburg, Erica and Orfield, Gary (Eds). (2012). *The resegregation of suburban schools: A hidden crisis in American education.* Cambridge, MA: Harvard Education Press.

Freedman, Samuel. (1994). *Upon this rock: The miracles of a black church.* New York: Harper Collins.

Freeman, Richard. (1976). *Black elite: The new market for highly educated black Americans.* Report prepared for the Carnegie Commission on Higher Education. New York: McGraw-Hill. Cited in Moss and Tilly, 2001 (p. 35).

Freeman, Richard. (1991). The earnings and employment of disadvantaged young men over the business cycle. In Christopher Jencks and Paul E. Peterson (Eds), *The urban underclass* (pp. 103–121). Washington, D.C.: Brookings Institute.

Freeman, Richard and Gottschalk, Petter. (1998). *Generating jobs: How to increase demand for less-skilled workers*. New York: Russell Sage Foundation.

Freire, Paolo. (1992). *Pedagogy of the oppressed*. New York: Continuum Press.

Frenkel, Stephen J., Korczynski, Maretk, Shire, Karen, and Tam, May. (1999). *On the front line: Organization of work in the information economy*. Ithaca, NY: Cornell University Press.

Frey, William. (2012, Second Quarter). The 2010 census: On the cusp. Milken Institute Review. Santa Monica, CA: Milken Institute, pp. 47–58.

Frey, William H., Berube, Alan, Singer, Audrey, and Wilson, Jill (2011, December 20). Five things the census revealed about America in 2011. State of Metropolitan America. Available at www.brookings.edu/research/opinions/2011/12/20-census-demographics#5.

Friedman, Joel. (2003, October 24). The decline of corporate income tax revenues. Center on Budget and Policy Priorities. Washington, D.C.

Fruchter, Norm and Hyde-Keller, O'rya. (2011). Parent power: Viewer's guide. Annenberg Institute for School Reform. Center for Education Organizing. Available at http://annenberginstitute.org/sites/default/files/PP_guide.pdf.

Fry, Richard. (2012, September 26). A record one-in-five households now owe student loan debt: burden greatest on young, poor. Pew Research Center. Washington, D.C. Available at www.pewsocialtrends.org.

Galbraith, John. (1958/1998). *The affluent society*. Boston, MA: Houghton Miflin.

Galbraith, James. (1998). *Created unequal: The crisis in American pay*. Twentieth Century Fund Book. New York: The Free Press, Simon and Schuster.

Gamson, William. (1990). *The strategy of social protest*. Belmont, CA: Wadsworth.

Gamson, William. (1992). *Talking politics*. Cambridge: Cambridge University Press.

Ganz, Marshall. (2000). Resources and resourcefulness: Strategic capacity in the unionization of California agriculture, 1959–1966. *American Journal of Sociology, 105(4)*, 1003–1062.

Gecan, Michael. (2002). *Going public: An inside story of disrupting politics as usual*. Boston, MA: Beacon Press.

Gecan, Michael. (2004). *Going public: An organizer's guide to citizen action*. New York: Anchor.

Genovese, Eugene. (1976). *Roll, Jordan roll: The world the slaves made*. New York: Vintage Books.

Ginwright, Shawn. (2003, February). Youth organizing: Expanding possibilities for youth development. Occasional Papers Series on Youth Organizing, No. 3. New York: Funders' Collaborative on Youth Organizing.

Ginwright, Shawn and Taj, James. (2002, Winter). From assets to agents of change: Social justice, organizing, and youth development. *New Directions for Youth Development, 96*, 27–46).

Giroux, Henry. (1997). *Pedagogy and the politics of hope*. New York: Westview.

Gitis, Benjamin and Brannon, Ike. (2011, August 15). The mortgage interest boondoggle: A better way to boost home ownership. National Housing Institute. *16(45)*.

Gittell, Marilyn. (1980). *Limits to participation: The decline of community organization and citizen participation*. Thousand Oaks, CA: Sage.

Gittell, Marilyn. (1997, January). *Building civic capacity: Best CDC practices*. Howard Samuels State Management and Policy Center, The Graduate School and University Center of the City University of New York.

Gittell, Marilyn and Gardner, Sarah. (1997). *The capacity of grassroots groups in the environmental movement*. Howard Samuels State Management and Policy Center, The Graduate School and University Center of the City University of New York.

Gittell, Marilyn, Gross, Jill, and Newman, Kathe. (1994). *Race and gender in neighborhood development organizations*. Howard Samuels State Management and Policy Center, The Graduate School and University Center of the City University of New York.

Gittell, Marilyn, Newman, Kathe, and Ortega, Isolda. (1997). *Building civic capacity: Best CDC practices*. Howard Samuels State Management and Policy Center, The Graduate School and University Center of the City University of New York.

Gittell, Marilyn, Newman, Kathe, Ortega-Bustamante, Isolda, and Pierre-Louis, Francois. (1999). *The politics of community development: CDCs and social capital*. Howard Samuels State Management and Policy Center, The Graduate School and University Center of the City University of New York.

Gittell, Ross and Vidal, Avis. (1998). *Community organizing: Building social capital as a development strategy*. New York: Sage.

Gladieux, Lawrence. (2004). Low-income students and the affordability of higher education. In Richard Kahlenberg (Ed.), *America's untapped resource: Low-income students in higher education* (pp. 17–58). New York: The Century Foundation Press.

Glaser, Edward, Kahn, Mattew, and Chu, Chenghuan. (2001, May). *Job sprawl: Employment location in U.S. metropolitan areas*. Center on Urban and Metropolitan Policy. Washington, D.C.: Brookings Institute.

Goering, John and Feins, Judith (Eds). (2003). *Choosing a better life? Evaluating the moving to opportunity social experiment*. Washington, D.C.: The Urban Institute Press.

Goetz, Edward. (2010). Desegregation in 3D: Displacement, dispersal and development in American public housing. *Housing Studies, 25(2)*, 137–158.

Gold, Eva and Simon, Elaine. (2004, January 14). Public accountability. *Education Week*.

Gold, Eva, Simon, Elaine, and Brown, Chris. (2002). *Strong neighborhoods and strong schools: The indicators project on education organizing*. Chicago, IL: Cross City Campaign for Urban School Reform.

Gottschalk, Peter. (1997, Spring). Inequality, income growth, and mobility: The basic facts. *Journal of Economic Perspectives, (11)2*, 21–40. Cited in Lafer, 2002 (p. 60).

Greene, Jay (2001, November). *High school graduation rates in the United States*. Washington, D.C. and New York: Black Alliance for Educational Options and the Manhattan Institute.

Greenhouse, Steven. (2012a, July 22). At Caterpillar, pressing labor while business booms. *The New York Times*.

Greenhouse, Steven. (2012b, October 27). A part-time life, as hours shrink and shift. *The New York Times*.

Greenhouse, Steven. (2013, July 27). Fighting back against wretched wages. *The New York Times*.

Gross, Jane. (2003, August 29). Free tutoring reaches only fraction of students. *The New York Times*.

Guerino, Paul, Harrison, Paige, and Sabol, William. (2011). Prisoners in 2010. NCJ 236096. Washington, D.C.: U.S. Department of Justice, Bureau of Justice Statistics. Available at www.bjs.gov/content/pub/pdf/p10.pdf.

Haberman, Martin. (1995). *Star teachers of children in poverty*. West Lafayette, IN: Kappa Delta Pi.

Hacker, Jacob and Pierson, Paul (2010). *Winner-take-all politics*. New York: Simon & Schuster.

Hagopian, Jesse. (2012, November/December). A people's history of the Chicago Teachers Union, *International Socialist Review, 86*, 5–11.

Hahn, Steven. (2003). *A nation under our feet: Black political struggles in the rural South from slavery to the great migration*. Cambridge, MA: Harvard University Press.

Hale, Janice E. (2001). *Learning while black: Creating educational excellence for African American children*. Baltimore, MD: Johns Hopkins Press.

Hall, Doug. (2012, July 19). Minimum wage increase helps working families and the economy: Characteristics of workers affected by proposed minimum-wage increase to $9.80 in 2014. Economic Policy Institute. Available at http://stateofworkingamerica.org/chart/swa-wages-table-4-40-characteristics-workers/.

Hall, Stuart. (1997). Culture, the media, and the 'ideological effect.' In James Curran, Michael Gurevitch, and Janet Woolacott (Eds). *Mass communication and society*. Beverly Hills: Sage.

Halsband, Robin. (2003, November/December). Charter schools benefit community economic development. *Journal of Housing and Community Development*, 34–38.

Haney, Walter. (2003, September 23). *Attrition of students from New York schools*. Invited Testimony at Public Hearing "Regents Learning Standards and High School Graduation Requirements" before the New York Senate Standing Committee on Education Senate Hearing Room, 250 Broadway, 19th fl., NYC, NY

Harrington, Michael. (1963). *The other America: Poverty in the United States*. Baltimore, MD: Penguin.

Harvey, David. (2007). *A brief history of neoliberalism*. Oxford and New York: Oxford University Press.

Hayasaki, Eerika. (2003, May 30). Schools see an awakening of student activism. *Los Angeles Times*.

Henderson, Anne and Berla, Nancy. (1994). *A new generation of evidence: The family is critical to student achievement*. Washington, D.C.: Center for Law and Education.

Henderson, Anne and Mapp, Karen. (2002). *A new wave of evidence: The impact of school, family, and community connections on student achievement*. Austin, TX: National Center for Family and Community Connections with Schools, Southwest Educational Development Laboratory.

Herszenhorn, David. (2008, September 19). Congressional leaders stunned by warnings. *The New York Times*.

Hilley, John. (2004, May). Teens taking action in Tennessee. *Forum Focus, 2(2)*, 7–8. Available at www.forumforyouthinvestment.org.

Hohn, Joshua. (2003). *Chicago neighborhood discovers delicate balance between success of community schools and resident displacement*. Available at www.communityschools.org.

Holusha, John. (2003, March 16). New vitality around old railroad stations. *The New York Times*.

Holzer, Harry. (1996). *What employers want: Job prospects for less educated workers*. New York: Russell Sage.

Holzer, Harry. (2011). *Where are all the good jobs going?* New York: Russell Sage.

Holzer, Harry and Stoll, Michael. (2001). *Employers and welfare recipients: The effects of welfare reform in the workplace*. San Francisco, CA: Public Policy Institute of California.

Holzer, Harry and Stoll, Michael. (2003). *The employment rate of adult African American men*. Washington, D.C.: The Urban Institute.

Hooks, Bell. (1994). *Teaching to transgress: Education as the practice of freedom*. New York: Routledge.

Hosang, Daniel. (2003). Youth and community organizing today. *Occasional Papers Series on Youth Organizing No. 2*. The Funders Collaborative on Youth Organizing.

Hosang, Daniel, James, Taj, and Chow-Wang, Mamie. (2004, February 9). *Youth organizing for public education reform: A preliminary scan and assessment*. Available from the Mosaic and Movement Strategy Center, Edward W. Hazen Foundation, and Surdna Foundation.

Houser, Robert, Brown, Brett, and Prosser, William. (1998). *Indicators of children's well-being.* New York: Russell Sage.

Hout, Michael. (1988). More universalism, less structural mobility: The American occupational structure in the 1980s. *American Journal of Sociology, 93(3),* 1358–1400.

Howell, David. (1994, Summer). The skills myth. *American Prospect, 18,* 84–87.

Howell, David and Wolff, Edward. (1991). Trends in the growth and distribution of skills in the U.S. workplace, 1960–1985. *Industrial and Labor Relations Review, 44(3),* 486–502.

Howell, David, Houston, Ellen, and Milberg, William. (1999). *Demand shifts and earnings inequality: Wage and hours growth by occupation in the U.S., 1970–97.* CEPA Working Paper No. 6. New York: Center for Economic Policy Analysis at The New School University.

Huang, Chye-Ching and Marr, Chuck. (2012, September 19). Raising today's low capital gains tax rates could promote economic efficiency and fairness, while helping reduce deficits. Center on Budget and Policy Priorities. Washington, D.C. Available at www.cbpp.org/cms/?fa=view&id=3837.

Hungerford, Thomas. (1993). U.S. income mobility in the seventies ad eighties. *Review of Income and Wealth, 39(4),* 401–417.

Hungerford, Thomas. (2012, September 14). Taxes and the economy: An economic analysis of the top tax rates since 1945. Congressional Tesearch Service. Service 7-5700, www.crs.gov, R42729.

Huston, Aletha, Duncan, Greg, Bos, Robert, McLoyd, Johannes, and Crosby, Danielle. (2001). Work-based anti-poverty programs for parents can enhance the school performance and social behavior of children. *Child Development, 72,* 318.

Huston, Aletha, Miller, Cynthia, Richburg-Hayes, Lashawn, Duncan, Greg, Eldred, Carolyn, Weisner, Thomas, Lowe, Edward, McLoyd, Vonnie, Crosby, Danielle, Ripke, Marka, and Redcross, Cindy. (2001). *Summary report, new hope for families and children: Five-year results of a program to reduce poverty and reform welfare.* New York: Manpower Development Research Corporation.

INCITE! (2009). *The revolution will not be funded: Beyond the non-profit industrial complex.* Cambridge, MA: South End Press.

Ingels, Steven J. (2002). *Coming of age in the 1990s: The 8th grade class of 1988 12 years later.* U.S. Department of Education, National Center for Education Statistics.

Internal Revenue Service. (2011, May 11). The 400 individual income tax returns reporting the highest adjusted gross income each year, 1992–2008. Available at www.irs.gov/pub/irs-soi/08intop400.pdf.

International Monetary Fund. (2006). Global financial stability report. Washington, D.C.: IMF.

Jacobson, Dennis. (2003). *Doing justice: Congregations and community organizing.* Minneapolis, MN: Fortress Press.

Jackson, Kenneth. (1995). *Crabgrass frontier: The suburbanization of the United States.* New York: Oxford University Press.

Jackson, Kenneth. (2000). Gentleman's agreement: Discrimination in metropolitan America. In Bruce Katz (Ed.), *Reflections on Regionalism* (pp. 185–217). Washington, D.C.: Brookings Institute.

Jargowsky, Paul. (1998). *Poverty and place: Ghettos, barrios, and the American city.* New York: Russell Sage.

Jehl, Jeanne, Blank, Martin, and McCloud, Barbara. (2001, July). *Education and community building: Connecting two worlds.* Washington, D.C.: Institute for Educational Leadership.

Jencks, Christopher. (1991). Is the American underclass growing? In Christopher Jencks and Paul E. Peterson (Eds), *The urban underclass* (pp. 28–102). Washington, D.C.: Brookings Institute.

Jencks, Christopher and Phillips, Meredith. (1998). *The black/white test score gap.* Washington, D.C.: Brookings Institute.

Jenkins, J. Craig and Halcli, Abigail L. (1999). Grassrooting the system? The development and impact of social movement philanthropy, 1953–1990. In Ellen Condliffe Lagemann (Ed.), *Philanthropic foundations: New scholarship, new possibilities* (pp. 229–256). Bloomington, IN: Indiana University Press. Cited in Bothwell, Robert O. (2000). Foundation Funding of Grassroots Organizations. Available at http://comm-org.uto-ledo.edu/papers2001/bothwell.htm.

Johnson, Charles. (1941). *Growing up in the black belt.* Washington, D.C.: American Council on Education. Cited in McAdam, 1982, (p. 90).

Johnson, Michael, Ladd, Helen, and Ludwig, Jens. (2002). The benefits and costs of residential mobility programs. *Housing Studies, 17(1),* 125–138.

Johnson, Nolas, Carey, Kevin, Mazerov, Michael, McNichol, Elizabeth, Tenny, Daniel, and Zahradnik, Robert. (2002, February 26). *State income tax burdens on low-income families in 2001.* Washington, D.C.: Center on Budget and Policy Priorities.

Johnson, Simon. (2009). The quiet coup. *The Atlantic.*

Johnson, Simon. (2010). *13 Bankers: The Wall Street takeover and the next financial meltdown.* New York: Vintage. Kindle Edition.

Johnson, Simon. (2012, July 19). The Federal Reserve and the libor scandal. *The New York Times.*

Johnston, David Cay. (1999, September 5). Gap between rich and poor found substantially wider. *The New York Times.*

Joint Center for Housing Studies of Harvard University. (2001). *State of the nation's housing.* Cambridge, MA.

Judd, Jason and McGhee, Heather. (2012). Banking on America: How main street partnership banks can improve local economies. Demos NYC.

Kahlenberg, Richard. (2003). *All together now: Creating middle-class schools through public school choice.* Washington, D.C.: Brookings Institute.

Kahlenberg, Richard (Ed.). (2012). *The future of school integration: Socioeconomic diversity as an education reform strategy.* Washington, D.C.: The Century Foundation Press.

Kanter, Rosabeth Moss. (1995). *World class: Thriving locally in the world economy.* New York: Simon & Schuster.

Kanter, Rosabeth Moss. (2000). Business coalitions as a force for regionalism. In Bruce Katz (Ed.), *Reflections on regionalism* (pp. 154–181). Washington, D.C.: Brookings Institute.

Katz, Bruce. (2000, Summer). Enough of the small stuff: Toward a new urban agenda. *Brookings Review, (18)3,* 6–11. Washington, D.C.: Brookings Institute.

Katz, Bruce. (2003, January 9). American cities: Federal neglect imperils their rise. *The Baltimore Sun.*

Katz, Bruce, Puentes, Robert, and Bernstein, Scott. (2003, March). *TES-21 reauthorization: Getting transportation right for metropolitan America.* Washington, D.C.: Brookings Institute.

Katznelson, Ira. (2005). *When affirmative action was white.* New York: W.W. Norton & Company.

Kelley, Robin D.G. (1990). *Hammer and hoe: Alabama communists during the great depression.* Chapel Hill, NC: University of North Carolina Press.

Kelley, Robin D.G. (1994). *Race rebels: Culture, politics, and the black working class.* New York: The Free Press.

Kelley, Robin, D.G. (2002, Fall). Building bridges: The challenge of organized labor in communities of color. *New Labor Forum*, pp. 42–58.

Keynes, John. (1926). *The end of laissez-faire*. London: Leonard and Virginia Wolfe.

Keynes, John. (1964). *General theory of employment, interest, and money*. New York: Harcourt.

King, Joyce. (1995, Rev. Ed.). *Black mothers to sons: Juxtaposing African American literature with social practice*. New York: Peter Lang.

King, Martin Luther Rev. (1999) Beyond Vietnam: A time to break silence. Speech delivered on April 4, 1967. Available at www.hartford-hwp.com/archives/45a/058.html.

Kingsley, Thomas and Petit, Kathryn. (2003, May). *Concentrated poverty: A change in course*. Neighborhood Change in Urban America Series. Washington, D.C.: Urban Institute.

Kirp, David, Dwyer, John, and Rosenthal, Larry. (1995). *Our town: Race, housing, and the soul of suburbia*. New Brunswick, NJ: Rutgers University Press.

Kitwana, Bakari. (2002). *The hip hop generation: Young blacks and the crisis in African American culture*. New York: Basic Civitas Books.

Klandermans, Bert, Kriesi, Hanspeter, and Tarrow, Sidney (Eds). (1988). *From structure to action: Social movement participation across cultures*. Greenwich, CT: JAI.

Klein, Kim. (2000, November). Why are big-money philanthropies afraid of community organizers? *City Limits*, 1, 2.

Klein, Naomi. (2007). *Disaster capitalism*. New York: Henry Holt.

Klerman, Lorraine. (1991; 2003 Reprint Ed.). The health of poor children: Problems and programs. In Aletha Huston (Ed.), *Children and Poverty: Child development and public policy* (pp. 136–157). New York: Cambridge University Press.

Kneebone, E. (2009, April). Job sprawl revisited: The changing geography of metropolitan employment. Brookings Metropolitan Policy Program. Available at www.brookings.edu/metro.

Kochar, Rakesh, Fry, Richard, and Taylor, Paul. (2011, July 26). Wealth Gaps rise to record highs between whites, blacks, hispanics twenty-to-one. Pew Research Center. Available at www.pewsocialtrends.org/.../wealth-gaps-rise-to-record-highs.

Kohn, Alfie. (1998). Only for my kid. *Phi Delta Kappan*, *79*, 568–577.

Korenman, Sanders and Miller, Jane. (1997). Effects of long-term poverty on physical health of children in the national longitudinal survey of youth. In Greg Duncan and Jeanne Brooks-Gunn (Eds), *Consequences of growing up poor* (pp. 70–99). New York: Russell Sage.

Kornrich, Sabino and Furstenburg, Frank. (2012, September 18). Investing in children: Changes in parental spending on children, 1972–2007. *Demography*. Population Association of America 2012. 10.1007/s13524-012-0146-4. Published online. Available at http://link.springer.com/article/10.1007/s13524-012-0146-4/fulltext.html.

Kotz, David. (1987). Long waves and social structures of accumulation. *Review of Radical Political Economics*, *19*, 16–38.

Kotz, David, McDonough, Terence, and Reich, Michael (Eds). (1994). *Social structures of accumulation*. New York: Cambridge University Press.

Kozol, Jonathan. (1992). *Savage inequalities: Children in America's schools*. St. Helens, OR: Perennial Press.

Krasting, Bruce. (2012, July 15). Soak wealth, not income? Available at www.zerohedge.com/contributed/2012-07-15/soak-wealth-not-income.

Kretzmann, John and McNight, John. (1997). *Building communities from the inside out: A path toward finding and mobilizing a community's assets*. Chicago, IL: Acta Publications.

Kripner, Greta. (2005). The financialization of the American economy. *Socio-Economic Review*, *3*, 173–208.

Krugman, Paul. (2009). *The return of depression economics and the crisis of 2008*. New York: W.W. Norton.

Krugman, Paul. (2011, November 4). Oligarchy, American style. *The New York Times*.

Krugman, Paul. (2012). *End this depression now!* New York: W.W. Norton. Kindle Edition.

Labaton, Stephen. (2008, October 2). Agency's '04 rule let banks pile up new debt. *The New York Times*. Available at www.nytimes.com/2008/10/03/business/03sec. html?pagewanted=all&_r=0.

Ladd, Helen (1994). Fiscal impacts of local population growth: A conceptual and empirical analysis. *Regional Science and Urban Economics, 24*, 661–686.

Ladd, Helen and Ludwig, Jens. (2003). The effects of moving to opportunity on educational opportunities in Baltimore. In John Goering and Judith Feins (Eds), *Choosing a better life?* (pp. 117–152). Washington, D.C.: The Urban Institute Press.

Ladd, Helen and Yinger, John. (1989). *America's ailing cities: Fiscal health and the design of urban policy*. Baltimore, MD: Johns Hopkins University Press.

Lahart, Justin (2008, April 28). Has the financial industry's heyday come and gone? *Wall Street Journal*.

Lafer, Gordon. (2002). *The job training charade*. Ithaca, NY: Cornell University Press.

Lam, Tina. (2009, May 16). High lead levels hurt learning for Detroit public school kids. *Detroit Free Press*. Available at www.freep.com/apps/pbcs.dll/article?AID=/20100516/ news01/5160413/1319/high-lead-levels-hurt-learning-for-dps-kids&&template=fullarticle.

Lardner, James. (1998, March 16). Too old to write code? *U.S. News and World Report*. Cited in Lafer, 2002 (p. 250).

Lareau, Annette. (2003). *Unequal childhoods: Class, race, and family life*. Berkeley, CA: University of California Press.

Lather, Patti. (1991). *Getting smart: Research and pedagogy with/in the postmodern*. New York: Routledge.

Ledebur, Larry C. and Barnes, William R. (1993). *All in it together*. Washington, D.C.: National League of Cities.

Lee, John Michael and Ransom, Tafaya. (2011). The educational experience of young men of color: A review of research, pathways, and progress. The College Board: Advocacy & Policy Center. Available at http://advocacy.collegeboard.org/sites/default/files/ EEYMC-ResearchReport_0.pdf.

Lee, Valerie E. and Burkam, David T. (2002). *Inequality at the starting gate: Social background differences in achievement as children begin school*. Washington, D.C.: Economic Policy Institute.

Lemann, Nicholas. (1994, January 9). The myth of community development. *New York Times Magazine*, pp. 27–31, 50, 54, 60.

Leonhardt, David. (2003, April 26). As companies reduce costs, pay is falling top to bottom. *The New York Times*.

Leonhardt, David. (2008, April 9). For many, a boom that wasn't. *The New York Times*.

Leonhardt, David. (2011, July 6). How to reduce the deficit. *The New York Times*.

Leopold, Jason. (2009, September 27). The republican war against ACORN. Truthout. Available at http://archive.truthout.org/092709A.

LeRoy, Greg. (2001). *Talking to union leaders about smart growth*. Sprawl Watch Clearinghouse Monograph Series. Available at www.sprawlwatch.orgnewsletterdec01.html.

LeRoy, Greg and Slocam, Tyson. (1999). *Economic development in Minnesota: High subsidies, low wages, absent standards*. Washington, D.C.: Good Jobs First.

Lester, William and Jacobs, Ken. (2010, November). Creating good jobs in our communities: How higher wage standards affect economic development and employment. American Progress Action, www.americanprogressaction.org.

Letwin, Daniel. (1997). *The challenge of interracial unionism: Alabama coal miners, 1878–1921.* Chapel Hill, NC: University of North Carolina.

Levin-Waldman, Oren. (1999). *Do institutions affect the wage structure? Right-to-work laws, unionization, and the minimum wage.* Public Policy Brief No. 57. Annondale-on-Hudson: Jerome Levy Economics Institute of Bard College.

Levinson, Mark. (2012, June 25). Mismeasuring poverty. The American Prospect. Available at http://prospect.org/article/mismeasuring-poverty.

Levy, Frank. (1999). *The new dollars and dreams: American incomes and economic change.* New York: Russell Sage.

Levy, Frank and Murnane, Richard. (1994). Skills, demography, and the economy: Is there a mismatch? In Lewis Solomon and Alec Levinson (Eds). *Labor markets, employment policy, and job creation.* Boulder: Westview. Cited in Lafer, 2002, (p. 52).

Lewin, Tamar and Medina, Jennifer. (2003, July 31). To cut failure rate, schools shed students. *The New York Times.*

Lewis, Charles, Allison, Bill, and the Center for Public Integrity. (2001). *Cheating of America: How tax avoidance and evasion by the super rich are costing the country billions – and what you can do about it.* New York: William Morrow.

Lewis, Earl. (1957, Summer). The negro voter in Mississippi. *Journal of Negro Education, 26,* 329–350. Cited in Payne, 1995, (p. 18).

Lewis-Charp, H. (2003). *Extending the reach of youth development through civic activism: Outcomes of the youth leadership for development initiative.* San Francisco, CA: Social Policy Research Associates.

Lipman, Barbara. (2006, October). A heavy load: The combined transportation and housing burdens of working families. Washington, D.C.: Center for Housing Policy.

Lipman, Pauline. (1998). *Race, class, and power in school restructuring.* Buffalo, NY: SUNY Press.

Lipman, Pauline. (2003). *High stakes education: Inequality, globalization, and urban school reform.* New York: RoutledgeFalmer.

Lipman, Pauline. (2011). *The new political economy of urban education: Neoliberalism, Race, and the Right to the City.* New York: Routledge.

Lippit, Victor. (2006). Social structure of accumulation theory. Paper prepared for the Conference on Growth and Crisis. National University of Ireland. Galway, Ireland.

LISTEN. (2004, March). *From the frontlines: Youth organizers speak.* Washington, D.C.

Liu, Cathy and Painter, Gary. (2012, April). Suburbanisation in the US: Is there a spatial mismatch? *Urban Studies, 49(5),* 979–1002.

Logan, John. (2001, December 18). *Ethnic diversity grows, neighborhood integration lags behind.* Lewis Mumford Center. Albany, NY: Suny Albany.

Logan, John. (2002a, July 24). *The suburban advantage: New census data show unyielding city-suburb economic gap.* Mumford Center for Comparative Urban and Regional Research. Albany, NY: University at Albany.

Logan, John. (2002b, October 15). *Separate and unequal: The neighborhood gap for blacks and Hispanics in metropolitan America.* Report by the Lewis Mumford Center for Comparative Urban and Regional Research. Albany, NY: University at Albany.

Logan, John and Stults, Brian. (2011). The persistence of segregation in the Metropolis: New findings from the 2010 census. Census Brief prepared for Project US 2010. Available at www.s4.brown.edu/us2010.

Logan Square Neighborhood Association. (2004). *Literacy ambassadors: A parent-to-parent approach to building literacy.* Chicago, IL.

Logan Square Neighborhood Association. (No Date). *A community-centered, holistic approach to immigrant families in public schools.* Chicago, IL.

Lopez, M. Elena. (2003). Transforming schools through community organizing: A research review. FINE Family Network, Harvard University Graduate School of Education.

Loprest, Pamela. (1999). *Families who left welfare: Who are they and how are they doing?* Washington, D.C.: Urban Institute.

Lowenstein, Roger. (2000). *When genius failed*. New York: Random House.

Lowenstein, Roger. (2008, September 6). Long-term capital: it's a short-term memory. *The New York Times*. Available at www.nytimes.com/2008/09/07/business/07ltcm. html?pagewanted=all

Lowrey, Annie. (2012, September 18). Who pays and who takes. *The New York Times*.

Lu, Hsien-Hen. (2003). *Low-income children in the United States*. National Center for Children in Poverty. New York: Columbia University, Mailman School of Public Health.

Luce, Robert and Luce, Stephanie. (1998). *The living wage: Building a fair economy*. New York: The New Press.

Ludwig, Jens, Duncan, Greg, and Ladd, Helen. (2003). The effects of moving to opportunity on children and parents in Baltimore. In John Goering and Judith D. Feins (Eds), *Choosing a better life?* (pp. 153–177). Washington, D.C.: Urban Institute Press.

Lundberg, Shelly and Rose, Elaina. (2004). Investments in sons and daughters: Evidence from the Consumer Expenditure Survey. In Ariel Kalil and Thomas DeLeire (Eds), *Family investments in children's potential: Resources and parenting behaviors that promote success* (pp. 163–180). Mahwah, NJ: Lawrence Erlbaum Associates, Publishers.

McAdam, Doug. (1982, Second edition, 1999). *Political process and the development of black insurgency, 1930–1970*. Chicago, IL: University of Chicago Press.

McAdam, Doug. (1988). *Freedom summer*. New York: Oxford University Press.

McAdam, Doug, Tarrow, Sidney, and Tilly, Charles. (2010). *Dynamics of contention*. New York: Cambridge University Press.

McArdle, Nancy and Stuart, Guy. (2002). *Race, place, and segregation: Redrawing the color line in our nation's metros*. Research Report to the Civil Rights Project, Harvard University.

McGirr, Lisa. (2001). *Suburban warriors: The origins of the new American Right*. Princeton, NJ: Princeton University Press.

McGrath, Daniel and Kuriloff, Peter. (1999, November). They're going to tear down the doors of this place: Upper-middle-class parent school involvement and the educational opportunities of other people's children. *Educational Policy, 13(5)*, 603–629.

McIntire, Mike. (2012, April 21). Conservative nonprofit acts as a stealth business lobbyist. *The New York Times*. Available at www.nytimes.com/2012/04/22/us/alec-a-tax-exempt-group-mixes-legislators-and-lobbyists.html?pagewanted=all.

McKenzie, Evan. (1994). *Privatopia: Homeowner associations and the rise of residential private government*. New Haven, CT: Yale University Press.

McLaren, Peter. (1997). *Revolutionary multiculturalism: Pedagogies of dissent for the new millennium*. New York: Westview.

McLaren, Peter. (2002). *Life in schools: An introduction to critical pedagogy in the foundations of education*. Fourth Edition. Boston, MA: Allyn and Bacon.

McLoyd, Vonnie. (1998a). Children in poverty: Development, public policy, and practice. In I. Siegel and K. Renninger (Eds), *Handbook of child psychology*, Fourth Edition. New York: Wiley.

McLoyd, Vonnie. (1998b). Socioeconomic disadvantage and child development. *American Psychologist, 53*, 185–204.

McLoyd, Vonnie, Jayaratne, Toby Epstein, Ceballo, Rosario, and Borquez, Julio. (1994). Unemployment and work interruption among African-American single mothers: Effects on parenting and adolescent socio-emotional functioning. *Child Development, 65*, 562–589.

McRoberts, Omar. (2003). *Streets of glory: Church and community in a black urban neighborhood*. Chicago, IL: University of Chicago Press.

Madrick, Jeff. (2009). *The case for big government*. Princeton, NJ: Princeton University Press.

Marable, Manning and Mullings, Leith. (2000). *Let nobody turn us around: Voices of resistance, reform, and renewal – an African American anthology*. New York: Rowan and Littlefield.

Marr, Chuck, Charite, Jimmy, and Huang, Chye-Ching. (2013). Earned income tax credit promotes work, encourages children's success at school, research finds. Washington, D.C.: Center on Budget and Policy Priorities. Available at www.cbpp.org/cms/?fa=view&id=3793.

Marris, Peter and Rein, Martin. (1973). *Dilemmas of social reform: Poverty and community action in the United States*. Chicago, IL: Aldive.

Martin, Martin. (No Date). A strange ignorance: The role of lead poisoning in failing schools. Available at http://detroitleaddata.cus.wayne.edu/.

Marx, Gary and Useem, Bert. (1971). Majority involvement in minority movements. *Journal of Social Issues, 27*, 81–104.

Massey, Douglas. (2012, May/June). Lessons from Mount Laurel: The benefits of affordable housing for all concerned. *Poverty & Race, 1*.

Massey, Douglas and Denton, Nancy. (1993). *American apartheid: Segregation and the making of the American underclass*. Cambridge, MA: Harvard University Press.

Masten, Ann and Coatsworth, Douglas. (1995). The structure and coherence of competence from childhood through adolescence. *Child Development, 66*, 1635–1659.

Mauer, Marc. (2003a, May/June). Some punishments begin after prison. *The Crisis*, pp. 16–17.

Mauer, Marc. (2003b). *Invisible punishment: The collateral consequences of mass imprisonment*. New York: The New Press.

Mayer, Susan. (1997). *What money can't buy: Family income and children's life chances*. Cambridge, MA: Harvard University Press.

Medina, Jennifer and Lewin, Tamar. (2003, August 1). High school under scrutiny for giving up on its students. *The New York Times*.

Mediratta, Kavitha and Fruchter, Norm. (2003, January 17). *From school governance to community accountability: Building relationships that make schools work*. New York: New York University Institute for Education and Social Policy, and the Drum Major Institute for Public Policy.

Mediratta, Kavitha and Karp, Jessica. (2003). *Parent power and urban school reform: The story of Mothers on the Move*. New York: New York University Institute for Education and Social Policy.

Mediratta, K., Cohen, A., and Shah, S. (2007). Leveraging reform: Youth power in a smart education system. In Robert Rothman (Ed.), *City schools: How districts and communities can create smart education systems* (pp. 99–115). Cambridge, MA: Harvard Education Press.

Mediratta, Kavitha, Fruchter, Norm, and Lewis, Anne. (2002). *Organizing for school reform: How communities are finding their voices and reclaiming their public schools*. New York: New York University, Institute for Education and Social Policy, Steinhardt School of Education.

Mediratta, Kavitha, Shah, Seema, McAlister, Sarah, Fruchter, Norm, Mokhtar, Christina, and Lockwood, Dana. (2008). *Organized communities, stronger schools: A preview of research findings*. Providence, RI: Brown University, Annenberg Institute for School Reform.

Medoff, Peter and Sklar, Holly. (1994). *Streets of hope: The fall and rise of an urban neighborhood*. Boston, MA: South End Press.

Melucci, Alberto. (1999). *Challenging codes: Collective action in the information age.* Cambridge, UK: Cambridge University Press.

Mendenhall, Ruby, DeLuca, Stefanie, and Duncan, Greg. (2006). Neighborhood resources, racial segregation, and economic mobility: Results from the Gautreaux program. *Social Science Research, 35,* 892–923. Center for Human Potential and Public Policy, Harris School of Public Policy Studies.

Merriam-Webster. (No Date). WPA: Works Progress Administration. Available at www.merriam-webster.com/dictionary/wpa.

Meyer, Rachel. (2002, August 17). Collective action and the making of interracial solidarity. Paper presented at the American Sociological Association Annual Meeting, Chicago, IL.

Meyerson, Harold. (2013, January 3). All hail Wall Street. The American Prospect. Available at http://prospect.org/article/all-hail-wall-street.

Michaloupolos, Charles, Tattri, Doug, Miller, Cynthia, and Robins, Philip. (2002). *Making work pay: Final report on the self-sufficiency project for long-term welfare recipients.* New York: Manpower Development Research Corporation.

Mickelson, Roslyn (2001a). Subverting *Swann:* First- and second-generation segregation in the Charlotte-Mecklenburg schools. *American Educational Research Journal, 38,* 215–252.

Mickelson, Roslyn (2001b, August). How middle school segregation contributes to the race gap in academic achievement. Paper presented at the meeting of the American Sociological Association, Anaheim, CA.

Mickelson, Roslyn. (2003, April). The academic consequences of desegregation and segregation: Evidence from the Charlotte-Mecklenburg schools. *North Carolina Law Review, 81(4),* 120–165.

Minsky, Hyman. (2008a). *John Maynard Keynes.* New York: McGraw-Hill.

Minsky, Hyman. (2008b). *Stabilizing an unstable economy.* New York: McGraw-Hill.

Mishel, Larry. (2011, January 12). Education is not the cure for high unemployment or for income inequality. Briefing paper 286. Washington, D.C.: Economic Policy Institute.

Mishel, Larry. (2012, January 12). False signals on the need for college graduates. Washington, D.C.: Economic Policy Institute.

Mishel, Larry. Quoted by Davidson, Adam. (2013, January 15). It's the economy: The smartphone have-nots. *The New York Times Magazine.*

Mishel, Larry and Teixeira, Ruy. (1991). *The myth of the coming labor shortage: Jobs, skills, and incomes of America's workforce 2000.* Washington, D.C.: Economic Policy Institute.

Mishel, Larry, Bernstein, Jared, and Allegretto, Sylvia. (2006). *The state of working America: 2006/2007.* Ithaca, NY: Cornell University Press.

Mishel, Larry, Bernstein, Jared, and Boushey, Heather. (2003). *The state of working America: 2002/2003.* Ithaca, NY: Cornell University Press.

Mishel, Larry, Bernstein, Jared, and Schmitt, John. (2001). *The state of working America: 2000/2001.* Ithaca, NY: Cornell University Press.

Mishel, Larry, Bivens, Josh, and Eisenbrey, Ross. (2011, September 22). Putting America back to work: Policies for job creation and stronger economic growth. Washington, D.C.: Economic Policy Institute.

Mishel, Larry, Bivens, Josh, Gould, Elise, and Shierholz, Heidi. (2012). State of working America. Twelfth Edition, Digital Edition. Ithaca, NY: Cornell University Press.

Monthly Labor Review. (2002, October). Editor's comments. *(121)*10. Quoted in Lafer, 2002, (p. 47).

Moore, Rosanna and Sandler, Susan. (2003). *Supporting the education organizing movement: An exchange between intermediaries.* San Francisco, CA: Justice Matters Institute.

Morcroft, Greg. (2008, May 19). Citi-run group wins Pa. Turnpike lease. *Market Watch*. Available at www.marketwatch.com/story/citi-run-group-wins-pa-turnpike-lease.

Morgenson, Gretchen. (2008, December 21). Just call this deal Hoosier baroque. *The New York Times*.

Morgenson, Gretchen. (2009, January 24). Time to unravel the knot of credit-default swaps. *The New York Times*.

Morgenson, Gretchen. (2010, August 5). Exotic deals put Denver schools deeper in debt. *The New York Times*.

Morgenson, Gretchen. (2012, June 9). Swaps and public transit. Money from taxpayers to wall st.; How Banks Could Return the Favor. *The New York Times*.

Morgenson, Gretchen. (2013, March 15). JPMorgan chase whale trades: A case history of derivatives risks and abuses: Permanent subcommittee on investigations. *The New York Times*.

Morris, Aldon. (1984). *The origins of the civil rights movement: Black communities organizing for change*. New York: Free Press.

Morris, Aldon and Staggenborg, Suzanne. (2002). Leadership in social movements. Available at www.cas.northwestern.edu/sociology/faculty/files/leadershipessay.pdf.

Morris, Pamela and Michalopoulos, Charles. (2000). *The self-sufficiency project at 36 months: Effects on children of a program that increased parental employment and income*. Ottawa: Social Research and Demonstration Corporation.

Morris, Pamela, Duncan, Greg, and Clark-Kauffman, E. (2005). Child well-being in an era of welfare reform: The sensitivity of transitions in development to policy change. *Development Psychology, 41(6)*, 919–32.

Morris, Pamela, Huston, Aletha, Duncan, Greg, Crosby, Daniell, and Bos, Johannes. (2001). *How welfare and work policies affect children: A synthesis of research*. Washington, D.C.: Manpower Development Research Corporation.

Moses, Bob. (2001, May/June). Quality education is a civil rights issue. *Harvard Education Letter*, pp. 1–2.

Moses, Robert and Charles Cobb, Jr. (2002). *Radical equations: Civil rights from Mississippi to the Algebra Project*. Boston, MA: Beacon Press.

Moss, Philip and Tilly, Chris. (1996). 'Soft' skills and race: An investigation of Black men's employment problems. *Work and Occupations, 23(3)*, 252–76. In Moss and Tilly, 2001, (p. 47).

Moss, Philip and Tilly, Chris. (2001) *Stories employers tell: Race, skill, and hiring in America*. New York: Russell Sage.

Mui, Ylan Q. (2012, June 11). Americans saw wealth plummet 40 percent from 2007 to 2010, Federal Reserve says. *The Washington Post*.

Murnane, Richard and Levy, Frank. (1996). *Teaching the new basic skills: Principles for educating children to thrive in a changing economy*. New York: Free Press.

Nash, Gary. (1979). *Urban crucible: Social change, political consciousness, and the origins of the American revolution*. Cambridge, MA: Harvard University Press.

National Center for Children in Poverty (NCCP). (2004, May). *Low-income children in the United States (2004)*. New York: Mailman School of Public Health, Columbia University.

National Center for Educational Statistics. (2003). *The condition of education: An annual snapshot, 2003*. Washington, D.C.: U.S. Department of Education.

National Center for Public Policy and Higher Education. (2002). *Losing ground: A national status report on the affordability of American higher education*. San Jose: CA: National Center.

National Employment Law Project. (2012a, August). New minimum wage bills would accelerate recovery and improve job quality. Issue brief. New York: NELP.

National Employment Law Project. (2012b, August). The low-wage recovery and growing inequality. Available at www.nelp.org/index.php/content/content_about_us/tracking_the_recovery_after_the_great_recession.

National Jobs for All Coalition. (2002, October). *UnCommon sense*. New York. http://www.njfac.org.

Natriello, Gary, McDill, Edward, and Pallas, Aaron. (1990). *Schooling disadvantaged children: Racing against catastrophe*. New York: Teachers College Press.

New York City Coalition for Educational Justice. (2010). Beyond school closings: Effective alternatives for low-performing schools. Available at http://www.nyccej.org/wp-content/uploads/2010/05/CEJ-Turnaround-PaperFinal.pdf.

New York Times. (2011, November 7). Editorial. Wall Street's repeat violations, despite repeated promises.

New York Times. (2012, October 21). Editorial. The myth of job creation.

Newman, Katherine. (1993). *Declining fortunes: The withering of the American dream*. New York: Basic Books.

Newman, Katherine. (2000). *No shame in my game: The working poor in the inner city*. New York: Vintage.

Newman, Kathryn and O'Brian, Rourke. (2011), *Taxing the poor*. Berkeley, CA: University of California Press.

Newman, Maria. (2002, August 2). Trenton court upholds law on moderately priced housing. *The New York Times*.

Niedt, Christopher. (1999). *The effects of the living wage in Baltimore*. Working Paper No. 119. Washington, D.C.: Economic Policy Institute.

Nolan, Kathleen and Anyon, Jean. (2004). Learning to do time: Willis' cultural reproduction model in an era of deindustialization, globalization, and the mass incarceration of people of color. In Nadine Dolby and Greg Dimitriadis (with P. Willis) (Eds), *Learning to labor in new times* (pp. 114–129). New York: RoutledgeFalmer.

Norris, Frank. (2007, October 26). Who's going to take the financial weight? *The New York Times*.

Oakes, Jeannie. (1990). *Multiplying inequalities: The effects of race, social class, and tracking on opportunities to learn mathematics and science*. Santa Monica, CA: RAND.

Oakes, Jeannie and Lipman, Martin. (2002). *Teaching to change the world*. New York: McGraw-Hill.

Oakes, Jeannie, Rogers, John, and Lipton Martin. (2006). *Learning power; organizing for education and justice*. New York: Teachers College Press.

O'Connor, Anahad. (2003, October 21). Rise in income improves children's behavior. *The New York Times*.

Offner, Paul and Holzer, Harry. (2002, April). *Left behind in the labor market: Recent employment trends among young black men*. Center on Urban and Metropolitan Policy. Washington, D.C.: Brookings Institute.

Oliver, Melvin and Shapiro, Thomas (Eds). (1997). *Black wealth/white wealth: A new perspective on racial inequality*. New York: Routledge.

Olson, Lynne. (2001). *Freedom's daughters: The unsung heroines of the civil rights movement from 1830 to 1970*. New York: Scribner.

Orfield, Gary. (1996, April). Metropolitan school desegregation: Impacts on metropolitan society. *Minnesota Law Review, 80(4)*, 825–873.

Orfield, Gary. (2001a). *Schools more separate: Consequences of a decade of resegregation.* Cambridge, MA: The Civil Rights Project at Harvard University.

Orfield, Gary. (2001b, April 3). *Housing segregation: Causes, effects, possible cures.* Cambridge, MA: The Civil Rights Project, Harvard University. National Press Club.

Orfield, Gary. (2009, December 1). Foreword. In Deirdre Pfeiffer, *The opportunity illusion: Subsidized housing and failing schools in California.* The Civil Rights Project.

Orfield, Myron. (1997). *Metropolitics: A regional agenda for community and stability.* Washington, D.C.: Brookings Institute.

Orfield, Myron. (2002). *American metropolitics: The new suburban reality.* Washington, D.C.: Brookings Institute.

Orfield, Myron. (2007). The region and taxation: School finance, cities, and the hope for regional reform. *Buffalo Law Review, 55,* 91–135.

Orr, Marion. (1999). *Black social capital: The politics of school reform in Baltimore, 1986–1998.* St Lawrence, KS: University Press of Kansas.

Osterman, Paul. (1995). Skill, training, and work organization in American establishments. *Industrial Relations, 34,* 2–13.

Osterman, Paul. (2001). *Working in America: A blueprint for the new labor market.* Cambridge, MA: MIT Press.

Osterman, Paul and Lautsch, Brenda. (1996). *Project quest: A report to the Ford Foundation.* Cambridge, MA: MIT Sloan School of Management. Cited in Moss and Tilly, 2001 (p. 259).

Pack, Janet Rothenberg. (1995). *Poverty and urban expenditures.* Philadelphia: University of Pennsylvania, Wharton Real Estate Center. Cited in Orfield, 2002 (p. 27).

Paletta, Damian. (2012, February 3). With tax break, corporate rate is lowest in decades. *Wall Street Journal.*

Parson, Gail. (2003). *Outside the law: How lenders dodge community reinvestment.* Milwaukee, WI: National Training and Information Center.

Pastor, Manuel, Benner, Chris, and Matsuoka, Martha. (2009). *This could be the start of something big: How social movements for regional equity are reshaping metropolitan America.* Ithaca, NY: Cornell University Press.

Pastor, Manuel, Benner, Chris, and Matsuoka, Martha. (2011, December 14). For what it's worth: Regional equity, community organizing, and metropolitan America. *Journal of the Community Development Society, 42(4),* 437–457.

Pastor, Manuel Jr., Dreier, Peter, Grigsby, Eugene III, and López-Garza, Marta. (2000). *Regions that work: How cities and suburbs can grow together. Globalization and Community,* Vol. 6. University of Minnesota Press.

Pawasarat, John and Quinn, Lois. (2001). *Exposing urban legends: The real purchasing power of central city neighborhoods.* Washington, D.C.: Brookings Institute.

Payne, Charles. (1995). *I've got the light of freedom: The organizing tradition and the Mississippi freedom struggle.* Berkeley, CA: University of California Press.

Perry, Theresa. (2003). *Young, gifted, and black: Promoting high achievement among African-American students.* New York: Beacon.

Persky, Joseph and Kurban, Haydar. (2001, November). *Do federal funds better support cities or Suburbs?* Washington, D.C.: Brookings Institute Center on Urban and Metropolitan Policy.

Pettit, Becky. (2012). *Invisible men: Mass incarceration and the myth of black progress.* Ithaca, NY: Cornell University Press.

Pettit, Kathryn, Kingsley, Tomas, and Coulton, Claudia. (2003, May 30). Neighborhoods and health: Building evidence for local policy. Washington, D.C.: The Urban Institute.

Philadelphia Children Achieving Challenge. (1996). *A first-year evaluation report.* Philadelphia, PA.

Phillips, Kevin. (1990). *The politics of rich and poor: Wealth and the American electorate in the Reagan aftermath.* New York: Random House.

Phillips, Kevin. (2002). *Wealth and democracy: A political history of the American rich.* New York: Broadway Books, Random House.

Phillips, Kevin. (2009). *Bad money.* New York: Penguin.

Phillips, Meredith, Brooks-Gunn, Jeanne, Greg, Duncan, Klevanov, Pamela and Crane, Jonathan. (1998). Family background, parenting practices, and the black/white test score gap. In Christopher Jencks and Meredith Phillips (Eds), *The black/white test score gap* (pp. 103–145). Washington, D.C.: Brookings Institute.

Phillips, Meredith, Crouse, James, and Ralph, John. (1998). Does the black/white test score gap widen after children enter school? In Christopher Jencks and Meredith Phillips (Eds), *The black/white test score gap* (pp. 229–272). Washington, D.C: Brookings Institute.

Pigeon, Marc-Andre and Wray, Randall. (1999). Down and out in the U.S.: An inside look at the out of the labor force population. Public Policy Brief No. 54. Annondale-on-Hudson, NY: The Jerome Levy Economics Institute of Bard College.

Pittman, Karen. (2002, July). Balancing the equation: Communities supporting youth, youth supporting comunities. In John Terry (Ed.), *CYD Anthology 2002* (pp. 19–24). Sudbury, MA: Institute for Just Communities.

Pittman, Karen. (2003, May). Youth consultants for change. *Youth Today, 12(5),* p. 43.

Piven, Frances Fox and Cloward, Richard. (1979). *Poor people's movements: Why they succeed, how they fail.* New York: Vintage Books.

Polanyi, Karl. (1944). *The great transformation: The political and economic origins of our time.* Boston, MA: Beacon Press.

Policy Link. (2000). *Community based initiatives promoting regional equity: Profiles of innovative programs from across the country.* Oakland, CA.

Policy Link. (2001). *Dealing with neighborhood change.* Oakland, CA.

Policy Link. (2002). *Regional equity success stories: Los Angeles.* Oakland, CA.

Pollin, Robert. (1998, November 23). Living wage, live action. *The Nation.* Cited in Lafer, 2002, (p. 84).

Polokow, Valerie. (2007). *Who cares for our children? The child care crisis in the other America.* New York: Teachers College Press.

Popkin, Susan, Katz, Bruce, Cunningham, Mary, Brown, Karen, Gustafson, Jeremy, and Turner, Margery. (2004). *A decade of HOPE VI: Research findings and policy challenges.* Washington, D.C.: The Urban Institute.

Popkin, Susan, Levy, Diane, and Buron, Larry. (2009, July). Has HOPE VI transformed residents' lives? New evidence from the HOPE VI Panel Study. *Housing Studies, 24(4),* 477–502.

Porter, Eduardo. (2012, March 27). The case for raising top tax rates. *The New York Times.*

Porter, Michael. (1995a, May/June). The competitive advantage of the inner city. *Harvard Business Review, 73,* 55–71.

Porter, Michael. (1995b, Fall). An economic strategy for America's inner cities: Addressing the controversy. *Review of Black Political Economy, 24(2/3),* 1–17.

Poterba, James and Sinai, Todd. (2008). Tax expenditures for owner-occupied housing: Deductions for property taxes and mortgage interest and the exclusion of imputed rental income. Available at http://real.wharton.upenn.edu/~sinai/papers/Poterba-Sinai-2008-ASSA-final.pdf. Cited in Glaeser, Edward. (2009, February 24). Killing (or maiming) a sacred cow: Home mortgage deductions. *The New York Times.*

Powell, John A. (2000). Addressing regional dilemmas for minority communities. In Bruce Katz (Ed.), *Reflections on regionalism* (pp. 218–248). Washington, D.C.: Brookings Institute.

Powell, John A. and Graham, Kathleen. (2002). Urban fragmentation as a barrier to equal opportunity. In Diane M. Piché, William L. Taylor, and Robin A. Reed (Eds), *Rights at Risk: Equality in an Age of Terrorism* (pp. 79–97). Washington D.C.: Citizens Commission on Civil Rights.

Proctor, Bernadett and Dalaker, Joseph. (2002). *Poverty in the United States: 2001.* U.S. Census Bureau, Current Population Reports (pp. 60–219). Washington, D.C.: U.S. Government Printing Office.

Pryor, Frederic and Schaffer, David. (1999). *Who's not working and why: Employment, cognitive skills, wages and the changing U.S. labor market.* New York: Cambridge University Press.

Puentes, Robert. (2003). *An intelligent transportation policy.* Washington, D.C.: Brookings Institute.

Raines, Howell. (1983). *My soul is rested: Movement days in the deep South remembered.* New York: Viking Press.

Rampell, Catherine. (2012, January 9). College-educated workers gaining jobs, high school grads losing them. *The New York Times.*

Ravitch, Diane. (2000 Reprint). *The great school wars: A history of the New York City public schools.* Baltimore, MD: John Hopkins University Press.

Ravitch, Diane. (2013). *Reign of error: The hoax of the privatization movement and the danger to America's public schools.* New York: Knopf.

Reardon, Sean and Bischoff, Kendra. (2010). Growth in the residential segregation of families by income, 1970–2009. US2010 Project. Russell Sage Foundation.

Reardon, Sean and Bischoff, Kendra. (2011, January). Income inequality and income segregation. *American Journal of Sociology, 116(4),* 1092–1153.

Reich, Robert B. (2002, November 23). Whose tax cuts? *The American Prospect,* 13.

Reich, Robert. (2011a, February 16). The republican strategy. *The Huffington Post.* Available at http://huffingtonpost.come/Robert-reich/the-republican strategy.

Reich, Robert. (2011b, May 17). The great switch by the super rich. Available at http://robertreich.org/post/5583016733.

Reich, Robert. (2012a). Beyond outrage. (Enhanced Edition). Knopf. Kindle Edition.

Reich, Robert. (2012b, July 7). The Wall Street scandal of all scandals. Available at robertreich.org/post/26708840314.

Reilly, David. (2012, January 4). U.S. tax haul trails profit surge. *Wall Street Journal.*

Reneé, M. (2011, Spring). The growing field of youth organizing for educational justice. VUE: Voices in Urban Education, Annenberg Institute for School Reform, pp. 2–4. Available at http://annenberginstitute.org/sites/default/files/product/197/files/VUE30.pdf.

Reneé, Michelle and Mcalister, Sara. (2011). The strengths and challenges of community organizing as an education reform strategy; what the research says. Nellie Mae Education Foundation, Annenberg Institute for School Reform.

Rheingold, Howard. (2002). *Smart mobs: The next social revolution.* New York: Perseus Publishers.

Robnett, Belinda. (1997). *How long? How long? African American women in the struggle for civil rights.* New York: Oxford University Press.

Rogers, John and Orr, Marion (Eds). (2010). *Public engagement for public education: Joining forces to revitalize democracy and equalize schools.* Palo Alto, CA: Stanford University Press.

Rolnik, Raquel. (2012). Report on the financialization of housing and its impact on the right to adequate housing. UN General Assembly.

Rooney, Jim. (1995). *Organizing the South Bronx*. Albany, NY: SUNY Press.

Rose, Kalim and Silas, Julie. (2001, February). *Achieving equity through smart growth: Perspectives from philanthropy*. Oakland, CA: Policy Link and Funders' Network for Smart Growth and Livable Communities.

Rosen, Jan. (2011, November 1). Tax rules allow an array of givers to be more generous. *The New York Times*.

Rosenbaum, James. (1991). Black pioneers: Do their moves to the suburbs increase economic opportunity for mothers and children? *Housing Policy Debate, 2,* 1179–1213.

Rosenbaum, James. (2001). *Beyond college for all: Career paths for the forgotten half*. New York: Russell Sage.

Roth, Jodi, Brooks-Gunn, Jeanne, and Murray, Lawrence. (1998). Promoting healthy adolescence: Synthesis of youth development program evaluations. *Journal of Research on Adolescence, 8(4),* 423–459.

Rothstein, Richard. (1999, October 27). Shortage of skills? A high-tech myth. *The New York Times*.

Rouse, Jacqueline. (2001). We seek to know in order to speak the truth: Nurturing the seeds of discontent – Septima P. Clarke and participatory leadership. In Bettye Collier-Thomas and V.P. Franklin (Eds), *Sisters in the struggle: African American women in the civil rights-black power movement* (pp. 96–120). New York: New York University Press.

Rubin, Herbert. (2000). *Renewing hope within neighborhoods of despair: The community-based development model*. Buffalo, NY: SUNY Press.

Rubinowitz, Leonard and Rosenbaum, James. (2002). *Crossing the class and color line: From public housing to white suburbia*. Chicago, IL: University of Chicago Press.

Rusk, David. (1993). *Cities without suburbs*. Washington, D.C.: Woodrow Wilson Center Press.

Rusk, David. (1998, July). *Abell report: To improve poor children's test scores, move poor families*. Baltimore, MD: Abell Foundation.

Rusk, David. (1999). *Inside game/outside game: Winning strategies for saving urban America*. Washington, D.C.: Brookings Institute.

Rusk, David. (2000). Growth management: The core regional issue. In Bruce Katz (Ed.) *Reflections on regionalism* (pp. 78–106). Washington, D.C.: Brookings Institute.

Saez, Emmanuel. (2010, July 17). Striking it richer: The evolution of top incomes in the United States. http://elsa.berkeley.edu/~saez/TabFig2008.xls. Updated January 23, 2013.

Sammartino, Frank J. (2001). *Designing tax cuts to benefit low-income families*. Washington, D.C.: Urban Institute.

Sampson, Robert, Morenoff, Jeffrey, and Gannon-Rowley, Thomas. (2002). Assessing 'neighborhood effects:' Social processes and new directions in research. *Annual Review of Sociology, 28,* 443–478.

Sanbonmatsu, Lisa, Kling, Jeffrey R., Duncan, Greg J., and Brooks-Gunn, Jeanne. (2006). Neighborhoods and academic achievement: Results from the moving to opportunity experiment. NBER Working Paper No. 11909. Cambridge, MA: National Bureau of Economic Research.

Sanbonmatsu, Lisa, Kling, Jeffrey R., Duncan, Greg, and Brooks-Gunn, Jeanne. (2011). Moving to opporunity for fair housing demonstration program. Final Impacts Evaluation. U.S. Department of Housing and Urban Development, Office of Policy Development and Research.

Sanders, Mavis and Adia Harvey. (2002). Beyond the school walls. *Teachers College Record. 104(7),* 1345–1368.

Sandia Laboratories. (1993). Perspective on education in America. *Journal of Educational Research, 86(5)*, 259–310.

Sassen, Saskia. (2001). *Global city: New York, London, Tokyo*. Princeton: Princeton University Press.

Savitch, H.V., Collins, David, Sanders, Daniel, and Markham, John. (1993). Ties that bind: Central cities, suburbs, and the new metropolitan region. *Economic Development Quarterly, 7(4)*, 341–358.

Sawicky, Max and Cherry, Robert. (2001, December 21). *Making work pay with tax reform*. Issue Brief No.173. Washington, D.C.: Economic Policy Institute.

Schemo, Diana Jean. (2003, July 11). Questions on data cloud luster of Houston schools. *The New York Times*.

Schensul, Jean and LeCompte, Margaret. (1999). *Ethnographer's toolkit*. Walnut Creek, CA: Altamira Press.

Schmitt, John. (2008, May). The union wage advantage for low-wage workers. Washington, D.C.: Center for Economic and Policy Research.

Schmitt, John and Jones, Janelle. (2012). Where have all the good jobs gone? Washington, D.C.: Center for Economic and Policy Research. Available at www.cepr.net/documents/publications/good-jobs-2012-07.pdf?.

Schmitt, John and Rosnick, David. (2011, March). The wage and employment impact of minimum-wage laws in three cities. Washington, D.C.: Center for Economic and Policy Research.

Schutz, Aaron. (2004. January/February). Rethinking domination and resistance: Challenging postmodernism. *Educational Researcher*, pp. 15–23.

Schwartz, Heather. (2010). Economic integration promotes academic success in Montgomery county New York: Century Foundation.

Scott, Janelle. (2009). The politics of venture philanthropy in charter school policy. Education Policy. Available at http://epx.sagepub.com/cgi/content/abstract/23/1/106.

Seeger, Pete. (No Date). Appleseed recordings, www.appleseedrec.com/petecd/bruce.html.

Sharatrand, Angela M., Weiss, Heather, Kreider, Holly, and Lopez, Elena. (1997). *New skills for new schools: Preparing teachers in family involvement*. FINE Forum. Available at www.gse.harvard.edu/hfrp/puts/onlinepubs/skills/chptr3.html.

Shaw, Hannah and Stone, Chuck. (2011, March 7). Incomes at the top rebounded in first full year of recovery, new analysis of tax data shows. Washington, D.C.: Center on Budget and Policy Priorities.

Shaw, Randy. (2001). *The activists' handbook: A primer*, Updated Edition. Berkeley, CA: University of California Press.

Shaxson, Nicholas. (2012). *Treasure islands: Uncovering the damage of offshore banking and tax havens*. New York: Palgrave Macmillan.

Shierholz, Heidi. (2009, January 9). *Job losses balooned in final quarter of 2008*. Washington, D.C.: Economic Policy Institute.

Shierholz, Heidi and Gould, Elise. (2012, September 12). *Already more than a lost decade: Poverty and income trends continue to paint a bleak picture*. Washington, D.C.: Economic Policy Institute.

Shiller, Robert. (2006). *Irrational exuberance*. Second Edition. Princeton, NJ: Princeton University Press.

Shirley, Dennis. (1997). *Community organizing for urban school reform*. Austin, TX: University of Texas Press.

Shirley, Dennis. (2002). *Valley interfaith and school reform: Organizing for power in South Texas*. Austin, TX: University of Texas Press.

Shirley, Dennis. (2004). Transforming urban education through the Massachusetts Coalition for Teacher Quality and Student Achievement. Available from the author.

Short, Kathleen. (2011, November). The research: supplemental poverty measure 2010. Current population reports, Nov. 2011, U.S. Department of Commerce Economics and Statistics Administration. Available at www.census.gov/prod/2012pubs/p60-244.pdf.

Short, Kathleen, Iceland, John, and Garner, Thesia. (1999). *Experimental poverty measures.* Washington, D.C.: U.S. Census Bureau.

Shulman, Beth. (2002, July 26). It's not just money: Thirty-five million workers in low-wage jobs. *Uncommon Sense,* National Jobs for All Coalition, www.njfac.org/us26.htm.

Shuman, Michael. (1998, January 12). Why do progressive foundations give too little to too many? *The Nation.*

Silverblatt, Howard. (2009, July). Standard and poor's market attributes. Snapshot S&P 500 standardandpoors.com.

Sklar, Holly, Mykyta, Laryssa, and Wefald, Susan. (2001). *Raise the floor: Wages and policies that work for all of us.* New York: Ms. Foundation for Women.

Skocpol, Theda. (1991). Targeting within universalism: Politically viable policies to combat poverty in the United States. In Christopher Jencks and Paul E. Peterson (Eds), *The urban underclass* (pp. 420–434). Washington, D.C.: Brookings Institute.

Smeeding, Timothy, Rainwater, Lee, and Burtless, Gary. (2001, May). *United States poverty in a cross-national context.* Paper prepared for the International Research on Poverty Conference, Understanding poverty in America: progress and problems.

Smith, James and Welch, Finis. (1989). Black economic progress after Myrdal. *Journal of Economic Literature, 27(2),* 519–564. Cited in Moss and Tilly, 2001 (p. 5).

Snow, David, Rochford, Burke, Worden, Steven, and Benford, Robert. (1986). Frame alignment processes, micromobilization, and movement participation. *American Sociological Review, 51,* 464–481.

Snow, David, Soule, Sarah A., and Kriesi, Hanspeter. (2006). *The Blackwell companion to social movements.* Malden, MA: Blackwell Publishing.

Social Policy Research Associates. (2003, December). *Lessons in leadership: How young people change their communities and themselves: An evaluation of the Youth Leadership for Development Initiative.* Executive Summary. Takoma Park, MD: Innovation Center for Community and Youth Development.

Southern, Eileen. (1971). *The music of black Americans: A history.* Second Edition. New York: Norton.

Spring, Joel. (2000). *The American school, 1642–2000.* Fifth Edition. New York: McGraw-Hill Companies.

Squires, Gregory D. (2003). Racial profiling, insurance style: Insurance redlining and the uneven development of metropolitan areas. *Journal of Urban Affairs, 25(4),* 391–410.

Steele, Claude. (2011). *Whistling Vivaldi: How stereotypes affect us and what we can do.* New York: Norton.

Stempel, Jonathan. (2008, August 1). Wall Street to privatize US infrastructure: roads, airports on the block as budgets tighten. *Reuters.* Available at www.globalresearch.ca/wall-street-to-privatize-us-infrastructure/?print=1.

Stiglitz, Joseph. (2008a). The financial crisis of 2007/2008 and its macro-economic consequences. Paper presented at the Financial Markets Reform Task Force Meeting July 2008. Manchester, UK: University of Manchester.

Stiglitz, Joseph. (2008b). *The three trillion dollar war.* New York: Norton.

Stiglitz, Joseph. (2011, May). Of the 1%, by the 1%, for the 1%. *Vanity Fair.* Available at www.vanityfair.com/society/features/2011/05/top-one-percent-201105.

Stiglitz, Joseph. (2013a). *The price of inequality: How today's divided society endangers our future.* New York: Norton.

Stiglitz, Joseph. (2013b, January 19). Inequality is holding back the recovery. *The New York Times.*

Stipic, Deborah and Ryan, Rosaleen. (1997). Economically disadvantaged preschoolers: Ready to learn but further to go. *Developmental Psychology, 33(4)*, pp. 711–723.

Stoll, Michael, (2005). Job sprawl and the spatial mismatch between blacks and jobs. Washington, D.C.: Brookings Institute.

Stoll, Michael. (2010, March 30). *Job sprawl and the suburbanization of poverty.* Metropolitan Opportunity Series. Washington, D.C: Brookings Institute.

Stuart, Guy. (2000). *Segregation in the Boston metropolitan area at the end of the 20th century.* The Civil Rights Project, Harvard University.

Stuart, Guy. (2002). *Integration or resegregation: Metropolitan Chicago at the turn of the new century.* Research Report to The Civil Rights Project, Harvard University.

Su, Celina. (2009). *Streetwise for Book Smarts: Grassroots organizing and education reform in the Bronx.* Ithaca, NY: Cornell University Press.

Suarez-Orozco, Carola and Suarez-Orozco, Marcelo M. (2002). *Children of immigration.* Boston, MA: Harvard University Press.

Sugland, Barbara, Zaslow, Martha, and Brooks-Gunn, Jeanne. (1995). The early childhood HOME inventory and HOME short form in differing socio-cultural groups: Are there differences in underlying structure, internal consistency of subscases, and patterns of prediction? *Journal of Family Issues, 16(5),* 632–663.

Suro, Roberto and Singer, Audrey. (2002, July). *Latino growth in metropolitan America: Changing patterns, new locations.* Washington, D.C.: Brookings Institute.

Swanstrom, Todd and Barrett, Laura. (2007). The road to jobs: The fight for transportation equity. *Social Policy,* (Summer).

Swanstrom, Todd and Sauerzopf, Richard. (1993). The urban electorate in presidential elections. Conference paper for the Urban Affairs Association, Indianapolis, Indiana, April 1993. In Manuel Pastor, Jr., Peter Dreier, and J Eugene Grisby (Eds), (2000) *Regions that work: How cities and suburbs can grow together* (p. 193). Minneapolis: University of Minnesota Press.

Swarts, Heidi. (2002, January/February). Shut out from the economic boom: Comparing community organizations' success in the neighborhoods left behind. *Snapshots: Research Highlights from the Nonprofit Sector Research Fund, (21),* The Aspen Institute.

Tabb, Bill. (2007). The centrality of finance. *Journal of World Systems Research, 13,* 1–11.

Tabb, Bill. (2008). Four crises of the contemporary world capitalist system. *Monthly Review, 59,* 1–13.

Tarrow, Sidney. (1998). *Power in movement: Social movements and contentious politics.* 2nd edition. Cambridge: Cambridge University Press.

The Education Trust. (2001, March). *The funding gap: Low-income and minority students receive fewer dollars.* Washington, D.C.

The Education Trust. (2004). *Trends in student aid.* Washington, D.C.

The Education Trust. (2005). *Funding gap 2005: Most states shortchange poor and minority students.* Washington, D.C.

The Education Trust. (2012). *Close the funding gaps in our schools.* Washington, D.C.

The Foundation Center. (2003). Highlights of the Foundation Center's Foundation Yearbook. *Foundations Today Series.* New York: Foundation Center.

The Initiative for a Competitive Inner City. (1998). *The business case for pursuing retail opportunities in the inner city.* Boston, MA: Boston Consulting Group.

The Staff of Black Star Publishing (Ed.). (1970). *The political thought of James Forman.* Detroit, MI.

Thorbecke, Willem. (2000). *A dual mandate for the federal reserve: The pursuit of price stability and full employment.* Public Policy Brief No. 60. Annondale-on-Hudson, NY: Jerome Levy Economics Institute of Bard College.

Thurm, Scott. (2012, April 9). For big companies, life is good: large corporations emerge from recession leaner, stronger—and hiring overseas. *Wall Street Journal.*

Torre, Maria Elena and Fine, Michelle. (2003, Summer). Youth reframe questions of educational justice through participatory action research. FINE Family Network, *The Evaluation Exchange. IX(2).*

Traugott, Mark (Ed.). (1995). *Repertoires and cycles of collective action.* Durham, NC: Duke University Press.

Turner, Margery Austin. (2002, November). *Discrimination in metropolitan housing markets: National results from phase I of HDS2000.* Washington, D.C.: U.S. Department of Housing and Urban Development.

Uchitelle, Louis. (2009, January 9). Jobless rate hits 7.2%, a 16-year high. *The New York Times.*

United States Conference of Mayors. (2002, June 6). *The role of metro areas in the US economy.* Washington, D.C.

U.S. Census Bureau. (2011). Income, poverty, and health insurance coverage: 2010- historical poverty tables, Table 2, Status of people by family relationship, race, and Hispanic origin. www.census.gov/prod/2012pubs/p60-243.pdf.

U.S. Congress. (1998). Federal Transit Act of 1998, Section 3002, Amendments to Title 49, United States Code, Congressional Findings.

U.S. Department of Education. (2000). *Digest of education statistics.* Washington, D.C.: National Center for Education Statistics.

U.S. Department of Education. (2003). *Overview of public elementary and secondary schools and districts: School year 2001–2002.* Washington, D.C.: National Center for Education Statistics, Common Core of Data, Local Education Agency Universe Survey, 2001–2002.

U.S. Department of Education. (2004). *The condition of education 2004 (NCES 2004–077).* National Center for Education Statistics. Washington, D.C.: U.S. Government Printing Office.

U.S. Department of Education. (2012). *The condition of education 2012 (NCES 2012–045), Indicator 48.* National Center for Education Statistics. Washington, D.C.: U.S. Government Printing Office.

U.S. Department of Transportation. (1998, June 6). Office of Small and Disadvantaged Business Utilization Press Release.

U.S. General Accounting Office. (2001, March). *Welfare reform: Moving hard-to-employ recipients into the workforce.* Report GAO-01-386. Washington D.C.: U.S. General Accounting Office.

U.S. General Accounting Office. (2004, February). *Comparison of the reported tax liabilities of foreign- and U.S.-controlled corporations, 1996–2000; United States General Accounting Office.* Report to Congressional Requesters GAO-04-358.

Valdes, Guadaloupe. (1996). *Con respeto: Bridging the distances between culturally diverse families and schools: An ethnographic portrait.* New York: Teachers College Press.

Valenzuela, Angela. (2001). *Subtractive schooling: U.S.-Mexican youth and the politics of caring.* Buffalo, New York: SUNY Press.

Venkatesh, Sudhir. (2004). *Chicago public housing transformation: A research report.* New York: Center for Urban Research and Policy, Columbia University.

Vidal, Avis. (1992). *Rebuilding communities.* New York: Community Development Research Center, New School for Social Research.

Vincent, Theodore. (1972). *Black power and the Garvey movement.* San Francisco, CA: Ramparts Press.

Voith, Richard. (1992). City and suburban growth: Substitutes or complements. *Business Review.* Philadelphia: Federal Reserve Bank of Philadelphia.

Voith, Richard. (1998). Do suburbs need cities? *Journal of Regional Science, 38(3),* 465–464.

Waldman, Amy. (1999, October 20). Long line in the Bronx, but for jobs, not the Yankees. *The New York Times.*

Waldron, Travis. (2013, March 27). Corporations pay historically low tax rates while lobbying to make them even lower. U.S. Securities and Exchange Commission, http://www.sec.gov/edgar.shtml.

Walker, Christopher. (1993). Nonprofit housing development: Status, trends, and prospects. *Housing Policy Debate, 4(3),* 369–414.

Wallace-Wells, Benjamin. (2004, April). There goes the neighborhood: why home prices are about to plummet – and take the recovery with them. *Washington Monthly.* Available at www.washingtonmonthly.com/features/2004/0404.wallace-wells.html.

Wallin, Denise, Schill, Michael, and Daniels, Glynic. (2002). *State of New York City's housing and neighborhoods.* Furman Center for Real Estate and Urban Policy, New York University School of Law.

Warren, Mark. (2001). *Dry bones rattling: Community building to revitalize American democracy.* Princeton, NJ: Princeton University Press.

Warren, Mark and Mapp, Karen. (2011). A match on dry grass: Community organizing as a catalyst for school reform. New York: Oxford University Press.

Weiner, Lois. (2012). *The future of our schools: Teachers unions and social justice.* Chicago, IL: Haymarket Books.

Weiner, Tim. (2001, August 14). In Tijuana, a new kind of drug peril. *The New York Times.*

Weir, Margaret. (1999). Power, money, and politics in community development. In Ronald Ferguson and Wiliam Dickens (Eds), *Urban problems and community development* (pp. 139–178). Washington, D.C.: Brookings Institute.

Weisbrot, Mark and Michelle Sforza-Roderick. (1998). *Baltimore's living wage law.* Washington, D.C.: Preamble Center.

Weiss, Mattie. (2003). *Youth rising.* Oakland, CA: Applied Research Center.

Weissbourd, Robert. (1999). *The market potential of inner-city neighborhoods: Filling the information gap.* Boston, MA: Shorebank Corporation.

Weissmann, Jordan. (2012, April 23). 53% of recent college grads are jobless or underemployed. *The Atlantic.*

Weitz, Jerry and Crawford, Tom. (2012). Where the jobs are going: Job sprawl in U.S. metropolitan regions, 2001–2006, *Journal of the American Planning Association, 78(1),* 53–69.

Wells, Amy Stuart and Serna, Irene. (1996). The politics of culture: Understanding local political resistance to detracking in racially mixed schools. *Harvard Educational Review, 66,* 93–118.

Wells Fargo Bank. (1996). *The underground economy: A California growth industry?* Cited in Weissbourd, 1999.

Whalen, Samuel P. (2002, April). Report of the evaluation of the Polk Bros. Foundation's full service schools initiative: Executive Summary. Chapin Hall Center for Children at the University of Chicago. Available at www.communityschools.org.

What Kids Can Do. (2004). *Youth organizing: An emerging model for working with youth.* Providence, RI: What Kids Can Do.

Wheeler, Wendy. (2003). *Lessons in leadership: How young people change their communities and themselves.* Tacoma Park, MD: The Innovation Center.

White, Karl. (1982). The relationship between socioeconomic status and academic achievement. *Psychological Bulletin, 91(3)*, 46–81.

Williams, Juan. (2003, July/August). A great day in Washington: The March on Washington for Jobs and Freedom was America at its best. *The Crisis*, pp. 24–30.

Wilson, Jill and Audrey Singer. (2011, October) Immigrants in 2010. Metropolitan America: A decade of change. Brookings, www.brookings.edu/metroamerica.

Wilson, William Julius. (1997). *When work disappears: The world of the new urban poor.* New York: Vintage.

Wimsatt, William Upski. (2002). In Jee Kim et al. (Eds), *Future 500: Youth organizing and activism in the United States.* New Orleans: Garrett County Press.

Wolff, Edward. (1994). Trends in household wealth in the United States, 1962–83 and 1983–99. *Review of Income and Wealth, 40(2)*, 143–174.

Wolff, Edward. (1995). *Top heavy: The increasing inequality of wealth in America and what can be done about it.* Washington, D.C.: Brookings Institute.

Wolff, Edward. (2002, Revised Edition). *Top heavy: The increasing inequality of wealth in America and what can be done about it.* New York: The New Press.

Wolff, Edward. (2003). *Recent trends in living standards in the United States.* Annandale-on-Hudson, New York: Bard College: Jerome Levy Economics Institute.

Wolff, Edward. (2006). *International perspectives on household wealth.* Cheltenham: Edward Elgar.

Wolff, Edward. (2013). *The asset price meltdown and the wealth of the middle class.* Russell Sage Foundation American Communities Project of Brown University.

Wood, Richard. (2002). *Faith in action: Religion, race, and democratic organizing in America.* Chicago, IL: University of Chicago Press.

Woodward, C. Van. (1966). *The strange career of Jim Crow.* London: Oxford University Press.

Wright, Caspi and Silva, Moffit. (1998). Early failure in the labor market: Childhood and adolescent prediction of unemployment and the transition to adulthood. *American Sociological Review, 63*, 424–451.

Yaro, Robert D. (2000). Growing and governing smart: A case study of the New York region. In Bruce Katz (Ed.), *Reflections on regionalism* (pp. 43–77). Washington, D.C.: Brookings Institute.

Youth Organizing. (2002a). *Youth organizing.* No. *3*, 2:1.

Youth Organizing. (2002b). *Expanding possibilities for youth development.* No. *3*, 10.

Zandi, Mark. (2008). *Financial shock.* Upper Saddle River, NJ: Financial Times Press.

Zandi, Mark. (2011, May 25). To shore up the recovery, help housing. Special Report, Moody's Analytics. In Stiglitz, Joseph E. E. (2012). *The price of inequality: How today's divided society endangers our future* (p. 302). Norton. Kindle Edition.

Zeldin, Sheperd and Price, Lauren. (1995). Creating supportive communities for adolescent development: Challenges to scholars. *Journal of Adolescent Research, 10*, 6–15.

Zellner, Wendy and Bernstein, Aaron. (2000, March 13). Up against the Wal-Mart. *Business Week*, p. 78.

Zepezauer, Mark and Naiman, Arthur. (1996). *Take the rich off welfare.* Tuscon, AZ: Odonian Press.

Zimmer, Amy and Mediratta, Kavitha. (2004). *Lessons from the field of school reform organizing.* New York: Institute for Education and Social Policy.

Zumbrun, Joshua and Chandra, Shobhana (2011, February 23). A U.S. recovery built on low-paying jobs; the economy is not creating opportunities at the high end. *Bloomberg Businessweek*.

INDEX

Note: "N" after a page number indicates a note; "f" indicates a figure; "t" indicates a table.

Lightning Source UK Ltd.
Milton Keynes UK
UKOW06f0803260417
299922UK00016B/248/P